Indian Trails
AND
Grizzly Tales

By Bud Cheff Sr.

Indian Trails
AND
Grizzly Tales

By Bud Cheff Sr.

Printed in the United States of America

Clothbound Edition, ISBN 0-912299-53-3
Perfectbound Edition, ISBN 0-912299-54-1

First Printing – October 1, 1993
Second Printing – November 20, 1993
Third Printing – July 1, 2000

STONEYDALE PRESS PUBLISHING COMPANY
523 Main Street • Stevensville, Montana 59870
Phone: 406-777-2729

Bud Cheff with the Mission Mountains in the background.

Lure of the Mountains

I have never been able to figure exactly what it is that attracts me to this place time and time again over the years. The Mission Mountains are a rough area on people and livestock. I am an old man of seventy-eight years now, and yet I am still attracted to them.

I was through there two summers ago with son, Buddy, grandsons Matt and Monty, a granddaughter, Laurie Jo, and a great grandson, Garrett. And last August my son, Buddy, his wife, Laurie, my granddaughter, Laurie Jo, and Eneas' granddaughter, Jeanette, and great grandson, Arnold, went with me on a trip through the Mission Range. I have always wanted to take some of Eneas Conko's descendants on this trip and let them see what it was like when I went in there with their grandfather.

We followed the route where the old Indian Trail used to be, camping in the same spots where I had camped with the old ones as a boy. It was a difficult trip, and before we returned, we were in snow and rain, and all had the chance to see how rugged these mountains are. I am sure that Eneas and Sofia's spirits were with us, guiding us and smiling their approval.

From Part Four, Indian Trails and Grizzly Tales

Dedication

This book is dedicated to my family, my friends, and especially to Eneas Conko.

The colorful Cheff camp on Holbrook in the Bob Marshall Wilderness, with the tepee and cook tent in the foreground.

Table of Contents

COVER PHOTO: The setting for this stunning scene of an encampment of Flathead Indians just after the turn of the century was the St. Ignatius, Montana, area, near where many of the stories in *INDIAN TRAILS AND GRIZZLY TALES* occurred. We thank the Mansfield Library at the University of Montana for permission to use the photograph.

WESTERN MONTANA
— *Setting of the Bud Cheff Story* —

Libby

Glacier National Park

Kalispell ● Martin City

Mission Mountains

Bob Marshall Wilderness

Ronan ● ● Great Falls

● Missoula

Helena
●

● Butte

● Dillon

Foreword

Many, many stories, some true, some not, have been written about the Old West. There are some pretty good factual records of the Indians, trappers, cattlemen and pioneers, but there's a part of history that has been neglected. With the ending of Indian uprisings, and all the Indians settled on their Reservations, the excitement and romance was seemingly gone. The Indians and the settlers were forgotten. This book helps fill in this neglected link from the old to the new. My father, Bud Cheff Sr., whose life has spanned those times, was a very important part of that link as you will see as you read this book.

In reading this you have to remember some of the happenings were a long time ago, and the standards were different then. Many things that were done would be illegal now. Hunting and fishing were a very important part of life and without it, many people would have found it impossible to survive.

My dad's early years were influenced strongly by the old fullblood Flathead Indians. His parents, although both of them had Indian blood, did not consider themselves Indian, and this was true of many families in the Valley who today are considered Indian. If you were one-half Indian, you were a halfbreed, and might be considered either one. If you were more than one-half, you were Indian, and less than one-half, you were white. Government regulations discouraged admitting any Indian blood at that time.

My grandparents, being from Canada and of French-Iroquois descent, found the Indians here quite different than those in eastern Canada, where the area was more settled. They were quickly accepted by the Flatheads and they, in turn, easily accepted their new life here. Some of our ancestors came into Montana from Canada in the mid-1800's and possibly even before that, as a band of the first known Iroquois came to this area from the Mission at Sault St. Marie in the St. Lawrence Valley, Ontario, Canada, where my grandparents came from. These early Iroquois were responsible for bringing the Blackrobes to this area.

There were few fences in the Mission Valley when my grandparents arrived, especially on the east side where they settled. The area stayed about the same until about the 1940's, and then it seemed to change rapidly. In the Swan Valley there was no highway, only a dirt road winding around the mud holes and big yellow (ponderosa) pines and tamarack (western larch) trees. There were no Forest Service roads leading up to the east foothills of the Missions as there are now. With the roads came the end of the remoteness of this range and the beginning of the end to the good hunting as it was back then.

When I was young there were still quite a few of the old fullbloods left who could remember the old ways, and had been on the hunting and gathering pack trips that my father experienced. When they talked about those old times there was a special light in their eyes and a longing in their voices. I loved to be with Dad when he visited with the old ones. They usually talked in Salish and although I could talk very little Salish, I could understand it pretty good. If I paid strict attention to them I could make out most of what was being said. I loved the old stories they told, and there is no doubt of the high regard they held for my father; they all had something good to say about him. Some of the older ones that I remember were Mr. & Mrs. Eneas Conko, Mary Catherine Mollman, Clara Paul and sons Mose John Peter Paul, old Mr. & Mrs. Redhorn, who were Joe RedHorn's mother and dad, Plassie Incashola, Adeline Sundown Adams, Elizabeth and Louie Hammer, Eneas and Tony Quequesah, Mary SmallSalmon, and Alex Beaverhead.

Alex Beaverhead rode up to our house one day with a gunnysack tied to his saddle and the sack was moving. He told Dad, "I have a gift for your little one. He is one smart dog." It was a puppy, and was the smartest dog I ever owned. Alex's son, Pete, and Pete's wife, Josephine, Beaverhead were our close neighbors.

The fine lady, Josephine Beaverhead, told me that my father was a very good traditional singer and one of the best dancers, and that he was one of the few who still knew how to dance in the old way.

Cecille Hewankorn had many funny tales to tell of Dad when he was young. She and most of the others named here are gone now.

Louise Adams Conko recalled when her father's (Pierre Adams) band met up with Eneas Conko's band in the mountains, and that was the time she first met her husband-to-be, Bill Conko, and my father. The two bands camped together for a few days until the horse feed got short. She said they had a grand time. She told me, "Those were the happy times. Everyone smiled and laughed all the time then. Now everyone is too serious, and they go around with long faces."

My father was super strong, and the hardest worker I have ever known. He, of course, expected us boys and girls to do our share. I look back to when I was too little to really be much help, but old enough to realize how hard he was working. Now I can hardly believe some of the feats he accomplished. He was lucky to have a wife and partner of old pioneer stock to help him. I was eleven years old before Mom finally had electricity, and it was a couple of years after that before she had indoor plumbing and water in the house. It was a time of hard work and a time of fun and laughter. We were fortunate to have such great parents whose example has been a challenge to all of us children to live up to.

Thank you for all you have taught me, the old and the new, and for sharing the story of those times and your friends with us...

Bud Cheff Jr.
Missoula, Montana
August, 1993

Introduction

I was born in 1915 on April 2nd, the fourth child of Ovila and Marie Cheff, who had come to Montana from Ontario, Canada, about the turn of the century. They were of French Indian descent, some of the first settlers along the St. Lawrence River.

On the day that I was born a neighbor lady who lived about two miles away came to be with my mother, as there was no doctor. She was Mrs. Joe Allard, who became my Godmother.

As the fourth child, I came into a family that included an older brother, the firstborn, named Leo. He died at a year old, so that left me as the third child. Rex then was the oldest, born in 1910, and Bernida in 1913. I was born in a new, two-story house that my father had just built on the old Teh Nom Finley place, near Finley Creek, later changed to Marsh Creek. Incidentally, we now own the land that I was born on; my sons, Buck and Mick, and I bought in 1966 and since then we divided our shares among our children.

My first memory is of our new house burning down. My folks were out doing the chores while we children were in the house. Bernida got scared and ran upstairs and hid under a bed. Rex, being a little older, ran after her. The only way he could get her was to get hold of her long brown curls and drag her out and down the stairs. I don't remember if I ran out, or if Rex got me out.

I do remember that we lost everything in the fire. My parents had just gotten all new furniture and they didn't get to save one thing. The kitchen range that was brand new at that time, about 1917, is still setting today where the house burned down.

Bud Cheff Sr.
Ronan, Montana
August, 1993

This 1930 photograph shows Bud Cheff (left) with Leo Page of Anaconda in the center and Bud's father, Ovila Edmund Cheff, at the completion of a hunting trip.

Part One

THE EARLY DAYS

My Folks Come To Montana

My father first came to Montana about the turn of the century to work for the Anaconda Copper Company, building on the smelter in Anaconda. Then the Company sent him and a few others to Cuba to build a smelter and on his way back he came via Ontario, where he married my mother. They came to Anaconda in 1906, where a son, Leo, was born in 1907. He died on his birthday, when he was a year old, and was buried there. They then moved to Ronan.

Dad worked for Andrew Stinger and Michel Pablo during the buffalo roundup in 1910. He was an Easterner, raised in Ontario, Canada, and was not a bronc rider. And the cowboys knew it! On his first morning he was given a horse to ride that was known to have bucked a lot of the good riders off. This was great fun for all of the old hands. As soon as Dad hit the saddle the horse was on his way. My mother was out there yelling, "Stay with him Vela, Stay with him, Vela!" About that time Dad had lost his stirrups and was flying through the air and onto the ground. Luckily, he was not injured, and was then given another horse. This was, and still is, done to a greenhorn on most ranches.

Dad did get to be a fair rider after working with all of these cowboys for a while, chasing buffalo day after day. Part of the herd belonged to Charley Allard Sr. and most of the buffalo were on the west side of the river, and they had to swim them to the east side. The cowboys tried to drive them thirty miles to the railroad at Ravalli, but were unsuccessful, so they built corrals and chutes at the river on what they call the Big Bend. They loaded them into wagons made with log crates and pulled with four-horse teams, and hauled the buffalo, one bull to a wagon, to Ravalli.

My father then started a bottling works where he made soda pop. He also had an ice cream and soft drink fountain in Ronan. Their place burnt down, and the water was polluted from so many ducks and geese in Spring Creek, so they moved out to Finley Creek, to the place where I was born. They built the pop factory right over the creek, which at that time was a large, clear-flowing stream. After our house burned down on this place, we lived for some time in the pop factory.

I can remember my father making breakfast for us and making great big pancakes, the size of the frying pan. I think this was when my sister Grace was born, and since it was kept secret from kids in those days we were told that they had found her inside a big pine stump right nearby. For the next two or three years we kids spent a lot of time chopping and trying to find another baby in that old stump.

We children were limited on the amount of pop we could have, so we would sneak out and hide it in the cold water along the stream. For several years after we moved from the place, we kids would go back there and find some of our hidden pop.

The Cellar
In those days everyone had a root cellar where they kept their vegetables, such as potatoes, carrots, turnips, rutabagas, cabbage, canned fruit and other things, and for cooling milk and such. They were made by digging back into the bank eight or ten feet and about six or eight feet wide, or as large as was needed. It was then logged up, or timbered up, and roofed over, usually with logs that were then covered over with straw, and then with the dirt from the excavation. An air vent was left on the top. These root cellars usually had double doors to keep them from freezing inside during the winter months.

My New Wagon
I was very proud when I got my first red wagon. My brother Rex and sister Bernida would pull me up and down the hill in it. One day I thought I could get into that wagon and go down by myself. I eased myself into my wagon and lurched and wriggled to make the wagon move. Not knowing how to steer the thing, I was hanging on with a hand on each side of the wagon. It began to move slowly and then, all at once, away it went. I had not taken the tongue in my hand to steer with, and didn't know how to use it anyway. I went flying down the hill with my eyes wide open and the wagon tongue jerking back and forth. We headed straight for the

Ovila Edmund Cheff in his very successful soda pop factory.

root cellar! Right on top, we went, head over heels, wagon and all, over the high part of the cellar. I managed to get up and run to the house screaming bloody murder, with cut lips and a bloody nose. But I had such a hard head and plump bottom that I wasn't hurt near as bad as I thought I was.

Dad Hauling Soda Pop

In those early days my father delivered soda pop as far north as Polson, and west as far as Hot Springs, and back south to Missoula with teams of horses and wagons. My parents would set up a stand and sell ice cream cones and pop at all the celebrations and the Indian PowWows. But sugar and extracts got so hard to get that he decided to go to farming.

Bill Conko Born

While we lived on this place, my Indian friend Bill Conko was born the same year as me, just one quarter of a mile from where I was born. When we got big enough we played together. I wore moccasins part of the time so there was a lot of little moccasins tracks between his place and ours. Most of our close neighbors were full blood Indians, so I played a lot with the Indian kids. My family all talked French, but through the years we also learned a lot of the Indian language.

Teh Num

Old Teh Num Finley, the man that owned the land that we lived on, made his home with us most of the time until he died. Quite often Teh Num would saddle Dick, his old white saddlehorse. I would get on behind him and we would ride off to town, eight miles away. We would tie Old Dick to one of the several hitch racks and then head for the store where he would buy me some candy. At that time the streets were just plain dirt with only a few short sidewalks made of plank, and they had rings on the edge to tie the saddle and buggy horses to. Nearly all the businesses had benches outside, in front of their stores, so people could sit down. Old Teh Num and I would sit on some of these benches and I would scoot right up close to him and eat my candy. But he would see to it that we saved some for the rest of the kids at home.

He seemed to know every person that came along and he told everyone that I was his boy; all of the old Indians called me Little Teh Num until they died.

Teh Num was sort of a medicine man, or doctor. He dug a lot of roots and plants, and kept his room in our upstairs full of them. I had the pleasure on several occasions to go with him to get more. He often would leave our home with a bunch of his roots and go from one end of the valley to the other to doctor different people. He was often gone for a week or two at a time. He usually stayed right at their places while doing the doctoring.

I still remember a lot of the roots that he used, and what they were used for, but as I was so young some of them I forgot, and others, though I know the plant, I don't remember what they were used for. Teh Num was always trying to adopt me as his son, but I would have been at home anyway, since he spent most of his time with us.

Bill Conko.

Louise Conko, Bill's wife.

My Dad Started To Make Moonshine

I think it was about this time that my father started to make whiskey, or moonshine, some of which he delivered in his pop bottles. He was supplying many of the prominent people in the valley and Missoula and he finally got turned in by someone. In those days if anyone wanted to turn someone in they could receive a $5.00 reward, so there were a lot of people who worked for that reward.

Our area then was in Missoula County and one of his best friends and also customer, Jim Green, the Missoula County Sheriff, had to come and pick him up. The County attorney, Dan Heferan, and Dwight Masson, another county official, were also old duck hunting friends and drinking friends of my Dad's, so he was never locked up, but got a fee for being the cook at the jail in Missoula.

Went To Canada

While Dad was serving time for his moonshine violation, my mother packed her kids up and we took a train ride — to Aunt Nellie's in Detroit, Michigan. It was an exciting time to ride that train, and I always liked to hear those old steam whistles blow.

Aunt Nellie was one of my dad's sisters, and her husband was a well-known musician. He taught me to say, "Kaiser Bill went up the hill to take a look at France. Kaiser Bill came down the hill with a bullet in his pants." This poem was one of my first words and poem to say in the English language, so I drove everyone crazy saying it over and over again. We were there a few days, then went into Canada, to Chatham, Ontario, and onto a farm where my grandparents, Grandma and Grandpa Caron, lived. We spent the winter there.

This is where I had my first fight. I had a cousin named Roland, a handsome, curly-haired kid. We were a pretty good match for each other in all aspects; we would play well, finally get into a fight.

His mother finally had enough of our fights, so she opened up a trap door in the kitchen and put us both down into an old, dried up concrete cistern, and shut the trap door. It was dark as coal all right. "Now fight all you want," she told us. Well, we couldn't even see each other to hit, but hitting left our minds. We were both afraid of ghosts, and they had told us that there might be some down in there. They called this place the Dungeon and approximately three times into that dungeon pretty well cured our fighting.

Antoine Finley Place

That spring we came back to Montana. My father was done with his cooking job and had a two-story log house that he had rented ready for us to come into about a mile north of where our other house had burned down. It belonged to Antoine Finley, some relation of Teh Num, and our buildings were in the woods to the east of Kicking Horse Reservoir.

This is where my father started farming. This was all dry land farming; he raised mostly wheat, and some hay, and all the farming was done with horses. We also had cattle, horses, pigs, chickens and geese.

While living on this place, two more children were born to our family, Floyd and Chris. I don't remember where Floyd came from, but Dr. Resner caught Chris in

Antoine Finley, at the far right, is among this group of Flathead Indians. (Photo courtesy Mansfield Center Library)

a big hole down at the creek on his fish pole. He did a lot of fishing at our place.

This made six children in the family. With this many children my mother didn't have enough to do, so she put in a very large garden! She also worked in the fields and I can remember her driving four horses on the grain binder while my dad shocked the grain bundles.

Rex And I Indian Singing and Dancing Around The Table

I remember one time when for some reason, perhaps because our folks had gone into town for early Mass, my brother Rex and I were left alone at home. Dad had left a nearly full quart of whiskey sitting in the middle of the dining room table.

I must have been about seven years old, and Rex was a little older. He and I each took a swig from that bottle and then started to sing Indian songs and do an Indian dance around the table. We would make a couple of rounds, stop, and take another drink out of the bottle. I don't remember how many rounds we made around that table, but the bottle got lowered quite a ways.

When the folks got home, our mother had not yet noticed that we were quite tipsy. She gave us a gallon pail and sent us upstairs to get her a pail of sugar from the hundred pound bag that was always stored upstairs along with the sacks of flour — nearly everything was bought in 100-pound sacks in those days. I think we first got into the flour sack and got a pail full, but decided it was the wrong sack! Then we tried to pour it back into the sack, and managed to get part of it in, the rest going all over the floor. We finally got the bucket full of sugar.

Rex started out with the bucket of sugar, but the drink had gotten to him. He started calling the chickens, throwing the sugar all over the house upstairs, just as we would throw grain to the chickens. Then he started down the stairs, still throwing the sugar everywhere. But about half way down he fell, spilling the bucket of sugar all over everything. When he landed at the foot of the stairway, some of his lower teeth were sticking all the way through his lower lip — and he still carries the scars. Back then you didn't go to the doctor unless you were about dead, so our parents had quite a job getting Rex's lip back up and over his teeth.

At first our mother thought that we had gone crazy, but Dad had seen that his bottle was almost empty, and told Mom that we were drunk. We were put outside on the porch where we laid on an Angora goat rug to sleep it off. I didn't get as sick as Rex did, and the worst part for Rex was knowing that the undertaker, Mr. Hoshen and his wife and four daughters were coming for Sunday dinner, and one of those girls had a crush on Rex. But all day long, he was too sick to even raise his head up, and she wanted to know what was wrong with poor Rex.

My First Camp Out

One summer Isadore Serall and family camped just a short ways from where we lived. He was not quite a full blood Indian, good sized and of husky build, a handsome man. Isadore had a son called Ernie that was about the same age as Rex. One day we decided to go out camping. We were already living in the edge of the mountains, so instead of going there, we went down to Kicking Horse Reservoir, a man-made lake about a three-miles walk away.

Rex and Ernie were going to initiate me but good to the out-of-doors; they were going to show me how to survive without taking any food or bedding. Of course we didn't have anything like a sleeping bag in those days and if there was such a thing, we had never seen one. But we did have a .22 caliber rifle with us, though we didn't shoot anything with it.

In the late afternoon when we all started to get hungry, Rex and Ernie put me to work helping them catch frogs as there were green frogs by the thousands any place there was water. We took the frogs to a spot that had a big rock about the size of a Volkswagon car, and several other smaller rocks near where the water entered the lake. Ernie and Rex got a good fire going from dry driftwood and then they took out their pocket knives and started cutting the hind legs off the dead frogs.

While they did this, they sent me after more frogs, but told me only to catch the big ones, which I did. We didn't have any pots or pans so we built the fire between some large rocks. When I came back with another bunch of frogs, they had the legs cooking on the hot rocks. We didn't have any salt, but we still thought the frog legs were great to eat — and I had my first meal of frog legs.

It was a good thing that it was a nice summer night as weed and grass don't make the best kind of bed. At the last part of the night we were all three shivering and by the time the sun came up I was thinking that home was not a bad place to live.

Ernie's father, Isadore, was quite a hunter and a good trapper. He was with us on one of my early pack trips with Eneas Conko. In the late Twenties, Isadore, who always checked his line on horseback, had a trap line that came quite close to where Rex and I were trapping. We noted that even though steel traps were cheap then, they still cost money and Isadore used homemade traps to catch his animals.

Fishing

While living at this place, having a stream on both sides of our place, Rex and I got to be pretty good fishermen. All that we used was a hook and line on a willow pole until we were grown up.

For bait we used what we called penny winkle, about an inch long, and grayish white with a fine sand and gravel shell around them, which we got from under the larger rocks in the bottom of the streams. We also used meat and wood worms, a big white grub found under the bark of rotten wood on a dead pine tree.

Pitch Gum, Monkey Rope and Flying Squirrels

In those days the woods consisted mostly of real big trees and we kids spent a lot of our time looking and gathering our chewing gum. We looked for trees that had old scars on the side of the trees where the sap had oozed out years before, gotten hard, and turned brown. We always had some in our pockets all of our years growing up.

If you never chewed it before, it was sort of tricky as you first started to chew it — it would all crumble up. We just kept it in the same place or "gathered" in your mouth, and kept on chewing. It would soon gather and turn into a gum.

Besides having all our pockets full of pitch gum, we always carried a supply of what we called Monkey Rope, to smoke. It was a vine that looked like a grapevine and grew way up into the bushes sometimes up to 20 feet high into other bushes or trees. It grew where it was sort of damp, from a match size to one or more inches in diameter.

Monkey Rope smoked best when the plant was dead or dry. It had joints in it about every six to eight inches and we would cut all of the joints out as they would prevent the smoke from coming through.

My sisters would also smoke Monkey Rope. It was not habit forming, but at first we all thought we were big as we smoked it. I would cut a lot of it and take it to my friends at school.

In these same big trees Rex and I spent a lot of time catching or trying to catch flying squirrels. If you haven't seen one, they seem to be getting scarce nowadays. They look on the order of a pine squirrel, but a lighter shade, and have a web from the front foot or feet, and it angles back to the back legs, and they have a wide, flat, bushy tail. They can't really fly like a bird, but can glide from one tree to another. They have a loud, coarse whistle and usually whistle in late evening or early morning. They sometimes sound like they are a long ways away, but still can be very close.

I haven't heard any for some time now. It was a pleasant and yet sort of an eerie sound. We used to hear them all the time, especially in the spring of the year, wherever there were trees. In those days the ruffed grouse were in abundance and we had a good grouse dog that would tree them. We had a .22 caliber single-shot Stevens rifle and Dad would give us just so many shells when I first started to hunt, telling us, "You better get a bird for every shell."

So in order not to miss I may have to try two or three trees to get the right rest before I would pull the trigger. From then until we were grown up, we shot an awful lot of grouse.

Pheasants — Geese

In those days there was no hunting season or we didn't know about a season. But we didn't shoot the birds until after the young ones were big enough to fry. There then were a lot of prairie chickens, as we called them, out in the valley. I think they were the sharptailed grouse. Rex and I would go with Dad, with our .22's, to hunt these birds.

We usually went west of the Mission, where there were grain fields and also big patches of brush. The birds fed in the grain fields, but when old Spoony and Sport, the bird dogs got close to them, up they would fly to the brush. I liked to stay by the brush as quite often some would land there, where I had a better chance to shoot them. Rex and I would get a few, but Dad got most of them.

In the mid-Twenties these birds all disappeared about the time the Chinese pheasants were brought in and I don't know if they killed them or ran them out.

During those days there were ducks by the thousands but we only saw geese when they were migrating. The Canada geese didn't start to nest here until about the 1940's. I believe they got started by a family by the name of Armstrong that raised a few domestic geese, and the wild ones started to mate with them. Now there are thousands of them in this valley and they are a problem for the farmers!

Ducks And Feathers

My father was an expert shot with a shotgun. He was also good with a rifle and in those days it would have been pretty slim picking without the wild game that we could get. During this period Dad owned an Overland pickup and I remember him coming home with so many ducks that there was hardly room for the dog.

The big job was plucking the ducks. The family would gather around a wash tub to pluck into and all the soft feathers went into the tub, the tail and wing feathers were put in an old box to be burnt. Some of the feathers from the Mallard drakes were saved separate by plucking the breasts in sort of clusters and put neatly into boxes like shoe boxes. The reddish-colored feathers from their sides went into another box, and the curly tail feathers went into another one. A few feathers from other ducks also were saved; these were sold and shipped somewhere back East, probably for use in making fish hooks.

Other feathers were used in making pillows, down quilts, and feather beds.

After the ducks were plucked and cleaned and washed, they were salted down into 55 gallon wooden barrels. We would put in a layer of ducks and then a layer of salt to preserve them. Then the ducks were taken to town and sold to the stores, or traded for other groceries — but we always kept plenty for the family to eat.

Fun and Fights

While I was growing up, with ten of us boys and three girls in the family, we had an awful lot of fun. But just like all families, we also had our fights, even though we still loved each other dearly. When my sister Bernida, who was just two years older than me, got mad, she was just like a cougar. She waited until I was not looking, then she would make a run at me from behind. She would jump with her knees up and hit me in the middle of the back with both knees, and grab me by the hair at the same time. Then she would pull me over backwards, and work me over.

Of course I never did have it coming. But what a relief it was when I finally got big enough that I was able to handle her.

All in all, my three sisters were sweet, loving gals. It just seemed that the fights were with the brother just older or the one just younger than myself.

It was so long ago that I don't remember for sure, but I do believe that my brother Rex and I got into a fight over a horse, which was what we usually fought over. Rex was older than I was, so I always got the worst of each fight. We were fighting on the back side of our log home.

Of course, again he was getting the best of me, but I happened to see a peavey standing against the yard fence and when I grabbed it, Rex started to run for the house. Now a peavey is a tool used to turn timbers or logs and it has a very sharp steel point and a sharp hook on the side. Rex turned a little to see what I was going to do just as I was throwing the peavey at him, just like a spear, with all of my might. The spear part went past his neck, the hook part was out to the side and grazed his neck a little as it passed over his jugular vein.

I had thrown that peavey with such force that it hit and stuck into the side of the log house and the wooden handle just quivered! It scared him and it also scared me. If that hook had caught him in the neck, it might have killed him.

Ovila and Marie Cheff are shown with their children and the children's uncle, Harry Marsh, in 1917. From left, the children are Grace, Bud, Bernida and Rex.

On another occasion, I had walked up to old Louie Mollman's house and taken one of his horses to ride, which I did quite often. I brought the horse home and tied it near our yard. My brother Floyd, who was a bit younger than I was, brought one of his horses too.

However, it was not as good a horse as the one I had so Floyd took my horse and tied his in its place. Someone happened to see him do this and told me, so I ran out to stop him. I was unable to catch him because the horse I was on was not fast enough.

There were two different winding roads through the woods that came into our home, with the roads being in a triangular shape, which made about half a mile distance by going out one road and coming back by the other road. I ran Floyd and the horse around this triangle three or four times but was unable to catch them. They would stay just far enough ahead of me to aggravate me.

In one place there was a sharp bend in the road around a big clump of thick bushes. I took a hard twist Manuela lariat rope and tied it across the narrow road between two trees, about waist high when on a horse. I then proceeded after my brother at a moderate speed until I got him going toward my stretched rope across the road. Then I whipped up my horse to full speed and he did the same with his horse. When he came around the sharp bend in the road, he was looking back at me, urging his horse to go faster. He hit my stretched rope, and I thought it knocked him clear off his horse. But it happened so long ago, and he says now that it didn't knock him clear off. Whatever, I did manage to get my horse back, even though as a kid I didn't give what I'd done a second thought. I could have caused Floyd to get hurt real bad.

Starting School

In 1921 I started school. My brother, Rex, had previously walked two miles when he started, and caught a ride with the McDonald kids. He rode with them in a horse and buggy to the country school of Leon, which is now a clubhouse. He then went to the Mission Boarding School.

When I started we walked three miles to the main road where we caught the bus and went five more miles into Ronan. It just happened that the bus driver, Mr. Shourds, was the grandfather of two of my daughters-in-law. He drove a team of mules pulling a covered wagon and in the winter time he used a sled with a little coal stove in it to keep the kids warm.

Sometimes we were so cold! I just loved some of the older girls that rode the bus, as often they would take me up on their laps, and warm me up under their big coats.

Kicking Horse Reservoir at that time was just half as large as it is today. When it was frozen over we would walk across it on the ice.

Several times we almost froze to death in blizzards. The girls and some of the smaller boys like myself always wore what we called muffs in the colder weather. They hung from a little strap from our necks and were made of different materials, but were always fur lined and were round so your cold hands could be tucked in on the fur from either end. They saved a lot of fingers from getting frozen.

Rex And I Trap, Skunk And Smell

About this time Rex and I started to trap. We trapped weasels, muskrats, mink, skunks, and coyotes. About a quarter of a mile from our house we found a skunk den where a big pine tree had blown over to expose a tanglement of roots. After setting the traps, we went the next day to check them and, sure enough, we had a skunk, but it was almost out of sight down in the hole.

Now the upper part of the hole was big enough for a person to climb down into it, so Rex, the wise one, said "Bud, you are the smallest, so you go down and get a hold of the trap chain and pull the skunk out. When you get it out, I will shoot it."

Well, I was not old enough to be skunk-wise yet, so I, the dumb one, agreed. I got down on my hands and knees and went down into the hole. I managed to get a good hold on the trap chain. We had caught the skunk well up on a back foot. I had to pull quite hard as it was digging in, trying to get away. I got it out far enough so that it could see me, but still not far enough for my skunk-smart brother to shoot it.

Yes, I had that old skunk by the back leg, and also, I was in just the position that the skunk wanted me to be. When I got him far enough out that he could get a look at me, I realized what he was going to do, but it was too late. His tail went up and he let fly right straight into my face, my eyes, my neck and my clothes. Rex killed the skunk, but not until after it had done the damage. I knew he was laughing, but it was not a funny matter until later years, as that yellowish mass was in my eyes and on my skin, and burnt as bad as fire.

I couldn't see a thing, so Rex had to lead me to the creek. By then I had some on him. He washed, I washed and re-washed several times, putting my face and eyes into the stream until I could see a little.

But that was not the worst of it, and after Rex carried that skunk home, can you imagine, Mom just would not let us come into the house! It was not the warmest time of the year to have to take our clothes off outside. Then we had to take soapy baths in an old-fashioned round wash tub, but even with all the washing, the smell was still on us. The next day was a school day, where I was not a popular boy. This was lesson number one in skunk trapping.

In later years after we moved to the Mollman place, Rex and I had a trap-line. We would leave home at daybreak on Saturdays and go down the west side of the big swamp, follow Finley creek as far as Post Creek, then go up Post Creek to the Big Ditch, and finally down the ditch to home.

The bigger animals like coyote we skinned on the trap-line, and sometimes we also skinned the smaller ones so it took us all day. Most of the time we didn't get home until way after dark and by the time we got close to home we would be so tired and hungry that we could hardly go.

Even at that age, we realized we didn't have any time to fool along. We had to hike a good clip all the way. As the snows got deeper we had to shorten our trap-line.

Overland Pickup

When we went anywhere we went in the old Overland pickup. My father had a couple of burlap sacks filled with straw in the back end for us to sit on, but we would much rather sit in the open back end with our feet dangling out.

At that time even the main roads were not graded up at all. They were just out on the bare, flat ground, and they wound around all of the ponds and there were few bridges so we forded the streams. The ford across Crow Creek was about one-quarter of a mile east of Highway 93. We forded the stream on a hard bottom. The little streams and low places that got real muddy were usually corduroyed, which was a lot of poles put cross-ways to the road so that the wagons and cars would not sink so deep into the mud.

When approaching the holes or bad spots in the road, Dad usually gave the Overland the gas in order to get through — and on several occasions I got bounced out of the back end onto the poles, or into the mud. I believe all of the kids at some time or another had their turns getting bounced out. But we adapted. When we felt Dad was pulling the gas levers down, we knew we had better get a good hold onto something solid because when you grabbed onto another person you would go out two at a time even though the top speed on this type of car was probably about twenty or twenty-five miles per hour.

My father usually carried one or two spare axles for the rig. I can't remember where we had been, but one time we were on our way home and were about one mile south of Post Creek, right near the foot of the mountains into a deep little draw. Pop! went an axle and this time we had no spare.

All we could do was to walk home, about four or five miles, Mom, Dad and five or six of us little kids. In those days there was no chance to catch a ride on this old wagon road with no cars, so we set out to walk home. We came to Post Creek at the old Ashley Ford and Mom and Dad took off their shoes and stockings and carried all the kids across the big creek. To save some steps we cut across through the woods but I got so tired, or thought I was, that I started to cry. I wanted to be carried.

My folks were already carrying the two or three of the little ones, so Mom said, "If you can't walk you can just stay right here." I got so mad I just laid down, but I kept at least one eye on them — when they got nearly out of sight, I easily found that I was still able to walk and even did a little trotting.

Horseback Ride And The Bear

One summer evening the three of us, Rex, Bernida and I, got on to old Teh Num's saddlehorse and went up into the woods on a horseback ride. We went on an old logging road, and about a half a mile away we came to a log bridge across the creek. We were all thirsty, so all got off the horse.

We let the horse drink first and then we each took turns holding the horse while the others drank out of the creek. Rex and Bernida managed to get back onto the horse, but about the time I was going to try to get on him, his ears went up and he shied. A real big bear with a fanny big enough that it looked like it took up half of the road was sitting just a little bit away, just watching us.

Lucky for us he was the opposite way from where we wanted to go. I took off running, not being able to get onto the horse without having a bank or stump or log to get up on, and none being close by, and not having that much time to spend anyway. Away we went!

This was my first race against a saddlehorse. The road was quite winding and I was leaning on the corners, and my heels were hitting my bottom. We were probably the first kids that this old bear had seen, and it was the first bear that this kid had ever seen! It was the right color for a grizzly, but we didn't know one bear from another at that time. We just knew that it was a BIG bear.

Sweat Bath

While we lived on this place, there was a good-sized pond which is now filled with dirt sediment. It was half-way between our house and Antoine Finley's house which were about one-fourth of mile apart. In the winter time Rex and I, on several occasions would go over and watch Antoine and some of his friends take their sweat baths.

Their sweathouses were made of bent willows, dome-shaped, about eight feet in diameter and about four feet high. They covered the frame with cedar bark or canvas, leaving a small doorway to crawl in through. Inside the sweathouse, they dug a hole in the ground about one foot deep and about fourteen inches wide. They would heat their rocks to red hot on an open fire outside and when the rocks were hot enough would fork them into the hole inside of the sweathouse.

They used flat boughs from the western cedar trees for a floor mat to lay on. They would all get inside. The last one in would bring a can of warm water and then shut the flap. A pine bough was used to dip into the can of water and sprinkle the rocks, which caused the steam.

Each person had a slender, hard stick about sixteen to eighteen inches long which they would use to pound or beat the rocks and sing their Indian songs while they were sweating. They would come out of the sweathouse and dive into ice water: they had chopped two holes through the ice a short distance apart and would dive into one hole and come out the other. It always concerned me then: "What if they couldn't find the other hole to come out through?"

Antoine Finley Burning His Wife

Antoine Finley came to our place one cold winter morning and my mother noticed that he was acting a little nervous. He didn't speak very plain English, so the talk went like this:

Mother: "What is the matter, Antoine?"

Antoine: "I burned all up my swuaw."

Mother: (all excited) "We will take her to the doctor!"

Antoine: "There a no use. Doctor she can no fix her. Already she's a all burn up."

Mother, still excited, ran out the door, put her hands to each side of her mouth and called as loud as she could, "*Ovela, Ovela, Viens t en, viens t en! De pe ches toi! De pe ches toi!*" In English it means "Ovela, Ovela, come on, come on, hurry up! Hurry up! Antoine burned up his wife."

Our father came running into the house. "What happened, Antoine, how did you do it?"

Antoine said, "I gotton no more some wood. I gotem to makem some wood. I can't makem some wood, we gonna all frozen. My swuaw she no like it to go. She too cold. I say it she got to go and make some wood. I gonna warm her some up. Den she can go. I makem fire under her, I gonna warm her up den she can go. Fire she's burnum good. I putum on more some sticks. All one time she's all go 'Poof!' Fire she go all over her. Shes a no more good my swuaw. My father realized that his "swuaw" was not his squaw, but his new wood saw that he had purchased not long before. His saw was what we called a woodpecker saw, a one cylinder gas-powered, with two big wooden arms that you set on the big logs, and drove two steel dogs into the log to hold the saw in place to cut the blocks of wood.

Digging Camas
Every summer or spring a few Indians would come and set their tepees up and camp on our land so they could pick their camas nearby. Some of us kids went along with the Indian kids and the women, and helped, or thought we were helping to dig camas, one of their main food supplies in the early spring. It grew very well in some of the ground that my father had previously plowed. In the spring of the year the women would come and gather the camas when it was in bloom. Sometimes there would be from ten to maybe twenty women at a time.

The camas was a plant about twelve to twenty-four inches high with a pale blue flower. The bulb was like an onion with the meat in layers. They grew about average of four inches underground. The root digging tools in the older days were made of a prong from a deer or elk horn, and were fastened with sinew to the bottom of a good sturdy stick that usually had a fork on top, or some kind of limb cut off short for a handle. The main stick was just long enough so that from a standing position they could push it down into the ground and under the roots, and then pry the camas out of the ground.

The stems were then cut off of the bulb. Afterward, the plants were gathered into a pile and this was a job we kids could do. We sometimes would take the women's digging tools and try to dig some ourselves. But the women would get after us, mostly because the larkspur, which was poisonous, grew in the same areas and they didn't want us to eat any of it. We kids didn't know the difference between a camas and a larkspur.

We always ate the camas raw. I liked it raw, but didn't care too much for it after it was cured. After the tops were cut off of the camas, we kids would gather and put the bulbs into birch bark containers to be carried back. They would preserve it by digging a pit, putting hot rocks in the pit and covering the rocks with skunk cabbage leaves. Then they would pour the camas in and cover them with more leaves, and put warm water through a hole they made in the middle with a sharp stick. This would steam and cook the camas.

Dave Finley Mauled by Grizzly
I was a small boy when Teh Num Finley's brother, Dave, came to our house and showed us the scars he carried after being mauled by a grizzly. He told us how it happened.

When I was a boy, the old Mollman Pass trail went on top of Mollman ridge to where the ridge gets real steep. From there the trail went to the creek bottom. Dave and a white man were hunting with only one gun between them. They were at the very steep part of the ridge when they saw a large grizzly above them.

The grizzly started to bellow at them and Dave told the other man not to shoot as the bear was right above them, but the fellow shot the bear anyway. It came right down after them.

Both men started to run and Dave was behind the other fellow. The bear caught Dave and Dave hollered for the other man, who had the gun, to come help him. But the guy kept right on running, leaving Dave to fight the grizzly barehanded.

The bear opened his big mouth to bite Dave in the face and Dave said all he could see was those big teeth and a big tongue. In order to protect his face, he stuck his hand right into the bear's mouth. The last thing he remembered was that he was still hanging on to the bear's tongue. When he woke up, the bear was gone.

When Dave didn't come in by evening, Louie Mollman and a nephew of Dave's called Moon Finley, went looking for him. They found him and took care of his wounds, and then brought him back. He undoubtedly would have bled to death if they had not come after him.

Dave was planning to kill the man who had left him alone with the grizzly, but the fellow was wise enough to leave the country. I remember Dave showing me his scars. One of his arms had been badly chewed on, the other was also scarred, but not as bad as the other. The bigger muscles in his back and the back of his shoulders had been torn out, leaving terrible wounds. These scars were horrible!

Dave and his oldest brother, August, along with Johnny and Dave Ashley, were on the first surveying crews in this part of the country. This group of Finleys, along with TehNum, all liked to prospect for gold and were close relatives of the ones that made the historic gold discovery, the first in Montana, on Gold Creek above Drummond.

Branding Horses

While living on this place, we had large corrals, and in the spring the Indians used to gather the bands of horses. They were the same as wild horses off of the prairies, as we called the valley in those days. As there were few fences, they would bring all the younger ones and the old ones that were not branded to our corrals.

Then the corralled horses were all roped by the front feet. The ropers would flip them down and someone was ready to sit on their head, and twist the nose upward while the legs were being tied. Then they were stretched out, branded, and the studs gelded unless they were special; then they were kept for a stallion doing their duty. A big share of the horses that are on our ranch today are descendants of some of those horses.

It was in those days that I decided that I wanted to be a cowboy when I watched the first cowboys ride bucking horses. For example, I saw Jackson Sundown ride one with a mane and tail hold, with the tail over one shoulder. At one time Sundown was the world champion bronc rider. Jim Grinder was also in the Valley, a well-known rider of this time.

During the roundup, a young stallion jumped one of the fences and broke its neck. The cowboys butchered it, the first and only time I know of that I ate horse meat.

When the roundup was over I really started to prance around on my stick horses after watching those beautiful stallions.

It was about this time I first started to learn how to milk a cow, too. I would run out to the barn with the bucket before my folks got there, and would be proud to be able to have a little milk in the corner of the bucket when they came. One time, after I got a little better, some Indian kids came. I was proud to take them out and show them how I could milk and I would squirt milk into their mouths, and also all over their faces, some of that being intentional.

As I grew a little older, it wasn't quite as much fun to have to milk several cows. Now, as a man, I enjoy milking cows by hand but in all my years I never saw anyone that could milk a cow faster than my mother — and that poor lady milked a lot of them. And my father was the world's poorest milker.

Almost Washing Down Over the Drops

This happened a little earlier in my life. One time we had to go to Teh Num Finley's place for something, I don't remember what. My mother took us with the team and wagon and we had the lower half of the grain box with its eighteen-inch high sides on the wagon.

Mom loaded all of us kids into the wagon. Then she got up into the driver's seat and we took off with several of us in the back part of the wagon. We went by Antoine Finley's place along the woods and as we came to the canal that fed Kicking Horse Reservoir, we discovered it was plumb full of water as it was high water time. However, we were facing a dilemma. Since we were only a half a mile from where we were going and since the old bridge downstream was out, we either had to go through the canal or go back around several miles.

The water was murky, so my mother couldn't see the bottom to see how deep it was and she debated a while about what to do. This particular canal had been built through old ponds and the crossing was located at one of them. The main part of the canal was only about 30 feet wide, but there was another 100 feet more of water to go through in the pond part — and the water was flowing fast down this canal.

Mom didn't realize how deep that water was, but after debating, or praying, finally she said ,"You kids all hang on tight, now." Which we did! I was scared, because I knew that there was a concrete drop about 100 yards downstream that the water just boiled and churned as it went down and over what everyone called "The Drops."

The bank was quite steep where we entered the canal and the horses hadn't gone very far until they were swimming. The momentum of the wagon coming down the bank helped push the horses on across far enough so they could get some footing, but as we hit into the deep and swift water, the back end of the wagon box sort of floated up, and came off of the back bolsters and started to go downstream.

I don't remember if anyone screamed or not, but I believe we were all too frightened. It was just a miracle that the kingpin didn't come out of the front bolster, or the front of the box would have come out, as it did in the back end. Whatever, the horses managed to pull us all to safety. We then had quite a job getting the wagon box back into place. I believe that before Mom put the team into the water, she had been praying. But a different route was taken to get back home.

Mollman

In 1922 or 1923 we moved from the Finley place to the Charlie Mollman place. It was just below the feeder canal and almost one-fourth of a mile south of the present day road. We first lived in two little log cabins until, later, we finally built a good-sized two-story log house.

This place had a large natural meadow and a nice stream ran by our house. We also leased Louie Mollman's land, which was a large meadow. The fences at that time were all fenced with split rails with the rails piled in a zigzag way on top of each other. It took thousands of rails to make the several miles of fence and we came to realize that those old Indians had done a lot of hard work to split all of those rails.

Charlie Mollman died shortly after we moved up there, but I've always been fascinated by their stories. Charlie and Louie were half Iroquois, and their father came west about the first part of the 18th Century. As we were told, their father was with a large party including several Iroquois Indians that left the eastern part of our country, or Canada, to come to the West. But it ended up, old Louie said, that only seven of the group got here.

I don't remember from what he told me if those who made the journey were all men, or if there were some women along. I only wish I had been old enough at the time to have been able to write down his stories. But I do remember that he said some died on the way and some were killed and others captured by other tribes they encountered on the way. Louie and Charlie both had Flathead wives; I never knew Charlie's wife, as she was dead before I knew him, but Louie's wife's name was

Charles Mollman.

Philomie.

Using Louie's Horses

He also had a small band of real good saddlehorses and a buggy team. I often went up to his place and got some of his horses to ride. He liked to have me ride them as they didn't get enough riding, because he was in his nineties by then.

He would put a jaw rope on his saddle horse, no halter or bridle or saddle. He would jump on his horse bareback from the ground, just like a young man, to round up his horses for me. I watched him while heading his horses off and riding at full speed. His saddlehorse would lean and turn like turning on a dime. He just fascinated me! What a sight to watch him — and I stood there just wishing that some day I would be able to ride like him!

He had two crude but neatly-built log cabins that he lived in and his yard had a nice, cold little stream running through it. The yard was natural ground with two or three huge rocks sticking out and his place sat on the edge of the valley at the foot of mountains that go up to 10,000 feet elevation.

From their home, he and his wife, Philomie, could look over all of the valley. During the summer months, they would sit out in their yard in the evenings and pluck the grass as far as they could reach, move over a little and keep plucking by hand. There was no such thing as a lawnmower in those days but they kept their whole place spick and span. What a yard, and what a sight! There were a lot of big, natural shade trees and Louie's corrals were good pole corrals with swinging pole gates. It was all enclosed with real thick chokecherry bushes that were tall and sort of hung over the corral fences — what a beautiful spot for the horses and cows!

I Smoke Louie's Pipe

At the edge of his meadow there were a few big pine trees and my father would cut one of these trees down every year for Louie, and then cut it up into blocks with our old woodpecker saw. Then old Louie would cut up every one of the limbs with a buck saw.

After the wood was all made up, he would rake up all the pine needles and cones, and little sticks by hand — and I often went up to where he was working and tried to help him.

He would work a while, then would sit down to rest. Each resting time, it seemed, he would take out his old stone pipe, fill it with his homemade tobacco made of kinnikinnick. His pipe had a long wooden stem and he would take a few puffs, pass it to me, and I would take a few puffs. We would pass it back and forth until the pipe was empty and then he went back to work.

I thought I was big stuff getting to smoke his pipe! But I think my brother, Rex, got to smoke on his pipe also.

Louie Mollman's Tobacco Pouch

I don't think that Louie ever wore any pants or at least I never, ever saw him with any on. He wore long leggings that came up to his groin. At the top was a buckskin string to tie to the belt to hold them up. He had a breech cloth on, with a skirt that came half way to, or near his knees. He always wore a loose-fitting blouse.

He always had a belt on, with a hatchet on one side. On the other side he had a buckskin pouch that was made about three or four inches wide, and about fourteen inches long. It was sewn all the way around on both ends, and the sides were sewn shut. The only opening was a little slit that was cut right in the middle of it, half way from each end of the pouch. He would put his tobacco and his stone pipe through that slit, into the pouch, with the tobacco at one end, and the pipe at the other end if he didn't have anything else to take with him. If he did, he would put his pipe and tobacco together in one end, and whatever else he had into the other end. Then this pouch was put, or slipped under his belt and pulled up halfway, with the rest of it hanging down over the belt. The slit was on the top; this made it impossible to lose anything out of it, as the slit was always closed.

Of course he always had moccasins on his feet and in the hot summer he often wore short leggings that came just above his calves. And, of course, he had long braids, and often wore a stiff brim, high crowned hat.

From left, Mrs. Louie Mollman, Louie Mollman, Mrs. Alex Beaverhead.

During those years, early on New Year's morning, my father would shoot three rifle shots high over the Mollman's house, which was three-quarters to a mile away. Then Louie would answer with three shots, or sometimes it would be vise versa, and he would shoot before Dad. It meant "Happy New Year". Then Louie and Philomie, his wife, would walk down and have breakfast with our family.

Bow and Arrows

I can only remember Louie and Philomie going to town for supplies twice a year, once in the spring and again in the fall with a team of horses and a spring wagon.

Louie was an expert maker of bows and arrows, and his brother, Charlie, may have helped him. They made the bows and arrows for the Flathead Tribe.

Louie at one time was one of the Tribe's top buffalo hunters. He was a good-sized man, with as powerful a build as a younger man. Old Louie gave me one of his older bows and a bunch of arrows. He had used this bow quite a lot and I was so proud of this gift — but, just like all kids, not proud enough! As my mother used to tell me, and ask me to put it up and to keep it. But at that age I didn't realize the value or what a keepsake this gift was. I would sneak it out and I finally shot all my arrows away, and finally broke the bow. Now I would just love to still have it.

Louie's Money

One time I went up to get one of Louie's horses to ride. In those days the Indians didn't knock at the doors like the White people did before coming into someone's house. As I went to see them, I just made the usual grunt, and pushed the door open, and stepped in. Louie and Philomie, his wife, were setting flat on the floor, which was common to the Indians.

When I opened the door, old Louie sprang to his feet as if he had been sitting on a strong spring. I know that my eyes must have bugged out because in the middle of a blanket on the floor was a large pile of money — to me the most money I had ever seen. There were different stacks of gold coins of different sizes, and a lot of silver coins and piles of paper money. I tried the best I could to apologize for surprising them. He told me which horse to take, but didn't come out to help me as he always had done before. Not too long after this, old Philomie died and was taken by horse and wagon to the Mission for burial.

Louie Falls Off His Roof

A year or two later my father was plowing with four horses in a field below our house. As he would make the turn at the lower corner of the field, he would get some flashes in his eyes — and he finally discovered they were coming from Louie's house. So, Dad felt there was something wrong. He quickly unhitched his horses from the plow, took them home and hiked up to Louie's place where he found Louie, with a broken hip, laying at one side of his house right near a big rock.

This was in the fall of the year and he had gotten on his house, which had a peaked roof, to repair a hole before winter set in. He evidently slipped, slid off the house and fell on top of that large rock. He had signaled to my dad with a little looking glass that he flashed into my dad's face every time that my dad made the turn in the field and was facing him.

Louie said he always carried this little looking glass with him and had previously used it to signal other Indians for different reasons, including while they were on some of their buffalo hunts. I always wanted to know where he got this glass, which he kept inside a stiff little leather container. He may have gotten it from some early trapper or pioneer, or it might have been brought out here by his father, from back east when he and the Iroquois group came west.

When Louie fell off of this house he said he was 94 years old. He lived for another year.

Going To School

When we moved up to the Mollman land we had two ways of getting to school: we could either walk five miles to the main road and then catch a school bus and go four more miles into Ronan to school, or we could drive a horse and buggy to school.

So, we drove an old mare named Queen for quite a long time. The road to our place was a real winding road through heavy timber and wound around ponds and trees and through two large creeks. We would drive through the woods and come out just one mile from town. When we would get to this point there were other kids that walked to school, so we would come along. The kids along the way would hitch onto our buggy and by the time we got to school, there would be kids hanging all over our buggy.

Queen Runs Away And Other School Escapades

Old Queen, our buggy mare, was sort of an unpredictable old horse. Sometimes she would balk on us, but on occasion she also would try to run away with us.

Sometimes to get her started, Dad would have to get into the buggy with us and get her to going good. Then he would give the lines to my brother Rex and jump out of the buggy and we went on with no problems. However, one evening a boy named Chester Cole who lived near town came home with us to stay the night. The next morning as we got ready to leave for school, my father loaded the five-gallon cream can into the buggy with us kids because about twice a week we took the cream can into the creamery as he sold this cream for grocery money.

Well, on this morning old Queen was acting quite frisky. We managed to get about a half a mile from home when away went old Queen on a mad run. Rex was unable to control her! She ran past the end of a big pine log, at which time an explosion occurred. As the two left side wheels hit and went over the log, kids flew in every direction — along with the can full of cream. The can and Chester, our friend, must have gone together right over the front of the buggy. As we all picked ourselves up, we spotted poor old Chester and the empty cream can laying together, both splattered with thick cream.

The buggy wheel had run right over Chester's neck, but luckily it hadn't broken his neck — though he had a buggy track and a stiff neck for a while.

Queen, after getting rid of all of us, stopped at a gate not far away. We all scraped thick cream off of each other and went down and all got back into the buggy, and went on to school.

When we didn't use the buggy to go to school, we used to walk to the main road

Antoine Chief Eagle.
Photo circa 1905.
(Photo courtesy Mansfield
Center Library)

and we had to leave home way before daylight in the morning. Then we had to walk back at night.

There were about five miles of winding road to cover and we went right through the middle of what is now the Job Corps camp, then down by the fence at the reservoir. At that time the reservoir didn't come up that far and there was no ditch like there is today. The road went up on the hill to the west and then wound around the ponds and stayed on the higher ground because it didn't get so muddy. Quite often it would be raining or snowing all the way and our clothes would often be soaked; sometimes our clothes or coats were not yet dry by the time we left the school to go home. Often, the road also would be real muddy and our overshoes were already heavy on our feet. Then the mud would stick to our feet, and we would try to kick it off about every other step. We would get so tired that we could hardly get home — and on occasion some of us fell asleep while eating our supper.

We always had to take our coats, as there was no such thing as a weather report in those days. It might be nice in the morning, but could be storming by night or vice versa so we carried our coats whether we needed them or not, and we also carried our lunch pails, which were usually a half gallon lard pail.

Antoine Chief Eagle Took Us Home in a Blizzard
One time just after we got off of the school bus, a bad blizzard came up and the road drifted over and we were having a hard time trying to see where we were going

as there were no fences and the road was not graded at all. It was just a flat road.

Antoine Chief Eagle, an old Indian, came and picked us up with a new bobsled and snappy black team that he had just bought a short time before. He lived about three quarters of a mile from our pathway and he'd come for us because he knew that we would be out there somewhere. He took us all the way home — and I've often thanked the Good Lord for Antoine as it may of been that he saved our lives. I wish now that I could have done a good deed for him before he died. Because our folks lived up in the woods, they didn't realize that it was storming so bad down in the valley.

Sofia Conko, Eneas' wife, is shown in the center holding her son, John. At left is Panameeh Pierre, Sofia's sister. The young woman on the right is unknown.

Part Two

INDIAN TRAILS

Polly's Lumber Company

In 1923 or 1924, Polly's Lumber Co. started to log the big trees through our woods. They bought most of the timber stumpage in the area, paying very little for it, and all of the timber, or logs, were hauled to the Bonner Mill by railroad and old steam engines.

The railroad spur started off the main tracks one and one-fourth miles southwest of Ronan. The tracks crossed Highway 93 about one mile south of Ronan and then went east across Crow Creek, and angled southeast to a little creek about four and a half miles from town. This is where Camp One was built.

From there the railroad went straight south to Finley, or Marsh Creek. Camp Two was set up where Barkers now live and a spur from that track took off the main track on the land just 200 yards east of the Job Corps. It angled east and south, up and onto some of the land that we had leased, which was three-fourths of a mile south of what is now called Mollman Pass Trail road, and one-half mile below the feeder canal. Camp Three was on the Jackson Sundown place, three-fourths of a mile from our house, and Camp Four was on Middle Crow Creek, right near where Ronan gets its water now.

I don't know how many men they had employed, but there was a great number. Everything was done by men, horses and railroad, and there were many spurs running off of the main tracks. Most of them ran parallel to each other, and all about one-half a mile apart. The loggers didn't want to skid the logs more than a quarter of a mile with the teams.

They had crews that just worked putting in the tracks. A crew went ahead and cleared the right-of-way for the tracks and then came the "Tie Hacks," who cut and hewed out all the ties and piled them along the way. My Dad did a lot of this kind of work.

After they were piled the dynamite crew came along and blew out all the larger stumps. Next the grade had to be put in, for which they used teams and walking plows. They would start by plowing one furrow down the middle of the grade and then, as they were coming back, plowed the second furrow onto the first one. They went back and forth plowing the dirt to the inside to form the bed for the ties to lay on. They also used a lot of Fresnoes and scrapers pulled by horses to move dirt — and a lot of pick and shovel work was done.

After the grade was put in, the trestle crews came along. A trestle was put across every stream and every low spot that was too low to fill with dirt. As the tracks were laid, a steam donkey engine followed along and laid the rails in place, and then picked up the timbers and placed them for the trestle. Each camp had what they called a coal dock, which were big bins built up on top of a trestle to store the coal. These bins were built high enough so that each morning the train engines could run under the dock and fill their bins full of coal for the day's work.

Also, at every stream there was a sump hole built and dug. Some were logged up as these were put in so the engines could keep their water supply up for their steam.

It seemed at the time that the woods were full of loggers. The timber fallers, I think, got 75 cents a thousand feet for falling trees, and the logs were all cut in sixteen-foot lengths. Everything was cut with the old cross cut saws.

I can remember a huge pine tree at the lower end of our meadow for which the fallers had to bring an extra long saw to fall. I can't remember the width of that stump, but us kids played on it a lot. I do remember that the logs were so big that the teams couldn't drag them in sixteen-foot lengths, so they rolled them with the teams all the way to the railroad, about 300 or 400 yards.

At Camp Three, inside of the woods a little ways, the loggers had tables and benches set up right near our road. They would come and eat the lunches that their cook supplied to them, and sometimes the loggers would leave canned milk, sandwiches or cookies on the table for us kids. They knew there would be some hungry kids that would come along and clean them up; the canned milk was a treat for me, as I liked it.

Each camp had a big horse barn made sort of simple from poles and a shake roof. I always enjoyed being at the camp early in the mornings to watch all those big, beautiful, well-kept horses coming out of the barn to be hooked onto their skidding rigging and would leave for the woods.

In some areas the fallers only fell and cut the logs in sixteen-foot lengths. Then the swampers, as they were called, came along and chopped the limbs off.

The woods boss was a big Frenchman by the name of Duchet. He would not fire a man as long as he was doing something. One big, tall man was not getting quite as much done as Duchet thought he should, so he tried to catch the man loafing. But each time he came upon him, he would always be sitting on a stump sharpening his axe, so he was always busy. Instead of firing him, Duchet just gave him a new name, Sharp Axe John.

After each area was logged off and the tracks were pulled up, we kids would take a horse and buggy, go along and pick up all the railroad spikes that were missed. We also picked up any splice irons — we got ten cents for them and one cent each for the spikes. We had to haul them all the way down to Camp One, but we thought we were making good money.

School and My First Inside Toilet
My father finally bought a new Model T Ford truck and got the first school bus route off of the main road in our direction. Dad built up the sides, put a wooden bench on each side, and covered the top with a canvas cover and sides that rolled up. Rex, my oldest brother, who was thirteen or fourteen at the time, was the new

school bus driver. What a happy bunch of kids we were to have a bus to ride in!

I started school in a two-room yellow government building and spent two years in the first grade, because I didn't understand English too well since we spoke mostly French at home. Then I went to a two-room school that sat where the Ronan Post Office is now located. Then I went back to the place where the schools are today.

At that time we just had outdoor toilets. The boys was a four holer with an upright board fence around the front part. There was a wooden trough for a urinal and a lot of the boys would try to see who could go the highest on the boards, or even go over the top instead of using the urinal. I even tried to compete a couple of times, but I was outclassed! Oh, what a smelly place that got to be.

After a while, a new, big, brick school house was built, and it had indoor plumbing — this was a really fancy school. I recall my first time to go on one of those stalls with the swinging door on the front and a fancy seat to sit myself on. I'd comfortably done my job and everything went very good until I started to lift myself up. A terrible growling noise started, so I sat back down. I tried to get up three or four times and each time that awful noise would start. I finally decided I couldn't stay there and hold that seat down all day, so I finally jumped up and slammed that swinging door open right into two high school boys — Kenny Egan and Frenchy Roullier. I knew Frenchy quite well and I was so excited that I asked him in French what was the matter with that thing? It makes a bad noise, and the water is going to get out of it, and go all over. But he assured me that it would be all right, so I watched it from a distance as the water came almost to the top, swallowed everything up and went down. That was my first time to see a spring loaded toilet seat that automatically flushed when you got up.

Playing Hookey

In our early years of school we missed a lot of school due to the bad weather and our language barrier. I flunked two or three grades while in the grade school, so it was quite embarrassing to be behind even though there were several kids older than me (some were up seventeen and eighteen years old).

One time Eddie Normandeau and I skipped school while we were both coming to school in buggies. We called it "playing hooky" and we stayed out for a full week, hiding in the school horse barn. One end of the barn was piled high with loose hay so we made a hiding place out of a few old boards that we put up on the ceiling. During the recesses and noon hour we would climb up there and lay as quiet as possible.

The following Monday we were afraid to return to school so we tried it again. About 10 a.m. we noticed John Nedrau, the city cop, walking slowly toward our barn. We scrambled up to our hiding place and laid on our boards, doing our best not to even breathe as we were scared half to death. He stood in the middle of the big, open doorway.

A big deep voice came out, "All right boys, come on down from up there. I have got a better place for you two boys." Still trying to hold my breath, I peeked down at him. He was not even looking up at us. "Come on, come on down from there," he said again. So, eventually, shaking and sucking in a good breath of air, we slowly climbed down.

He called us to him and with his big hands picked up two little trembling hands and led us to the school house and into the basement. Then our teacher came down. I didn't cry like Eddie did, but I was still fighting a few tears. They asked us what we would rather do, go to jail or go to school — we could take our choice. What a great relief when our teacher put her arms around us and took us up to our class!

Bitterroot and Camas Festival

One year in late spring or early summer I was invited to go with the Conko family over to Camas Prairie to where they gathered with other Indians to have their annual festival, a celebration to start the digging of the Camas and Bitterroot. They had a big feed of these two plants, along with Indian bread and meat.

We kids played an Indian ball game that is something like hockey. We had a ball about eight inches in diameter made of buckskin and stuffed with deer hair. Each player had a stick for hitting the ball and you could only hit the ball with this stick. The kids were divided into two equal sides. Each team was about fifty yards apart with a well-marked line cut in the dirt, about thirty feet long, for the goal line. Another line was made halfway between each team.

At the start of the game, the defending team came to the center line and an older person would oversee the game. To determine which team started the ball, this individual had two identical bones, but one was marked just like the bones used in the stick games. He concealed the bones, one in each hand, and a player from each side picked a bone. The team with the marked bone was the first to play. They started the ball from their goal line and the other team met them at the center line. Each team tried to get the ball to their goal line and the games got pretty rough, and there were a lot of skinned shins and bruises.

In the evening the stick games were played, and the camas dances were danced and during the celebration day they also had foot races and horse racing. The next day the digging of camas and bitterroot was started in earnest.

Indian Medicine Dances

In the old days when the Indians had their medicine dances, the sick ones would come or be brought to this place to be healed of whatever was wrong with them. The medicine ground was only about two miles from where we lived and they would be there for several days. Often, from our house, we could hear them singing and drumming.

Only full blood Indians were allowed to attend these ceremonies. Although I am more French than Indian, I am probably the only one not a full blood who was allowed to attend. I went with the Conko family.

Everyone had to be dressed in Indian clothing. The medicine men were all painted up, some sort of hideous looking. One of the medicine men had a grizzly bear outfit and looked like a real bear as he performed mostly around the sick people. He was on his hands and feet part of the time, then at times on his feet only. He grunted and growled like a bear. He crawled around the sweat lodge where the sick people were inside sweating. He'd growl and dig and roll around on the ground, and then would sit and sing his medicine song, which was very mournful. It was a scary feeling for a young kid.

Each person had his own medicine costume, or outfit, as they called them, and sang their own medicine songs. Phillip Pierre was one of the medicine men who was also a great hunter. His dance outfit was adorned with many grizzly claws and elk teeth.

They had poles fashioned and tied high up in the air where some performed, much like trapeze artists. They would cut all kinds of capers on the poles, in the air and also on the ground. I don't understand how they did it, but I saw them pick up red hot rocks, roll them over their bodies, and walk on them. They had several sweat houses built and they would put most of the sick ones in to sweat while they performed around the sweat house and the fire. Then they would put the sick ones into the cold creek. I didn't see any die from this, but some did.

We Find Hidden Indian Medicine Bag

Those that came to be healed brought one of their most precious garments to be put into the medicine bag before they could be healed. Then two Indians of good health, and reliable, (I don't remember how they were chosen) would take the bag somewhere to hide it where they thought it would never be found. Sometimes these Indians would be gone for two, three or more days while hiding the bag. They were never to reveal where they had hid it. Sometimes, I think, they may have put them into deep holes in the Flathead River, or the lake, or maybe the deep ponds, or high in the mountains.

One time Rex and I went to Susanne Creek, which was a remote area then, located straight east of where my son Buck now lives. Old Sport treed a grouse in a tall, bushy spruce tree. We looked way up into the tree at what looked like a huge hornet nest. Upon climbing the tree, we found a big bag about three or four feet in diameter made of several layers of canvas. We tore a hole in it, and it was plumb full of beautiful beaded moccasins, vests, leggings, and armbands. A few of the pieces had rotten spots on them. What we took out, we neatly folded and put back in and tried to close the hole as best we could — we realized that it was an Indian medicine bag that had been hidden there some years before.

My good friend, Bill Conko, had told me before that if a person ever found one of these, he should not touch or bother it because the spirits would cause you to get all the diseases that the medicine man had taken from the sick ones when he made up the bundle.

The following Monday when I went to school I proceeded to tell all the kids on the school bus about what Rex and I had found. A week or so later we were going to show our dad what we had found, but when we got there it was gone. Everything had been taken.

I had described to several of the kids exactly where we had found it and one bunch of kids were real interested. They were about one-fourth Indian and I believe their father went there and got the contents.

Going Into The Mountains With The Indians

In 1924 when I was nine years old, I was invited to go on my first pack trip with the Conkos. Bill Conko, my close friend, had asked his dad, Eneas, if I could go with them into the most remote area of the Mission Range and this trip was one of the most exciting times of my life.

I left home early in the morning, riding Old Babe, a remarkable mountain horse. I had a blanket under my saddle, on top of the pad for my sleeping blanket since there was no such thing as a sleeping bag in those days. I had a box of shells and a .22 caliber rifle with me.

I went to Conko's place, which was by the lower canal on what is our road today. They were putting the packs on the horses when I got there.

The women had just as much to do with the packing as the men did. They used saddles that they made themselves out of two wooden boards hewed out to fit the horse's backs, called the plates of the saddle. Then the women sorted through many of the large deer or elk horns to find some with prongs shaped with the right curving to use for hoops. Holes were bored through the horns and the plates, and then tied tightly together with rawhide strings. This framework was covered with sheets of wet rawhide and sewed with sinew. After the rawhide dried, the saddles were ready to use. They were very efficient and durable.

Riding saddles were made in the same way with a little different shape. The Indians were very proud of their saddles and from what I've seen, they should be.

The food and gear was loaded into parfleche bags, which were made out of hide and would fold something like an envelope. These containers were laced up with heavy buckskin string and were shaped like a pillow when filled. This would enable the horses to squeeze through the brush and trees without bumping the packs, since the Indians cut as few trees as possible on their trails. Each pack had a stick about one and one-fourth inches in diameter inside, the entire length of the pack. Two square buckskin ropes were put into the pack through a hole in each end of it, and were wrapped around the stick. This stick suspended the pack and kept it from tearing. Then the buckskin rope was fastened to the fork of the saddle.

Then they put a top pack over the parfleches, tied with what they called a "Squaw Hitch," which was a cinch made out of buckskin or canvas. A rope was tied to the end, which went over the pack and then back over again before being tied. Then a stick fourteen inches long was put under the rope and twisted to tighten the pack. If the pack loosened up, they simply took another twist.

After everything was loaded onto the horses, we all mounted and headed toward the mountains with Eneas in the lead. What a sight for me to see! We followed an old wagon road that wound around the trees and came to the upper canal where my son Mick's field is now. Then we crossed through the canal, which was quite high, and hit a brushy trail that was just about fifty yards north of where our house is now sitting. About a mile up the trail, we crossed Eagle Pass Creek to the south side and then continued up the canyon all the way to the top.

The trails were very rugged compared to what they are now and the horses had to be good stock in order to make it up there; even so, we had to rest them quite often because the trail was so steep.

A large grizzly was seen about two-thirds of the way to the top of the mountain as we came to a beautiful alpine area, but I only got to see it as it was leaving, going into the woods. When we got about a mile from the top, we all stopped to let the horses have a rest. We walked up the bank and got a drink of water from a small spring under the foot of a little cliff. Then we all mounted and continued through an open, meadow-like slide area. The last quarter of a mile was very steep and the horses had to dig in to get to the top, but what a sight when we reached the top of the mountain.

We all dismounted and then started down the back side following Eneas, who went ahead a ways to see if we could get through the snow that was left from the previous winter. This was a high experience for me at nine years old; looking back down over the valley gave me a feeling of being on top of the world. Looking down the other side, into Summit Lake, appeared to be a long, steep way — which it was. We had to be very careful not to roll any rocks down or they might have hit someone below us.

After getting to Summit Lake the horses were unpacked and unsaddled before we turned them loose to feed. The tepee poles were taken down from where they had been stored the year before, upright against a big spruce tree (a common practice because it kept the poles straight and kept them from rotting as they would have on the ground and because they would not have to cut more poles as often). So I also have done this with my tepee poles throughout the years.

The tepees were made of light canvas, though sometimes they were made out of flour sacks which were light and thin but still they held the rains. If the weather was bad, the cooking was all done on the inside on the open fire.

As we were setting up camp, we saw four big grizzlies sitting on their haunches on a sidehill about one hundred and fifty yards away, watching us. I asked if they were going to shoot them, and an old Indian answered me. "Sumka, she don't makem trouble for us, we don't makem some trouble for Sumka." It was at this time that I learned that the grizzly bear was sort of a sacred animal to the Tribe. They would not kill them unless they were forced to.

While Bill and I helped two of the women gather limbs for firewood, the men were active in cutting willows and erecting a frame for a sweathouse.

Bill and I had about an hour to do whatever we wanted to do. This was something I had never done. We each cut ourselves a willow for a pole, got some cotton string from his mother and a tiny piece of rag which we tied onto the end of the string. We tied the string to our willow pole and we were ready to start fishing without a hook. Although there was no fish in this lake at that time, it was alive with frogs. (Fifteen years later I stocked it with fish.) We would swing our line with the little rag bait over the frogs and they would jump and grab the rag, hanging onto it, and we would bring them right up into our hands. Their mouth or jaws seemed to lock right onto the rag and we would swing them around, though once in a while one would turn loose. We had a lot of fun catching these frogs and I learned that frog legs are quite tasty.

Bill and I carried limbs for the fire to heat the rocks for the sweathouse. These sweathouses were built by punching holes in the ground with a sharp stick to form a circle six to eight feet in diameter, depending on the number of people that were going to be in it at one time. The willows were each stuck in these holes and then bent into a dome shape to the hole on the opposite side. The dome was three to four feet high and was covered with canvas. Rocks were heated on the open fire until they were red or white hot and then placed in a hole about a foot deep that had been dug inside of the sweathouse. The hole had to be free from any wooden roots or burnable material because that would cause smoke.

After everyone was inside, the doorway was closed and the rocks were sprinkled with water to cause the steam. This made the dirt and sweat roll out of your skin. After you had enough, you ran out and jumped into the lake to wash off and Bill and I got to be the first ones to try out the new sweat house. The men were next and when it started to get dark the women took their turns. The Indians liked to have a clean body before they started to hunt.

At dark some of the horses were picketed for the night.

My First Raw Kidney For Lunch

Early the next morning after we ate, the tepees were taken down and the poles put back and up against that same old tree, the horses saddled and the pack horses packed. We left for Fish Lake, later called Hemlock Lake. In several places the Indians kept the trail camouflaged by spreading the horses out so they didn't make a visible trail whenever we could; this was a rugged trail and still is today. I named this Goat Foot Pass because the Indians always said the horses had to have feet like goats to make it through.

About halfway to the lake, we ran into a large bunch of mountain goats. The men shot a bunch of them and after cleaning them they got them back to the trail where they loaded them on the horses. As we got ready to go on, they threw each of us a raw kidney from the goats. Of course I didn't know what it was at that time, but everyone ate their raw kidney as we went along horseback. It was sort of chewy, not too bad. The paunches also were saved and washed out that evening and they, too, were eaten raw.

On one of these trips, Bill and I and his mother, Sofia, got behind the rest of the party when we stopped to shoot some blue grouse. As we got to the top of the divide on Hemlock Pass, Sofia went ahead of us a ways where the divide is all solid rock and there was no visible trail. Her horse must have heard or smelled the other horses and tried to cut across to get to the rest of them, but he came to a very high cliff and was standing on a rock that was slanted toward the edge.

Sofia got scared when she noticed the edge of the cliff! In those days the women wore long skirts that almost touched the ground. She jumped off her horse but the hem of her skirt got caught on the saddlehorn; her dress was up under her arms as she hung from the saddlehorn. She started to holler, "Eneas, Eneas," (her husband) but Eneas was already a long ways down the mountain. She was short and stocky and was unable to free herself. For me it was sort of embarrassing, but there was nothing else we could do but run down there and free her from the horse.

We camped that evening at what is now called Conko Lake about one-fourth of a mile above Hemlock Lake. That night we had the worst thunderstorm that I can remember; the lightning would hit the big flat rocks on all sides of us and really sound off. I was rolled up in my blanket, and tried not to see it, but it still would light everything up. I spent part of that night wishing I was at home.

Going Fishing

The next morning Bill, his mother and another Indian lady, and I got ready to go fishing. Sofia pulled some hair out of one of the horse's tail. The two women each had a stick in hand, about three or four feet long, that they used, as we went along, to knock the water off of the bushes to keep their long skirts from getting too wet.

We cut our fish poles about a quarter of a mile from camp and since there were no willows in this area, we had to settle for poles about five or six feet long and big at the butt end. Really, they weren't much more than a club. We tied our line on the end and put a plain hook on it, without a leader. The women baited our hooks with goat meat tied on with a horse hair so the fish couldn't get it off so easy.

We were not able to cast with this type of gear so we both waded out to our waist and threw our line out. Nearly every throw we caught a trout about fourteen inches long. Each time we caught one, we heaved it back to the bank and the women would take the fish off of our hooks and rebait them if needed. It didn't take long for us to catch all the fish that we four could carry back to camp in burlap bags.

When we got back to camp, some of the others had built a big drying rack and were drying the goat meat. So, they built another rack for the fish.

The racks were made with four poles stuck into the ground for posts, with four more poles tied onto them about four feet above the ground. Each fish was split all the way through and from the head almost to the tail and then strung onto poles and hung over the fire to dry. A fire made from dry wood without pitch was built under the fish or meat. Bill and I had the job of supplying the wood, which was mostly alder and cottonwood. With a little guidance from the women, we soon learned what kind of wood to use and what not to use. It usually took about twelve hours to dry good enough to keep without spoilage.

Bill and I Had Some Fun

I often think of where and what two little boys only nine years old did when we first started going on these trips. Today I look at my little nine- and ten-year-old grandsons and I would be worried to death to turn them loose and let them go into the area that we did, one of the most remote and inaccessible parts of this country. Bill and I would each fill a pocket with dried meat and take off with our .22 caliber single shotguns that we mainly used for grouse.

On one of the many long hikes we little guys took, he and I left camp at Conko Lake and went in a northeasterly direction down to Hemlock Creek where there were a few little meadows, past the spot where the horses were grazed. Then we started to climb the side of the mountain through thick brush and then heavy timber and downed trees. We kept right on climbing without taking much time for resting until we finally got to the top of the ridge not far from Hemlock Peak. The higher we got, the more open the area was — and this is where we started to see and shoot a lot of blue grouse. After getting to the crown of the ridge we shot another grouse or two and then we sat down with our backs against a big old log that had fallen many years before. We got out our dried meat and started on our lunch of only meat, but it was good. While sitting and admiring all of the beautiful flowers of all colors all over the sidehills and looking down into North Hemlock Lake, it seemed as if we both got very thirsty about the same time. After sweating all forenoon and then eating the dried meat we were very thirsty — we decided that although it was a long ways down there we would try to go down the other side to a stream. We gathered our grouse, piled them in the shade of a big rock and left our rifles nearby. Then we started to run down into the canyon, slipping, falling, getting up and running again.

When we got quite close to where there was a little stream running toward the lake, we thought we heard something. The area was quite open, but we didn't see anything, but when we got to the water's edge we both noticed that the water was a little murky. We got ourselves a good fill of that cold water. Then we noticed that just a short ways below us was a big hole about six feet in diameter dug into the stream.

"A bathtub for the grizzlies!" said Bill. I had never seen one up close, but his dad had told him about them and the hole had been freshly used as the ground around it was still all wet. It was a good thing we already had our drink because we may not have taken the time to get one!

We scrambled back up the mountain. I stopped for a breath of air and happened to look across the little canyon. About 400 yards away, I saw two grizzlies, one real large and the other smaller, probably a yearling. Thank the Good Lord they were moving away from us, so it really didn't bother us too much. We must have scared them out of their bathtub.

When we got back to the top of the ridge, we discovered that there were several big rocks that all looked alike. While looking for our guns and our grouse, we saw a little dark animal with something in its mouth and discovered that was one of our grouse — this was the first martin that either one of us had ever seen. He was so pretty and so friendly! He came right up close to us. We found our other grouse and the guns easily then, and debated whether or not to shoot him. But we decided to let him live, and gave him the bird he had already partly eaten. The marten got sort of excited when we picked up the rest of the birds and started off; it must have thought they were all his.

After going a short distance up this ridge, we decided to take a different route to get back to camp. Although we couldn't see where camp was, we knew that it was in this big canyon.

As we looked up along the sky line of the main ridge that led to Hemlock Peak, just above North Hemlock Lake where we had gotten our drink of water not too long before, we saw a beautiful sight — a large band of mountain goats were going along the rocky divide, all in single file. We sat down on a flat ledge of rock with our feet dangling over the edge and watched the goats for quite a while.

There were several of this year's kids in the bunch and the little ones were so cute. They were constantly running, bucking and challenging each other for fights. They would run up to their mother and also to the big billies and pretend they were going to butt them all off the mountain. Two little boys sat there and made big plans on how we were going to catch a couple of those little ones and take them home with us. But we decided it was too far and too late in the day to try to get to the goats then; maybe we'd try it the next day, and maybe, too, we would try to talk Whispering Charlie, one of the men, into coming to help us. Charlie was always quite willing to help us with anything we wanted.

We decided we had better start for home, or camp. We were above all of the heavy timber and around the head of Hemlock Canyon. So, we decided to go until we hit the horse trail where we had come through the canyon a couple of days before when coming to this camp.

On the way, we ran into a couple more coveys of grouse, and shot a few more and by now we had so many grouse we were having a hard time carrying them. We stopped and tied their legs together with some buckskin string that we had with us. Our knot tying was probably not very good, but it made it a lot easier to carry the grouse. I am sure, though, that when we got back to camp we had lost a few of our chickens. While walking on these steep sidehills, it got strenuous as we were slipping and falling as we stepped on the slick bear grass. And we were both starting to wonder if we were in the right canyon when we finally found the horse trail — it was a lot farther than we thought. We would have been better off going back the way we had come.

While walking down the horse trail toward camp, we tried every way to carry our game. We would put them on one shoulder, then change to the other. We even hung them around our necks but that didn't work very well either. And even this horse trail seemed like an awful long way after coming down it on horseback two days earlier; we were two tired little boys when we finally got back to camp.

After getting all the praises from the rest of the Indians for what we had brought in, I think we both felt like big heroes. Bill's mother had cooked us each a big fish by putting them on a stick about two and a half feet long, which was poked through the fish the full length. Then the sharpened stick was stuck in the ground near enough to the fire to cook all day. A piece of goat tallow was placed over the fish to drip onto it while it cooked and, oh, was it ever good!

Not much food was brought on these trips. Fish and bread were all that was really needed, and many times on these trips all we had for a meal was meat or fish, and bread. Sometimes we had huckleberries, sometimes plain, sometimes with a little sugar on them. The utensils brought along consisted of one or two gallon cans, one pot for cooking, one big frypan, a little tin dish, a spoon, and sometimes a tin cup for each person, plus a big spoon and several butcher knives.

Flour, salt, and baking powder was always brought along to make more bread. It was mixed right in the frypan into a very heavy dough shaped like a big patty about two to two and one half inches thick. It was baked in the same fry pan. The campfire coals were heaped up in a pile and then parted into two piles with a sort of trench between them. The pan with the dough in it was put into the trench on the coals at about a 45 degree angle. The bread was turned real often with a long forked stick, and turned over once in a while.

The heat came from both the piles of coals. The bread had to be watched continually while it was cooking in this long handled fry pan. Once in a while we would have fry bread, which was dough fried in deep fat from the animals that had been killed. We sometimes had pancakes with a little bit of sugar sprinkled on them. There was never any butter and the breads were eaten plain. It was always heavy and chewy, and would never be smashed down like the bread today.

Sometimes they brought along oatmeal, rice, potatoes, sugar, coffee, and beans, but there was never any cans or litter left at our camp site because they never brought any canned goods along.

Whispering Charlie Helps Us

After we told the others what we had done this day, and about all the mountain goats we had seen, and about the little ones cutting all their capers, we began to ask Whispering Charlie if he would go and help us catch some of the little ones the next day. With a little bit of coaxing he agreed to go with us.

Early the next morning we started out for the high peak. We followed the horse trail nearly to the divide and then angled off to the east and onto the top of the ridge rim. We hadn't gone too far along the divide until we could see a few of the goats right near the top of the peak, still a mile or more away. The old goat trail along the divide was well matted with their tracks from the day before.

When we got quite close to the peak we came to a very narrow place with rock cliffs on both sides of the ridge. Charlie agreed with us that this would be the place to do our catching. He showed us where we should hide, me on one side of the goat trail and Bill on the opposite side, a little further up as we each had to have a rock to hide behind.

Now, Charlie had the hard part. We could only see about a third as many goats as we had seen the day before and Charlie said they would all be there some place, and he told us he would be the chaser. He told us it would take him a while to get behind them. He went into the edge of some trees, going below some ledges to keep out of sight of the goats. It seemed like he was gone forever before finally we saw four or five goats appear on the very top of the peak, and here they came.

None of the little ones were playing this time; they were close by their mama's sides. Bill and I ducked behind our rocks. I don't know about Bill, but my heart started to really pump! I was only about three feet to one side of their trail and several went by me when I saw two babies on my side of their momma.

This was my chance! As they came by, I jumped for the first one but my hands landed on the second. He exploded, just like a firecracker, right out of my hands. Bill took after the other one and though he was a pretty good runner, he wasn't gaining a bit. It was incredibly exciting as several of them came quite close to us and stopped to look at us before taking off again.

Then a few of them stopped again after getting by us, taking another look. I suppose we were the first two-legged creatures they had ever seen.

We finally saw Whispering Charlie coming. When he got close, we could see that he had a big smile on his face. He wanted to know where we had our goats tied up. I think he knew all along that we were not going to catch any of those babies.

It was a good thing, too, that we didn't catch one, as they probably would have died. But we were still young enough to have big dreams and we hadn't thought about how we were going to care for one of them. It was an episode that provided a lot of fun and good memories. And Charlie had to have been a pretty good guy to take his time and hard effort to go along with a couple of little boys with big plans.

Work as Well as Play

On these pack trips we prospected, fished and hunted, only killing enough game to keep the camp supplied with meat. We picked nuts and dug roots that were used for medicine, including one that was called Haask. It only grew in a few places in high elevation, just under the surface of the ground.

I enjoyed helping the women dig it, and then clean and dry it. When they got back home, they would trade it to other Indians, including other tribes. It was valued just like money and a small amount was worth a lot in a trade.

This root varied in size from one-fourth to three-fourths of an inch in diameter and up to about fourteen inches long. It had lots of fine hair roots that grew all around the outside of the main root. This hair was scraped off and the root washed free of dirt; then it was laid in a spot to dry. We usually had two or three pack loads to take out.

Nuts were also an important food. We called them pinion pine nuts, but later when I looked them up in a book, they were called Limber Pine nuts. They are a five-needle pine, and grow along the timberline at about 6,000 to 8,000 elevation.

In the days that I went on the trips with the Indians, these trees were loaded with cones. The small trees would be bent over with the weight of the cones and it took no time at all to pick two or three packhorse loads.

The cones have quite a large seed in them, in comparison with other pine seeds. They are delicious and after they were dried, I am sure they were very high in food value. The Indians would take these home and dole them out to the children and grown-ups, just like we would today with candy.

In the early Thirties, this seed started to disappear, with fewer being found on the trees each year. In the last 40 years or so, I haven't been able to find enough of these cones to get a handful of seeds. This year, my wife, Adelle, and I saw about three cones up by Mollman Lakes.

When it was time to go home, we would kill and dry a good supply of meat to take home, depending on how many packhorses we had. Usually, that would include three or four deer and elk. Eneas Conko and Philip Pierre were known as the Tribe's two best hunters and mountain men of that time and they made sure that every horse was fully loaded for the return trip.

I may have mentioned before that Bill and I were expected to help tend the horses and gather wood for camp, but our main job was to supply the camp with fish and grouse. Bill's mother always enjoyed going fishing with us and we liked to have her come along, as she was the perfect hook baiter! She tied the meat on our hooks with horse hair from the horse's tails. I can still see her proud, pleasant smile when we pulled in a big trout, or when we came into camp with a bunch of grouse. We were taught that if we didn't have any game we should bring in an armload of wood for the fire, which we always did and I still do today.

I wish I could have had a video camera at that time, but then I hardly knew what a camera was and no one thought of taking pictures back then. Some of the sights are still vivid in my mind, and it leaves me sort of sad to think that a lot of other people didn't get to see all that I did.

My older brothers and sisters got to see a lot of activities here in the valley, such as watching Indians on horseback going to the mountains to pick huckleberries, or bunches of Indian women digging camas and slocum, but I was the only one who shared the experiences in the mountains with them.

Nearly everyone traveled in buggies and on horseback then, and many Indian women rode horseback as well as the men did. We would see very large women fitting snug in their saddles, riding proudly with their blankets around their legs and their brightly colored shawls on, and their silk scarves on their heads. It was common to see old ladies carrying big loads of limbs gathered from the woods for fuel on their backs, and to see women working their hides. The scenes still burn brightly in my memory.

My First Elk

I was ten years old when I killed my first elk. It was early September in 1925. I went with Eneas Conko, his son, Bill, and Peter Paul Pierre, a nephew who was a couple of years older than Bill and I. We had come over Eagle Pass in the Missions and were camped at Summit Lake. At the time there was no trail down McDonald Canyon. Late in the afternoon, Eneas asked me if I wanted to go with him for a little hunt and I quickly jumped at the chance.

We went along the bottom of the steep ridge on horseback. There was very little downed timber in the canyon at that time, so it was possible to ride a horse almost anywhere in the area. We were coming along a little bench above Frog Lakes when we heard a bull elk bugle by the far lake. We rode to the lower end of the lake, tied our horses up and then started along the edge of the lake on foot.

I was thrilled when the bull bugled again. What a sight! It was a huge bull and had swam out to a big flat rock that was submerged under the water, so that it stood belly deep in the lake. Eneas quickly took my little .22 caliber single-shot out of my hands and handed me his long, octagon barreled 30-30 caliber rifle. He told me, "This is your elk to kill."

Well, I was unable to hold the gun up steady, so he told me to crawl to a big spruce log that was just ahead of us. He whispered, "Right behind the shoulders." I felt nervous and shaky, and when I finally got the sights where I thought they should be, I pulled the trigger. I guess it was by luck that that was where I hit him. The big bull jumped up in the air and came down again, and then went up and down a couple more times before falling over in the water. Eneas gave me a pat on the back and said, "You shootum good." I sure thought I was a big Indian hunter and I suppose I sure strutted after that. I do know I was thrilled.

The elk was lying about thirty or forty yards out in the lake and the next step was to get it out of the water. We went back and got the horses. Eneas tried to ride his horse out to the elk, but the water was too deep, so we went around the point of the lake and tried from that side. This time Eneas managed to get close enough to throw a long rope out and lasso the bull's antlers, and pull the carcass to shore.

It was common practice then for the Indians to move their camp to the kill if there was a lot of meat, and that is what we did. After we set up camp again, we built racks to dry the meat on and built fires under the racks. We skinned the upper side of the elk and cut the meat off of the bones in chunks. Then we would take a good-sized chunk of meat and cut around and around the chunk until it was a long slab; then we would hang it on a rack to dry. After the meat was removed from the upper side of the carcass, it was turned over onto the bones that were already stripped. We then skinned, cut up and dried the remaining half of the elk.

It was a beautiful night. The moonlight shone down on our little group, on the pretty lake and the towering peaks. The four of us worked all night long cutting meat and gathering wood to keep the fire going. We three boys took turns gathering the wood, which was quite a job, because it had to be free of pitch or the meat would taste. We dried the meat only enough so it would not spoil before we got it home. When we got it home it would have to be re-dried until all the moisture was gone from it.

Eneas Conko,
whom Bud Cheff considers "his
teacher."

When we finished, we laid down for a couple of hours sleep while the sun was rising in the morning sky. This was when I first learned that a hunter's work doesn't start until after he kills his game. On this morning I carved 1925 into the bark of a standing tree; I don't know if it is still there or not. Then we packed up and went home.

Around Christmas-time the following winter, Eneas gave me that old 30-30 caliber gun, as he had gotten himself a new 30-30 caliber half-octagon barrel gun. How proud I was to get that well-used gun. I used it as a single-shot as it didn't eject the shells right and I used that old gun all of my life. It had killed a lot of game before I got it, and a lot since.

How Lost Moccasin Lake Got Its Name
The small lake I am talking about, Lost Moccasin Lake, lies directly east of McDonald Lake but on the east side of the mountain just below where a big square slab of rock had slipped out of the side of the mountain.

One time we were camped in Crazy Horse Canyon, but I don't remember if it was the same year that we chased the goats or if it was the next year. But Bill and I were out exploring again. His dad had told us about this lake so we decided to go up there. After playing and skipping a few rocks on the water, we decided to follow the little stream on our way back.

We hadn't gone too far when we came to a place where a little logjam had blocked the stream and during high water had caused a flat, good-sized bed of sandy silt. We went out onto it but as soon as we got there, we noticed a lot of bear tracks.

Bud Cheff holds a cherished gift, the 30-30 rifle given him by Eneas Conko. Cheff has used the gun ever since Conko gave it to him in 1925.

Several of them were little cub tracks and Bill said, "I'll show you how to make some of those bear tracks." He took one of his moccasins off and laid it down some place and was making bear tracks with his bare foot when we heard some grumbling voices, the first time I heard this kind of sound, but one I've heard many times since. We looked up at the same time to see five little bundles of gray-blue fur, and it sounded like they were jabbering to each other and to their two momma grizzlies.

We wasted no time and, grabbing our .22 rifles, took off. Neither Bill nor I thought of his moccasin until we had run quite a distance, but there was no going back so we proceeded to go on to camp. After we told our story, Bill's mom said maybe we had better not play in the little bear's playground.

However, once again we approached Whispering Charlie Finley, asking him to go back with us in the morning to retrieve Bill's moccasin. He agreed. When we got back up there, however, we saw no sign of grizzlies but Bill's moccasin had been mauled around some. Maybe the little bears had tried to put it on, to try to make some moccasin tracks like Bill had tried to make cub bear tracks. Whatever, the little lake that we were at had no name, so I started to call it Lost Moccasin Lake.

Some of the people who were in that group were Whispering Charlie, Philip

Pierre, Mary Katherine Mollman, Mrs. Peter Paul, Frank Ashley, Antoine Finley, Baptiste Nickolas, Peter Paul Pierre, his mother, Mrs. Pierre, Baptiste Hewankorn, Cecille Hewankorn, Louie Camille, Isadore Sorrelle, and of course, Eneas Conko, the leader, and his wife Sofia, and sons Leo and Bill. Several times we met up with Pierre Adam's party, and camped together for a time.

On Pack Trips With The Full Bloods In My Young Life

Nowadays I can look back and think how I would of liked to have some pictures or colored movies of the groups of all full blood Indians along the trails and in the beautiful meadows and hillsides covered with all different colors of beautiful flowers, and also of the camps and what went on. The group of Indians that I went with were all a group of good-natured, jolly people always doing a lot of kidding and laughing.

On most of the trips it seemed as there were more women than there were men. The women were needed to take care of the meat after it was killed, and to dig the roots. It seemed that the Indian women were all good riders, and could handle their horses just as well as the men.

The Indians all liked bright colors. The women always had brightly colored silk scarves or bandannas for their head covering. They rode sitting on a blanket folded in a manner on their saddles so part of the blanket could be folded over their legs, which protected their legs from heat and cold and also from being scratched while going through the brush. It also helped a lot to keep them from getting saddle sore from their legs rubbing on the saddles.

They were also vain about having any part of their bare legs showing, so they wore long skirts that came down nearly to their ankles. Some of the men also rode in a blanket if they were going a long distance, as did the kids. Nearly all of the men wore high-crowned, stiff-brimmed hats with brightly colored, silk neckerchiefs. Many of their shirts and blouses were of bright colors and all were hand sewn, made by the women. Both men and women wore moccasins and they sometimes had low-cut rubbers to slip over the moccasins in wet weather. At the time I started going with them, the men were all starting to wear pants instead of leggings and breechcloths.

What a thrill it was for me to be able to be among all these joyful, happy Indians on these pack trips. I was always treated royally, especially by my friend Bill's mother, Sofia Conko. She treated me just as if I were her own. What a dear lady! Bill's dad, Eneas, was nearly always in the lead of the group. He always sat so erect on one of his best horses with his big hat bobbing back and forth as he lead the procession up the mountains. My friend, Bill, his mother and I were usually in the back end; I suspect she wanted to keep an eye on us.

We each had a little .22 caliber single-shot rifle. We thought we were big and we did shoot a lot of grouse and caught a lot of fish. We felt that this was our duty, along with gathering wood. We also helped some with the gathering of roots and washing them.

A Trip To The South Fork Of The Flathead

In 1925, we were going into the South Fork of the Flathead and had gotten to a big beautiful meadow, but at that age I didn't know one place from another so I don't know what it was called. The Indians had only killed enough game to survive on and this meadow had a lot of good high grass for the horses to feed on so we planned to get a good rest before going on. Every Indian was busy doing something, repairing saddles, and other chores when a rider appeared at a distance.

We boys were escorted into the main tepee and everyone went inside except two or three of the men. Bill and I peeked out and saw a stocky built man with a full mustache. He wore a low crown hat with a stiff brim, and was riding a big, beautiful white horse. To me he had the appearance of a Mounted Police, although at the time I had never seen one.

Conko and all of the other Indians suddenly forgot how to talk English. They were answering him in Indian and making all kinds of sign language even though Eneas Conko and Louie Camille could both speak English quite well. Bill and I were listening the best we could, but the women were keeping us inside the tepee for fear that we might say something that we shouldn't. The Indians were told by this man that they could not kill any game during the summer months.

Early the next morning, the camp was torn down and loaded onto the packhorses and the party proceeded in a northerly direction to Basin Creek, I think, then onward just south of Big Prairie Ranger Station, and finally on to Salmon Forks. In later years I got to hear about all these different places. I heard about the Danaher Meadows and about old Henry Morgan, the game warden who had patrolled that area in the early days. The Indians were quite careful about how much game was killed until they were ready to leave for home. Then they would kill enough game to be able to have a full load on all the horses after the meat was dried.

About twenty some years later a man with a big thick mustache came to my base camp at Holland Lake, in the early 1940's. He asked a few questions about our hunt. I recognized him as the same man who had been at that camp in the South Fork when I was a boy; I asked him if he used to ride a big white horse.

"Oh, yes," he said. "One of the best horses that ever walked on a mountain trail." I said, "Do you remember checking on a bunch of Indians at the Danaher?" "Yes," he said. I told him I was in one of those tepees peeking out at him. It was Harry Morgan, the game warden that had been around for many years.

The Price of Skipping School

During the times that we had to walk to the main road, which was four and one half miles from our house, we were often very tired by the time we got to school. Consequently, we would fall asleep upon going into the warm rooms and because of getting up so early in the morning.

And I would be ashamed when I didn't have my assignments ready and didn't want to go to school, so every chance I got I would still skip, not realizing that made it that much harder for me. This usually meant another year of not passing my grade.

The Hazards of Plowing

Two different years when plowing time came, Dad put me on the plow with four horses, using a two-bottom disc plow with a seat on it. Now the field was rocky with a lot of real big, solid rocks and I would watch close for the big rocks that showed at ground surface so I could jump off of the plow when we were about to hit one of them. After we had passed the rock, I would get back on the seat, but real often I would hit some that were not visible.

Many, many times I was bucked off of that old plow, and part or most of the time I landed on some of the metal or wheels. Several times I was thrown clear up into the horses heels. I would cry a while and then drive the horses while walking behind the plow. When I would get tired of walking and the hurt would slack off, I would get back on, sometimes going quite a long time, while other times I would only go a short distance when that old plow would hit another rock, and jump up into the air, and over the rock, and here I would go again! I had black and blue marks all over me.

By evening and quitting time I was so nervous from being thrown off so many times, I was always relieved when I saw that white flag waving at the house. That meant it was time to unhitch the horses and come in.

Hauling Hay

When I was quite small I went with Charley Brush, who worked for us, to get a load of hay for Dad. We went with a team and sled out to the Valley and just as we got there, a hard snowstorm hit us, so Charley took me to Thurkol's house, about one quarter mile west of Highway 93 where he left me because it was so cold.

Charley went on to Ninepipes and got the hay, and then picked me up on the way back. He dug a deep hole in the hay and put me down in there; it was nice and cozy and that was the first of many times of burrowing down into the hay to keep warm.

After I got older, my brother Rex and I fell to the job quite often of hauling hay. Some years we ran short of hay so Dad had to buy more and he sent us after it. We sometimes went with two teams and it was fine using the bobsleds as they went along so smoothly, but some times the roads would get muddy and freeze real hard so we would have to use the wagons. Sometimes, too, the road would be so rough that when you hit the frozen ruts and holes it would almost jar your pants off!

We would take along ropes and a green pole and after we got the hay all loaded onto the wagons one of us would hold that green pole up at an angle while the other one tied the end of the pole down to the front of the hay rack. Then we would pull that pole down over the top and the middle of the load of hay to bind it down tight. We tied the back end of the pole down to the bottom of the back of the hay rack to keep that loose hay from bouncing off the wagon.

It was a special art to put the hay onto the wagon, get a big load and not lose it as we went over the rough roads. Regardless of how good a load was put on, however, the roads were so rough that we would lose our load and have to pitch that hay back on and retie it down. A few times we had to re-load two or three times before getting home.

Sometimes it would be real late in the evening before we got home, and both us and the horses would be terribly tired. I remember one time the road was so bad that the neck yokes got to swinging and slammed back and forth against the horses' shoulders and neck, and the collars would wear the hide right off the top of the horses' necks. We quickly learned, when the weather was bad, to dig down and cover ourselves with hay. Sometimes just our arms and faces were out, to drive the horses.

Haying

During haying time in mid-summer, we used two horse-drawn mowing machines as soon as the hay was dry enough. A team with a dump rake was put into the field to rake up the hay. There were two foot levers on the rake and when the rake got full we stepped on a lever that tripped the rake and it would come up and dump the hay out. We always dumped at the end of each windrow that was being made as we went around the fields.

After the field was all raked up we would bunch it and did this by straddling each windrow with a dump rake pulled by a horse on each side. When the rake was full we dumped it. Then we had to shock it and most of the time the shocking was done in the evening after the horses were put away and supper was over.

All of those in the family who were able to handle a pitchfork went out to the field. Each bunch of hay that had been bunched that day was made into a nice, round mound of hay and the hay was placed on the top of the shock in such a way that it would shed the water if it should rain.

While we were mowing the hay, the sickles had to be sharpened at least twice a day. This was Dad's job and he sharpened them on an old grinding stone that was turned by one of the kids using a crank on one side, though sometimes it was turned by foot peddles. I once thought that maybe Dad was shirking as he would be gone from the fields for long periods of time and the stone was under the shade of a big tree. Well, one day Dad said, "It's time that you start learning how to sharpen the sickles." It didn't take me very long to find out how much Dad had been shirking under that shade tree as the sweat poured off of me. I would have rather been in any part of the field than sharpening the sickles!

My older sister, Bernida, did quite a lot of the hay raking, but she always wanted the wildest team that we had. It didn't take her long to rake up a field because she went around on a high trot. If Dad hadn't got after her, I think she would have galloped around.

Putting Up The Hay

While haying we had a lot of hard work, some fun, and at least one fight between Rex and me. I don't remember what our problem was, but it probably was because he laughed at me for losing part of my load of hay, as I did once in a while. He was a better loader than me, but I didn't want him to think he was. I stopped my team a little way from his and went over and socked him a good one, and then turned and ran.

One of Rex's driving reins was a lot longer than the other and had a metal snap on the end, and he was quite good at popping his reins. He flipped that rein out there at me. When it got out there, just over my head, he gave it a snap, a good one, and put me flat down. I am still carrying a knot on my head.

We were putting up hay above the canal at a place now called the Beaverhead place and all of our family was there working in the field. We had three hay boats bringing the hay to the stack, and my mother was driving our wildest team on one of the hay boats. This team liked to run away when coming in with a big load of hay and something scared the team; they took off running away with Mom doing her best to hold them and keep them under control. They ran into one of the guy-lines and anchors that held the stacker up and when the anchor got pulled up, the whole stacker fell over. Luckily no one was hurt, but when the stacker went over it scared the team that much more.

When the horses ran into the anchor, the hay boat was flipped up in the air and that tipped the load of hay right on top of my mother. Talk about a wild family! Big kids, little kids, everybody ran to the overturned load of hay and started to dig her out. We finally found her on the bottom of the hay pile and, fortunately, she was not hurt bad. But I can tell you there was an excited bunch of kids when they saw their mother getting buried!

After the haying was done, the grain harvest came next. We cut the grain with four horses on the binder. Dad usually drove that, and Rex and I did the shocking of the bundles. Rex would take one side and one end of each field, and I would take the other side and end. We worked like beavers putting up the shocks, running from one windrow to the other, but the binder would eventually get ahead of us and then it would get discouraging.

Ice and Water on the River

My mother, in her later years, told us stories until late in the night of happenings in this valley during her and Dad's younger life. One stands out in my mind because it was about the Flathead River, which is a fast-flowing, treacherous stream. She said that they and several other couples, most of them Ronan business people, chipped in and rented a sharp-shod (which meant they were shod to stand on ice) four-horse team and bobsled from one of the three local livery stables equipped with a teamster. She couldn't remember the teamster's name, but he was a daredevil bucking horse rider.

I said to her, "That sounds just like Hector McCloud." I knew Hector well as a boy because I also wanted to be a cowboy. She said, "Yes, that was him but before he got his arm shot off." When I knew Hector, his arm was gone, but he was still riding bucking horses. He was a good horse teamster, and also a good square dance caller.

Anyway, the group of people all loaded into the bobsled with the prancing team of four horses on the main street of Ronan. Their minds were all set for a dance and their destination a little outpost called Sloan's located just on the other side of the Flathead River about halfway between Ronan and Hot Springs, a distance of about twelve or fourteen miles. In those days they did not plow the snow off of the roads as they liked to have the hard-packed snow on them to make it better for sledding.

This was either 1910 or 1911 and they had a good heavy snowpack and the group had a great time singing songs and telling stories all the way. At a hill just before going into the river bottom, the road was very steep for about a half mile and by the time the horses got to the bottom of the hill they were running at full speed, a thrilling ride for all of the young couples. There were no dams on the river upstream at this time, so the water fluctuated very little and when they reached the river it was frozen over. There was no bridge at that time, but Sloan had a little ferry that only ran in the summer months.

Away they went on the ice, across the river at Sloan's. The horses were unhooked and fed and the group had a great time dancing and kicking their heels up in the square dances.

When daylight came and it was time to go home, it was starting to rain. They hooked up the team and everyone hurried into the sled and they started for Ronan and home. As they went from Sloan's to the river, about a quarter of a mile, it was raining very heavy upstream and on the lake, so when they got to the river there was another river on top of the ice, rushing downstream.

Part of the group didn't want to try to cross, but Hector, the daredevil, said, "I brought you here and I will bring you back."

The horses didn't want to go into the water and onto the slick ice, but thank goodness they were sharp shod — Hector put the whip to the horses and finally got them down on the ice and water. The women all started praying and so did some of the men. My mother said she had seen several of the men drinking heavily, but they all sobered up quickly as they crossed the river, with some of the water coming almost into the sled. What a relief they experienced when they got to the other shore and they all swore they would never try that again. That same afternoon the ice came up and all went out.

My Brother Louie Almost Drowned

One day while I was shocking a field above the feeder canal, I was quite a distance above the canal when just by luck I noticed my little brother, Louie, who was about two years old, come up onto the canal bank toward the place where we had a narrow foot bridge made of two logs side by side, with a plank walkway.

He disappeared from sight so I ran as fast as I could to the spot. When I got there, he was nowhere in sight. The canal was plumb full of swift water, but I noticed a few bubbles coming up from under a log raft that we had tied to the foot bridge. As soon as I saw the bubbles coming up, I dove under the raft. I was far from being a champion swimmer or diver, but I found him under the raft, with his clothes caught onto a piece of barbed wire. I pulled him free from the wire and took him to the top of the canal. Then I laid him down with his head downhill and a lot of water ran out of his mouth and nose.

I didn't know anything then about artificial respiration, but I had heard about it, so I started to pump on him while I was also calling for help. But after I had pumped on him for a while, he gave a few gasps for air and it was not long until he came to.

I realized that if I had not seen him come up to the canal, we probably would not have found him for long time. I doubt that anyone would have thought to look under that raft for him.

Incidentally, the old ditch was a wonderful place to fish. The fish were all native cutthroat, and there were lots of big ones. After the new ditch was built, it took a year or so before the fishing was good again, and that is when I first saw an eastern brook trout. I liked to catch them as I thought they were so pretty but it didn't take too many years until that was all we could catch. The native fish were gone and it's too bad that someone had to bring the brook trout into these waters.

Dam At McDonald Lake

About 1911, the dam at McDonald Lake was built and the ditch following along the foot of the mountains was put in as far as Pablo Reservoir. At that time it was just a small ditch, about one-third as large as it is today. In about 1922 or 1923, the Reclamation started a reconstruction and put up a steam shovel at Post Creek and started to rebuild the feeder canal.

This was an old antique shovel that was run by steam and had rope controls. A man by the name of Mr. King was the operator and a man by the name of Hunter was the fireman on this big rig. It sat on the upper side of the ditch and went backwards as it dug.

A crew of men went ahead and cleared the trees and logs out of the way and they cut wood at the same time, leaving the wood in piles to feed the steam shovel when it came along. After the canal was finished they had to come back and put all new head gates at every stream. When the canal was finished, the old steam shovel was abandoned at the Pablo Reservoir and I think it could still be resting there.

Getting Our First Sheep. Times Were Tough

In those days it was hard to make ends meet. I don't remember the year my Grandmother Caron died, but my mother got about a thousand dollars from the estate, not a lot of money but at that time it meant a lot. She put it in the bank and soon after the bank went broke, so she lost it all.

My folks milked a few cows and we had a small herd of beef cattle and a few horses. In about 1924, my father was looking for a way to make a better living. Dad learned that the Lane Sheep Company, from the east side of the mountains, had sheep to put out on shares; so, Dad ordered a bunch, about 500 head of young ewes that had never lambed before. These sheep came into the Ronan stockyard by railroad in the spring when the grass was nice and green. All of the kids in our family who were big enough to help went out early at daybreak to drive the sheep home as there was no such thing as trucks or trailers. Not one person in the family, not even Dad, knew anything about sheep. But we started to learn.

We didn't even have a sheep dog and when we opened the gate to the pens, the sheep all wormed out of there like a bunch of bees out of a hive. They were hungry from their long ride and they started running for the first field they saw. We finally got them out of the farmer's field and onto the road and from there all the way home we had kids on both sides of the road trying to keep them out of the fields. With Dad and someone else driving them the first day, we only got half-way home, about four miles, by nightfall. Everyone was tired, and I don't think any of us wanted to be in the sheep business anymore.

Herding Sheep

The next day we managed to get them home — and now it was time for us to learn to be sheepherders. As yet, we didn't have any fences designed to hold sheep, so they had to be herded. And we finally got a sheep dog — Dad visited several sheep ranches to get as much information about sheep as he could and he learned that a good dog was one of the main helpers.

My brother Rex and I started herding together at first. As we had to herd in the timber and mountains, it was quite a job to keep from losing some — and to keep the bears and coyotes from getting them. It was a common thing to have to shoot bear and coyotes in order to protect the sheep from them.

It didn't take long to find out that sheep are not as dumb as we first thought they were. Each evening we brought them home and when evening came we would holler, "Home, home." After a few times of this the sheep would all bunch up and would start off the mountain just like soldiers.

Rex was older than me and was put to other kinds of work, so I herded by myself. For some time I had always carried a 30-30 long barreled octagon barrel rifle. One day two men came by where I was sitting on a log watching my sheep and asked where my Dad was. I said he was home. "You are all alone with that big gun, yes?" They told several people after they got to town that they had seen a kid herding sheep up in the woods with a gun bigger than he was; a little later it turned out that I got to be good friends with the sons of one of these men, the Leighton boys.

The Big Dark Grizzly

During the late Twenties and early Thirties, before I was married, my folks were still raising a lot of sheep. One spring morning when my father went to turn the sheep out of a little pasture where he kept them at night, he found that a bear had come in and killed four or five sheep.

My brother Rex and I started tracking the bear southeast across the canal and straight up the big mountain on the south side of Mollman Canyon.(This was before anyone lived up along the mountain). The bear knew we were following him and while we got to see him several times, we never got a shot at him.

We followed him all day up to the top of that mountain where the snow got so deep we finally played out and had to turn back. That old bear must have turned and followed us right back down, because even though Dad penned the sheep in a smaller pen closer to our house, the bear came back that evening and got into the pen. The sheep couldn't get away from him and he must have hit them left and right; he killed about twenty-five sheep.

The next night we moved the sheep about a half mile from our house to the sheep shed, thinking the bear would not be able to get into the building. This shed had been a big horse barn for the logging camp's skidding horses and we had extended the roof on down and out so it was three feet from the ground, and covered the roof with cedar shakes.

Dad fixed a bed up on top of the platform where we sacked the wool and slept there for a couple of nights so he could watch over the sheep. Then he asked me to stand watch for a night. I agreed and went to bed on the wool sacking platform. The next morning when I woke up and opened the shed door to let the sheep out, I discovered three sheep lying there dead. I looked around and found that the big bear had climbed up onto the roof about fifteen feet from where I was sleeping, tore a bunch of shingles off the roof, and either jumped or let himself down about seven or eight feet to the ground inside the shed.

He killed four sheep and took one back with him through the hole in the roof. I still don't understand how he managed to get out through that hole with the sheep, but he did it and I must have been sleeping awful sound, because he didn't even wake me up!

I hurried back to the house to tell dad, who by then was getting pretty frustrated, what had happened. We went to the shed and got one of our two old bear traps and some tools, and then found where the big fellow had taken the sheep to the edge of

Young Bud Cheff (at right) and his father, Ovila, with a sheep-killing grizzly that went over 800 pounds.

what we called the swamp to have his feast. He had eaten the biggest part of it.

We cut a bunch of logs from six to eight inches in diameter and about six or seven feet long, from which we built a V-shaped pen by stacking the logs on top of each other, securing them with spikes and wire. The top of the structure was also covered with logs, while a doorway was left open at the front. When we finished, we put the rest of the sheep carcass inside the far end of the pen. Then we had to put screw clamps on the trap's springs and screw them down to open the trap in order to set it. We laid the trap at the foot of the open doorway, and fastened its chain to a wooden toggle made from a green log about six inches in diameter and seven feet long. This is done so that when a bear is caught it can drag the toggle with it; if the trap is fastened to something solid, a big bear will often break the trap or get out.

After fastening the trap to the toggle, we cut and sharpened both ends of fifteen little pegs about fourteen inches long and drove them halfway into the ground, all around the trap. We then covered the trap with small pieces of cedar boughs to make it look like a perfect place to step — bear will avoid the sharp pegs, stepping on the pad first with a front foot to get to the bait inside the V-pen.

Early the next morning, my dad went to check the trap, which was about a half mile from the house. He soon returned to tell me the bear was gone with the trap. I got my old 30-30 caliber rifle and we went back and started to follow the marks where the toggle had been dragged. We had only gone a short distance when that old grizzly let out a beller, and stood up facing us with the trap on a front foot. My father shot him between the eyes with his 6mm navy rifle, and the bear went right down.

I started to take the trap off of his foot, but my father said to wait, we'd go home and get the team of horses to pull the bear out, as he was so heavy that both of us together couldn't move him.

We had caught up with the bear just past the end of a narrow opening that we had cleared so the sheep could get in to water at a big spring there. We went back to the barn and hooked the team to the wagon, and for some reason I laid my gun in the wagon box instead of leaving it in the barn, were Dad left his. My mother came out with two of my little brothers, one whom was just starting to walk and the other who was only a little bigger, and said she would like to go along.

While we were getting the wagon as close as we could to the area where the bear was, Dad told Mom that if she went ahead of us, following the sheep trail on past the end of the clearing a ways, she would come to the bear. So she took off with the two little boys, while Dad and I unhitched the team from the wagon, taking the doubletree and a chain to use to drag the bear.

We were just leaving with the team when a bear started to beller and my mother started to holler. I thought of my gun in the wagon and rushed back to get it and then ran into the woods after Mom. As Mom had gotten close to the bear with the boys, it had jumped up and started after her, dragging the toggle with it. When I came in sight of them, Mom was trying to get back to us, carrying one kid in her arms and half dragging the other one, and I couldn't shoot because they were in the line of fire. The bear stood up as I got past her and I shot him under the chin.

When it was all over, everyone was shaking. I don't care how big or tough anyone thinks he is, when those old bears start to beller, I think most anyone's hair would raise on end.

I don't remember for certain what the bear's weight was when we weighed it, but it seems to me that it was eight hundred and some pounds. When Dad shot the bear, he hit him just a little off center and the bullet followed around the contour of the skull without penetrating it, just knocking him out.

We had that skull for a long time and it always reminded me that this was when I learned to never shoot a grizzly in the head because the grizzly's skull is tapered from any direction that a man would shoot from, and the bullet would glance off instead of penetrating and killing him.

Wood Hauling

During the 1920's and 1930's nearly all the farmers and people who lived out in the valley burned wood for heat and for cooking. Most of them got their wood in during the winter months and most of the time they would get together about six or seven teams and sleds and would come out to our area in a group. They would help each other cut the trees and logs with crosscut saws, then roll their logs up on skids and onto their sleds.

It was a lot easier to haul on sleds than it was on wagons. In those days, most of the sleds had logging bunks that could be put on the sleds while the wagons had to be special made for hauling logs.

No one had a chain binder such as you see nowadays. The logs had to be fastened down by pulling a chain around at each end of the logs. Each log chain had a rounded hook and the loose end was put through the hook and the chain tightened around the logs by using what we called a fit hook. This was a flat hook with a handle from ten inches to two feet long that fit onto a chain link. The chains were tightened up by prying up one link at a time with the fit hook.

When the load was secure the fit hook fit against the rounded hook and was left there. When the load was released, the fit hooks were knocked loose from the chain by hitting them up and off with a hammer.

Sometimes it was so cold, especially after working all day in the snow, getting wet and sweating, that the farmers would hook their lines on the load and walk behind the sleds on their way home so they could beat their arms and keep warm.

Packing on Fires

During fire season I was able to make a little extra money by fighting forest fires. When I was only 14 years old the Indian Department hired me to pack for their fires.

We always had extra horses around and from then on, each time a big fire started, they hired me to pack. At that time I am quite sure that fire fighters got thirty-five cents an hour and they paid me $1.00 a day for each horse that I used.

My Runaway Horses, Ted and Betty

When I was about fourteen or fifteen years old I was raking hay one hot summer day with a team of horses named Ted and Betty, using a dump rake. I had just finished raking a patch of hay uphill on the upper part of the Mollman land and I became thirsty so I stopped my team of horses near this nice clear stream of water that came across just above the upper part of this field.

This was a good gentle team that always stood well after being stopped. I got off of the rake to get a drink of that good, clear, cold water that came right out of the mountains about fifty feet from the team and rake. I went to the stream and laid down at the side of the water and got my drink. But because of the noise of the fast-flowing stream, I did not hear my team of horses start out with the hay rake toward home.

I suppose that old team of horses knew they had finished that hay field and that it was also quitting time, so they just started for home. When I got up they were already a short ways down the field. I hollered "Whoa" but instead of stopping while I was running after them, they started to trot. I hollered "Whoa" again, but this time they broke into a gallop. About that time the little catch lever that held the rake teeth up in the air off of the ground while not raking, came loose and let the rake teeth hit the ground. The momentum of the team running let the rake teeth strike the dirt and caused the teeth to fly right back up to hit the back of the rake, and flip right back down so the rake teeth were constantly flying up and down, scaring the horses that much more.

This field was on a fairly steep grade for about a half a mile and when the horses got almost to the lower part of the field the end of the wooden tongue came out of the neck yoke. The tongue rammed right into the ground, which caused the hay rake to flip way up into the air and come down right on top of the team of horses. Then the rake went end over end three or four times.

When the horses finally ran over a large rock pile, the double tree came loose from the rake and freed the team from the rake. Then they stopped.

This team was a sad pair. Ted finally recuperated, but poor Betty was never any good after that; her back looked like a camel's from then on. The rake was ruined too; there wasn't a straight piece of iron on it and it stayed on the rock pile for many years.

Big Grizzly Near Lost Moccasin Lake

In about 1930, I and two friends, Harley and Andy, Andy being part Indian, went on a hunt going horseback with packhorses. We crossed over the top of the mountains to the east side of the Mission Mountains into a very remote area where we put up our camp.

On this particular day, I went out hunting on horseback, riding one of the best horses that I ever owned. As I was riding along in a very small draw on the side of the mountain, using a good game trail, I heard a bull elk bugle somewhere ahead of me. I got off of my horse and tied him up, took my old single-shot 30-30 and started out for him.

I thought the bugle sound came from a little meadow directly ahead of me, so instead of going directly to the meadow I climbed up the side of the mountain a ways so I would be high enough to be able to look down over that meadow. I was about

Louie Camille (left)
and Eneas Conko
in Washington, D.C.

halfway there, standing still and trying to locate that bull elk and hoping that he would bugle again when, all of a sudden from out of the timber, I saw something that looked like a blue rock. It appeared to be slowly rolling across this meadow — it was one of the largest grizzlies that I have ever seen.

It was the same color as all the other rocks in this area. At this time there were no restrictions on grizzly and I decided I would shoot this big bear. So, I took a good aim and pulled the trigger. This big feller started to beller and jump up and down, grabbing himself. I reloaded my gun and about that time he took off running right toward my horse, which I had tied with a good strong rope and I felt that he could not break loose.

The bear and I had about the same distance to go to get to my horse, which I didn't want hurt, so I took off running as fast as I could to save him. I was surprised when I got there, the bear was not there yet. So I untied my horse as fast as I could and jumped onto him with my gun ready to shoot. I waited there for quite sometime, but the bear never did come so I rode over to where I had shot him. There was a small amount of blood, but those fat bear do not bleed much. I was not able to find this bear.

The other two boys came back with me to look for it but no luck. Sometime later I came back into this area with the Indians to get our winter meat. I had told Eneas Conko, my old hunting teacher and my friend Bill's dad, about the blue bear. He and I rode up to where I had shot him and I showed Eneas where my horse had been tied and where I was at when I shot and where the bear had been. Eneas went almost directly to where that bear had gone. He said that if the bear hadn't gone to my horse he must have gone toward a little ridge or bench.

We were able to smell the bear before we found him. It seemed as Eneas had a natural instinct to where that bear had gone. I had a deep feeling that I didn't want to ever hunt again after losing that big nice animal, but since losing that bear I've learned a lot about finding a wounded animal.

Conko With Nine Grizzlies

That same vicinity is where Eneas, while hunting for elk, rode horseback right into a bunch of nine grizzlies.

The bears were all around him before he realized that they were there and he said his horse just froze and stood still and started to tremble.

Eneas sat with his rifle in his lap, later saying there was nothing he could do except to start to pray. He said that every grizzly there was standing on his hind feet and looking at him. But they finally all got down and walked away slowly.

I have seen a lot of bear in my life, but Eneas, this old Indian, had seen so many more than I ever have. He told me that those bear were the most beautiful and most thrilling sight that he had ever seen, all of those grizzlies standing and looking at him at the same time. What a picture this would have made!

I have heard some biologists say that grizzlies are never seen in bunches. I don't know where they studied their bear, but I do know that since 1924 I've seen evidence and their tracks where there were several grizzlies in a bunch in the same area that we used to see them. And I hope that they continue to be there. I felt real good to see all of this bear sign recently, especially when people are saying that they are almost extinct.

But what has happened to the Montana grizzly? This is a question that has bothered many of our outdoorsmen.

I believe that a large number have died during hibernation. From the time I was a small boy I have spent all of my spare time in the wildest part of the wilderness areas, and have studied the grizzly for about seventy years. The first trips into these areas were with the Indians, as they hunted, fished, prospected, picked huckleberries, dug roots and picked pine nuts from the limber pine trees. On my first trip, we saw four big grizzlies sitting on their haunches on a sidehill, watching us as we unpacked.

Being a Hobo

One summer (about 1931) and about mid-July, Adelle's brother Jess (we all called him Junior) and I decided to try to be hoboes. We decided we would catch the freight train the next day at the Ronan Depot.

The evening before, Adelle had some of her girl friends visiting. Junior and I found some live bats in their attic and we thought we would have some fun. We caught the bats and took them down in the yard where the girls were; it was great fun to chase girls and to hear them scream.

The next day we went out to the railroad. We managed to catch our freight train and headed west. We got off at Paradise as we were on a local train that went to Missoula and we wanted to see Spokane over in Washington. That evening we chopped some wood for some people for a nice big sandwich and a piece of cake for each of us.

Now Paradise was a small, little town, but there were several tough looking hoboes around there and we didn't have any money, only a few pennies in our pockets. I discovered I was a very poor beggar, but Junior was good at it.

That evening we went into a place with several men sitting around and Junior gave them a hard luck story. One man gave us two tickets to get our breakfast with at the local cafe and I think Junior got a quarter and a dime from some other man. We went out feeling quite rich.

There was a field of freshly shocked hay across the road from town and we decided to spend the night there. We didn't trust some of those rough looking guys and thought we might need something for protection, so we each found a nice-sized round rock, which we each put in the toe end of an extra sock. If something should happen, we would have something to fight with. Sleeping in the hay without a blanket was something new for Junior, but I had done it before. We had a good night's sleep.

In the morning we re-shocked the farmers hay the best we could with our hands and then went to use our breakfast tickets, got a good breakfast, and with the dime bought two candy bars for our lunch.

Soon the whistle from the steam engine started to blow and we realized the train to Spokane that we wanted to catch was coming in to Paradise to stop and take on water for steam. A bunch of hoboes started jumping off the train — running for a beautiful garden a distance from the tracks. A lady came out of a nearby house, hollering and screaming, with a broom in her hand but as she tried to chase some out, others came in right behind her and pulled up everything they could get a hold of. I really felt bad for that poor lady — when the train left, her garden looked very sick.

We got onto a tanker or oil tank car with a walkway on the edges. It was a nice warm day and we sat on this walkway with our feet dangling down, enjoying the ride. However, it was sort of scary, at first, when the train went over the high trestles or rivers and through the tunnels.

We got to Spokane quite late as the train stopped many times along the way. We found some good-sized pieces of paper and went down to the river, where we curled up in that old paper under a tree and spent the night, and it was good thing it was a warm summer.

We were invited to go to the jungles with the hoboes and eat some of their vegetables and share a couple of chickens they'd picked up along the way, but we declined. We preferred to be by ourselves. We hid what little we had with us in some weeds and called this our home while we were there. And I noticed that Junior was starting to smell quite bad by now.

We went into the main part of town. Junior was a good bum; he was a nice looking boy and always had a sad story. He was wise enough to hit up the men and women that were well dressed and it didn't take him long to have enough to get something to eat and to go to the zoo for the day. By then I thought he was smelling terrible, and he had nerve enough to start accusing me of stinking! It was starting to get awful!

We got back to our camp in the evening. It was sort of chilly so I put my jacket on. "Boy, Ju, you stink!" I said. I put my hand into my pocket. Lo and behold, I pulled out the rottenest, slimiest, stinkingest bat that anyone could ever imagine. If Adelle had been there, she would have been chased again, this time with a rotten bat! She had put it in my pocket before we left home a few days before to get even with me for chasing her.

After about four days of hoboing I was ready to start for home. We were not able to catch a train out of Spokane during that day as the yard bull was too tough; he threatened to shoot us off if we got on. So, we waited until it was getting dark, walking around the railroad yard and up the track a ways. Finally, a train was getting ready to leave and when the whistle blew we hid behind a little bank. As soon as the engine passed us and the train was rapidly gaining speed, we made a run for it and each managed to catch a box car.

There were no gondolas or open cars on this train. Every car was full, a completely loaded train, so we had to ride on top of the cars all night long. At times we both got very sleepy, but didn't dare go to sleep or we might have fallen off since we had no rope to tie ourselves on with. We tried to hold our breath as we went through the tunnels because the smoke was so bad on top of the train.

The train stopped in Frenchtown the next morning and we jumped off, ran to the store, and used my last dime to buy a loaf of bread. We ran back, got on the train and ate that loaf of bread; it had been about 24 hours since we'd eaten. We got off the train in Missoula, hit the soup line at the Salvation Army, and then started walking for Ronan. We had wanted to ride the Galloping Goose, a self-powered trolley car that ran between Missoula and Polson, but got caught as we tried to ride on the steps and they chased us off. It was probably a good thing as there was nothing to hang onto, and we probably would have fallen off. We caught a ride about five miles out of Missoula and our days as hoboes were over.

Things That We Did

A lot of our recreation was hunting, fishing and running wild bunches of horses. When we were kids, we did a lot of fishing.

In the early days all we had for poles were long, slender willows. We had a hard time finding money for fish hooks or line, let alone being able to buy a pole.

Mother would have fish on the table about twice a week and we kept our poles hid at the canal. When Mom wanted fish for a meal, she would tell us beforehand. Sometimes, and real often, Rex and I would come out of the field for lunch, grab our poles and in about fifteen minutes we would have enough fish for the family's supper. When we bought fly hooks, we got only two kinds — the grey hackle and royal coachman. Rex would try one kind and I would take the other. If we thought the fish followed one type rather than the other, we would both use that kind.

Often Dad and we boys would hike down to Crow Creek to fish. We would fish down the creek about three miles to the Chief Eagle Meadows at the edge of the woods and Mom, the girls and the little ones would come in the car, bringing a picnic lunch. By the time we got there, we would have all the fish we could carry.

On other occasions, we would go down Finley Creek or Post Creek and do the same thing. In August, after the ruffed grouse got big enough to fry, at least once a week Mom would say she would like to have grouse for the next day. Rex, old Sport and I would go out with our .22 caliber rifles — and Sport was always all wiggles when he saw us with our guns. He would tree the grouse and then bark to let us know where he was so we could come and shoot the birds. We considered it almost a sin to miss a shot. We used .22 shorts as they were a little cheaper to buy.

The best places to find grouse were along the creeks, where it was brushy and where there were more berries.

Team of Horses Run Away From Swimmers

One time my brother, Rex, and two friends (I think it was Jim Scofield and Alton Ingraham) were coming home through the woods on an old road. They had a team and spring wagon, with a load of groceries and a few other items.

It was a warm day and as they crossed the bridge at North Crow Creek they decided to take a swim. There was a nice, deep hole there, just right for swimming.

The boys were about eleven or twelve years old at the time and they had a good, reliable team of horses so they didn't take time to tie the horses to a tree; they just let them stand there. The boys peeled off their clothes and put them into the back end of the wagon box.

All three jumped into the water and didn't notice the horses as they took off for home, up the old wagon road through the woods. When the boys came out of the water, there were no horses, no wagon, and no clothes, in sight. Bare naked, they started running to try to catch up with the horses. Now that road went right through the middle of a logging camp and in addition to the loggers in the camp, there were several families that lived in tent houses not far from the road. The boys streaked through as fast as they could, finally catching up with their team and wagon about a half mile past the camp. The horses had given the locals a good show; they stayed on the road all the way.

A Russian Hermit

They called him Andrew Leo, but I don't know if that was his real name or if anyone knew his real name. He lived in a little log cabin near the creek right where Rick Jore built his new log house. At that time this was sort of a wilderness up there, with only a narrow wagon road to get there.

He and his dog lived there alone. He had escaped from Russia during the Bolshevik revolt. He had stolen passage on a ship from Russia to the United States and I think he lived up there in hiding. He never did give out too much information. Besides, he was hard to understand as he talked very broken English.

He would cut wood and fence posts for what little cash he needed and once in a while he did work for my dad. One time he came to work in the hay field for a couple of days and he didn't have any crotch in his pants, and didn't have any shorts on, so Dad had to let him go as there were too many little kids around.

Andrew Leo smelled so bad that when we met him in the woods, we could detect him before we ever saw him. Many times while I was out hunting, I would run across him, or I would hear him cutting wood, and I would stop and visit with him. This one evening when I was between fourteen and sixteen, I came down from high on the mountain and thought I would stop to visit Andrew for a few minutes. He asked me into his cabin. I had been in there before, but someone else was always with me.

I stood my rifle against the side of the cabin, next to the door, and went in. He was rolling dough to make bread on his rough table-top. He would roll the dough a while and then would scrape the dough out of the cracks in the table top with a knife. He was scraping out dirt and all, and rolling it into the bread dough. The next time he rolled it out, he got a big bunch of black dirt. I said, "You got a little dirt into your dough that time."

He kept right on rolling for a minute and then laid it down. He was talking about Russia and the Bolsheviks. I had seen him get riled up before on this subject. He took a knife with quite a long blade off a shelf and started sharpening it on a stone. I told him I had to go, but he beat me to the door, and blocked my way. I started to get a little nervous as he started waving his arms and prancing back and forth and I couldn't understand what he was talking about.

The cabin had only two very small windows and I knew the only way to get out was through the small door. I couldn't see a thing that I could use to defend myself if he tried to use that knife on me. I made several attempts to get to the door, and each time he beat me there. I was getting more nervous. As he ranted and raved, I watched him closely, waiting for him to take two or three steps away from the door, thinking that when he did, I would hit it. I knew the door swung to the inside, which I didn't like, but maybe that helped me. As he took one or two steps away from the door, I was there. I grabbed the door, swung it into him, and was out. I grabbed my gun. I was so nervous that if he had come out I would have shot him. I said goodbye and I never stopped there again. I warned my brothers not to go there.

I have thought of this instance so many times during my life. I wondered if I made him mad about the dirt in his bread dough, or was he off his rocker a little. In those days I didn't even know that there was such a thing as a homosexual — and I sometimes wonder if he had something like that in his mind. Anyway, he was not very sane on that day.

The last time I saw Andrew, about 1943, he and another old guy named Jean Doyle, who was staying with him, were on their way back from Ronan. They had pushed a wheelbarrow ten miles into town, where they bought a 100-pound sack of potatoes and a 50-pound sack of flour. I don't know what else they bought, but whatever it was, they had the wheelbarrow full.

They were leaving Highway 93 to go up Mollman road, which was only a dirt road at that time and real muddy. Jean Doyle had a rope over his shoulders and fastened to the wheelbarrow. He was pulling and Andrew Leo had the handle and was pushing and yelling at poor old Jean. He was cursing him to "Pull harder, you old S.O.B."

I didn't know if old Doyle was drunk, or sober, but he was slipping and staggering all over. About a year later, Andrew Leo was found dead in his cabin.

Hunting Bees

In those days we did a lot of mountain hiking and climbing the peaks. We boys and most of our friends used sling-shots instead of guns when we were not hunting for real. We had them hanging around our necks, or in our hip pockets, and always had a pocket or two of rocks to shoot. We got quite good with them.

One summer the Matt boys, Joe, Bud, Bob, and Bee lived where our son Buddy and his wife now live, or on part of the same land. Rex and I played with them a lot.

One day we were hunting bees, or black hornet nests, with our sling-shots. We found a real large nest hanging on a tree about head high. Bee and I were the youngest in the group and the bigger boys told us that we could have first chance. "You two go right up close so you can be sure to hit it," they said. "Be big, and tough! Get closer."

Well, I wanted to be big and tough, so I got closer. Just as I raised my sling-shot to shoot, the nest flew apart All the other boys had been ready and shot ahead of me. Who did the bees see first? I didn't feel like I was so big and tough after being stung several times. When those old black hornets hit you, it feels like you have been hit with a shotgun.

One time I was fishing all by myself, by Hammer Dam on south Crow Creek. I pulled a fish out and swung it around me, and right into a black hornet nest just about four feet from my face. I hadn't noticed it before. As the fish flopped into the nest, those old hornets came boiling out. They must of thought I had an ugly face, but they should have seen it when I got home! By the time I got there, I could hardly see. I was hurting from several stings in my face, but my family had to laugh at me anyway.

Things That We See No More — Crows & Magpies

During the 1920's and early Thirties, sometime in October, I think, the crows came. They came by the thousands; they followed along the edge of the woods first. We could hear them cawing for miles. As far as we could see both ways it would be crows, all going in a southern direction. There was a steady stream that lasted two or three days, and then after they were gone the magpies came and it was the same thing.

Some of the birds would land in the trees, but only for a few minutes and then they would be gone again. It would have been fun to be able to follow them, to see where they went. You can't imagine how many birds there were. When I tell of this nowadays, some people don't seem to want to believe it.

During the Twenties and Thirties, there were so many Columbia ground squirrels that it was dangerous to ride a horse at full speed anywhere in the valley or around the reservoirs because of the gopher holes everywhere.

I had several horses fall with me before I finally realized that a good horse is always watching for the holes so it is a lot better to give the horse the reins. He will very seldom ever step in a hole. When trying to rein the horse around the holes, they are more apt to fall, as they may step in one that they had not seen, or you had not seen. So I learned to let my horse have his head when running bands of horses in squirrel infested areas.

In the late Thirties, during W.P.A. times (Work Program Administration), the Indians had a program to poison the squirrels because they were taking all the grass and the grain and there was little left for cattle and horses. This program had ten to twelve men on horseback who rode side-by-side and covered the valley floor from the foot of the mountains. They each had a bag of 10-80 poison hanging on their saddlehorn and would throw a pinch of poison to each gopher hole. It was a good project as they killed almost every gopher in the valley, but high up in the mountains there are still a lot of the ground squirrels and they are starting to move back into the valley.

Other Birds and Flying Squirrels

Also in the 1920's and 30's there was an abundance of meadow larks and bluebirds. When the many fields and patches of yellow bells and shooting stars were in bloom the birds would be singing their best. In those same years the woods were full of yellow canaries and chickadees. I haven't seen a yellow canary for many years now.

The little green frogs used to be around the streams and ponds and reservoirs by the thousands. In the evening you could hear them croaking everywhere. What music at night! We never hear that anymore and I think the blue heron crane got the frogs.

Another thing we don't hear or see anymore is the flying squirrel. I miss the sound of their evening whistle. If you were in the woods anywhere in the evening, you could hear them calling each other — a beautiful sound it was! It was hard to determine where the squirrels were. Sometimes they sounded like they were a long ways away, but would be very close to you, and sometimes you thought they were close by but they would be far away.

Animals & Plants Disappearing

When I was a boy in the winter time we often saw cute little owls that were about

—71—

the size of a robin. They were always around the barns and the hay and straw stacks and would sit on the fences, and their little heads would turn so fast that they appeared to be on a swivel. It looked like their heads turned all the way around.

They had spots on the back of their heads that looked like their eyes so it was very hard to tell if we were looking at the eyes or the spots. Whenever a mouse appeared they would have it.

I thought they were extinct because I had not seen one for about sixty years, but in December of 1992, one of my sons, Happy, saw one in his barn. This gave me a big thrill as I thought they were no more.

Another animal that we used to see all the time was the weasel. I haven't seen one in several years. They have always been such good mousers. The mice today number in the billions and they are taking over the cropland. Rabbits, too, used to be all over these woods and I used to snare and shoot a lot of them but I haven't seen a cottontail in these woods for a long time. We still see a snowshoe rabbit once in a while and, of course, the bear are way down in numbers, and also the porcupine.

When I was a kid, there were frogs and pollywogs everywhere. Now I never see them. In the late 1930's, the Blue Heron crane came to the area. It is illegal to kill them now and I think they cleaned out the frogs, which were important as they ate many bugs, mosquitoes and larva. The Blue Heron are now following the fish, even the bull trout, all the way to their spawning beds and into the wilderness areas.

There are also a lot of plants that are disappearing. When the wild strawberries were on we all went out to pick them and have our first fresh fruit of the year, strawberries and cream. Now there are not many left, certainly not enough to go picking them. Next were the sarviceberries. My mother made a lot of pie out them, and canned them with rhubarb; they were not so flat tasting with the rhubarb.

Picking Berries

After sarviceberries came the huckleberries. When they were ripe the whole family, except the very little ones, went up in the mountains to pick them. Sometimes we went along with bands of Indians, often on horseback, and sometimes just our own family went.

We had several patches we picked from and my mother canned hundreds of quarts of them. Adelle, my wife, also canned a lot of them after we were married.

Raspberries ripened next. They were plentiful along the canal. Then came chokecherries. Each fall we made gallons of syrup for our pancakes and ate them with thick cream spooned over them.

One fall when I was still in school I made a fifty-five gallon barrel full of wine. I had a few steady customers I sold wine to get spending money and I had to keep the wine hidden in jugs and ten-gallon kegs. One day our dad disappeared and mother said, "Bud, go down and check your wine keg."

I had one hidden by the stream and I found Dad laying on his back along side of my wine keg, where he had passed out. He had a little siphon hose and had been sucking my wine. My keg was about empty because he had fallen asleep while sucking and the wine siphoned out onto the ground.

Our old huckleberry patches now have no huckleberries and the chokecherry bushes and other berry bushes also are almost gone, or are deformed and sick looking.

In the days of growing up and during our young married life, being able to get these berries was very important as the biggest part of our living came from the land. The main things we bought were flour and sugar. As long as people had bread, meat, potatoes and fruit they were happy, but, of course, milk and cream were also nice to have.

Going to School and Fishing

When I got old enough to start getting interested in different activities at school, our family had no such thing as allowances or money for a show or candy. The only money that I remember getting was at Christmas time. Mom would give us fifty cents or maybe a dollar. What money I got I always spent on nuts, oranges and bananas, and I brought them home for the family, as these things were rare for us.

I earned nearly all my money fishing in Spring Creek, which runs through Ronan. I started snaring fish at a very young age, using a copper wire with a loop in the end. In those days the best wire I could find was from the inside of an old Model T Ford coil. It was strong, flexible and bright. I would twist a small eye about one-fourth of an inch in diameter in the end of a piece of copper wire about two and a half feet long. Then I put the other end of the wire through the loop, and pulled the wire on through until the wire formed a loop about three or four inches in diameter.

Then I fastened the wire onto the small end of the pole with two half hitches, leaving the loop about twelve or fourteen inches from the end of the pole, bringing the remaining wire on down the pole as far as it would come, where I would fasten it. This way, if the end of my pole broke off, I still had my wire and my fish.

Usually I would find the fish first, looking for them in the largest, deepest and quietest hole in the stream. I would walk slowly, stepping softly, looking into the water. The fish would usually be at the deepest part of the pool, about one to four inches from the bottom.

It was important not to make any quick movement or the fish would disappear. Next, I made the loop just a little larger than the fish so it could go around the fish without touching it. If the fish touched the wire, it was gone. Very slowly, I would put my pole into the water a few feet in front of the fish with the wire almost touching the bottom. Then I would start the pole downstream toward the fish, making sure I did not scare the fish. Because the wire was bright and shiny, I could see it when it was around the fish and when the wire was past the gills and front fins I gave it a jerk and I would have a fish.

I kept two or three poles hidden along the creek. Thursday was usually my big day, as I had some Catholic customers. At our lunch hour I would run for the creek and start snaring fish. When I caught what I needed, I would hide my pole and run as fast as I could with the fish to my customers, and then run back to the schoolhouse and try to get there before the bell rang. I don't remember what I got for my fish, but I thought I was making pretty good money at the time.

I also used this type of snare to catch squirrels and grouse. The Franklin grouse (called foolhens) are easily caught by just slipping the loop over their heads, giving a jerk and pulling them to you. The ruffed grouse is a wilder bird and harder to get, but the big blue grouse often will let you get close enough to snare it. Sometimes I caught snowshoe rabbits this way, using a little heavier wire than was needed for fish.

I taught my Indian friends how to snare as they had not seen it done before. At the time, none of us paid any attention to game laws because we didn't even know that there were such laws. It was a great life.

Getting to School and Home Again

I didn't realize at the time that I must have caused my mother a lot of worry because whenever there was something going on at school or in town, I would have to walk eight miles home at night or stay with friends.

When I walked home, a lot of times not even one car would come along the road. If one did, they nearly always picked us up. Sometimes the car would already be loaded with people, but they would let us stand on the running boards on the outside until we got to our corner. Then we had to walk four and one-half miles more to our house.

One night a friend, Charlie Barker, came home with me on a very dark and rainy night and we couldn't see anything. We were on the Plassie place, which now belongs to my son, Buddy, and were feeling our way along with our feet when, all of a sudden, a coyote that was quite close started to howl, and others started to answering from all directions. Well, poor Charlie grabbed me around the neck, and I thought he would choke me to death before I could get him pried loose. I had a hard time convincing him that they were not after us. But he still hung onto me the rest of the way home and Charlie never did walk home with me in the dark again.

One winter night as I was walking home alone, I was very tired and I had no gloves and wasn't dressed for a bad storm. I was out of town about two and one half miles when it started to snow and it kept getting worse, coming right into my face. There was a haystack not too far ahead, and not that far from the road, that I knew about and I managed to find it and get on the back side of it, where the wind and snow was not so bad. In those days the hay was all stacked loose, so I got down on my knees and started to dig a hole into the stack, about one foot from the ground level. At first my hands were so cold they didn't work too well, but they soon warmed up. I dug back into the stack the length of my body and then I climbed into it and put a little loose hay at the entrance to close it up. I slept as well as if I had been at home in my bed; when daylight came, the storm was over and I walked on home.

Stanley Scearce had a big hitchrack and an open-faced horse barn for the customers for his store in Ronan. People could put their horses in out of the weather while shopping or staying overnight in town and there was usually some hay left over in some of the mangers where the people had fed their horses. On several occasions when I was tired and it was late at night, I would sleep there. I had a little piece of canvas just big enough to go around my body that I left hidden there. When I wanted to go to bed I would rake part of the hay to one side of the manger, wrap my tarp around myself, and crawl into the manger. Then I would pull the rest of the hay over myself, and I would sleep good and snug.

This shed had four stalls and was walled in on three sides. It had a good roof on it, so I was always dry and the hay kept me warm. It was a very handy place for me on several occasions. When I had my horse with me, I would put him in the stall at the far end so I didn't hear him chewing all night.

My Trick Horse

We used to have a lot of fun trying to be cowboys. Of course, since I thought I was Hoot Gibson I had to try everything that he did in the movies. I had one horse that had been a race horse. I called him my trick horse, and I used to try all kinds of capers on him.

I would hang down on his sides at full speed, let myself down, hit my feet on the ground, and fly back up into the saddle. This horse was the only horse that I could do a decent job on by riding at full speed standing straight up in the saddle, sometimes with one foot on the horn. When this horse ran, he was very hard to hold back; all I had to do was to rear back on the reins to keep my balance.

One time on a dare I rode the full length of main street in Ronan standing in my saddle with three or four other kids pretending they were chasing me. When I got near the end of the street by the theater, two ladies were walking across the street and they started to run into a vacant lot, but when they started to run, my horse turned and went after them before I could get down into my saddle. Quick as a flash, the horse galloped across the gravel sidewalk and very nearly ran over the two frightened ladies. Well, I wasn't very popular for awhile with Mrs. Resner and Mrs. Krensberger.

In those days there was very little traffic on the streets and the street was clear when we started. But after losing my popularity with the two nice ladies, I didn't try any more of that in town.

Andy Disatel, a young feller a little older than I was, and who had run away from his home in Washington because his stepfather was so mean, worked for us in the hay. After the hay was finished, my mother felt sorry for Andy and told him if he couldn't find another job to come back. He did come back, and made his home with us for about three or four years. He got along well with all the family and he and I did a lot of riding together.

We liked to run in bunches of wild horses. Most of these horses were owned by someone, but some were not. There were not many fences then, and sometimes we would run one band into another band and the stallions would get to fighting. You could hear them squealing and bawling for miles.

Sometimes it was a hard job to get these horses through the woods so we could get them to our place. We had to keep track of where the other person was at so we could head the horses off accordingly. We used cowboy yells and Andy had a good one! I could hear him for a long ways; maybe being part Indian, he might have inherited his ability to yell from his ancestors. This way we could keep track of each other and where the bunches of horses were going.

If we saw some good looking horses we would catch them and ride them. Some would be broke to ride, and others were wild as they could be. In those days any two-year-old that was not branded could be claimed by anyone that caught them. It was a lot of fun.

After Kicking Horse Reservoir was enlarged, a bunch of us were playing follow the leader, which we liked to do. We would do everything we could think of with our horses.

One day I happened to be the leader and we decided to take our horses to the reservoir, a body of water about one half mile wide and two miles long. We went into the water to two or three of the islands, swimming our horses a short ways and then wading the rest. There was a bigger island that was quite a ways out and, being the leader, I thought I should be more daring than the others so I started out for this island. I got about half way there and my horse started to go under. I was trying to hang onto a stirrup, but he kept going up and down, then tried to get on top on me. I tried to get away from him.

On this particular day, I had one of the smallest horses. No one offered to help — I guess they thought that anyone this foolish didn't need any help. I started to swim back as fast as I could to get away from my horse but was not doing too good. My pockets were all filled with water and I finally managed to kick off one of my boots, but couldn't get the other one off. I thought for awhile that I was going to drown.

Finally I got back to where I could reach bottom. My poor old horse was coming back with just his ears and nose sticking out of the water. When he came out, he was on his knees. We left him there until the next day.

One time I stayed with some friends, the Leighton boys who lived north and east of Ronan, above the canal. Again playing follow the leader, several of us took off for town on our horses. We were following an old winding road along the bottom near North Crow Creek and I was in the lead again. The ground was quite wet, too wet for any speed on a horse or anything else! I came around a sharp curve in this old road and my horse slipped and lost its footing. Over we went with the horse rolling right over the top of me.

He got up, but I didn't. I was laying flat out on my stomach with my arms and legs stretched out like a pancake. I couldn't move or say a word. The other boys thought I was killed, and so did I. I could feel blood, or water running out of my stomach and onto the ground. I slowly got a little feeling in one hand and then I was able to move it. Finally, I was able to reach down to feel how much fluid had run out of me onto the ground. I was very surprised and so relieved when the ground felt dry. It wasn't long until my whole body was again getting feeling and I was able to talk, and with a little help was able to get back onto my horse. There was no more fast riding on that day for me! I was bruised up, but had no broken bones.

Playing Deer and Hunter

When we played deer and hunter, we played right where Buddy's house is now and to the east between the creek and the swamp. At that time the timber was thick and there were lots of logs.

We would have two hunters and the rest of the boys were deer. The hunters each had a BB gun. I don't think they were quite as powerful as they can be today, but boy, they sure did sting when you got hit. The hunters counted to fifty while the deer got a head start into the woods and this was when I learned to run, jump logs and duck through the thickest brush, especially when John Conko was a hunter. He was a fast and powerful runner, and didn't show much mercy on the poor deer.

I remember one day when he was a hunter. I thought I would hide, so I secreted myself by laying flat against a big log with a few bushes around me. I thought I had a good place until I could hear him walking nearby. Then my heart nearly stopped, for he jumped up onto my log, right over me! I tried hard not to breathe in any air or let any out while I pressed my body hard against the log. I may have left the print of my body in the side of that log, I pressed so hard. He was standing on that log right over me, and looking around for a deer. I don't think he heard me breathing, but I think he must have heard my heart thumping.

"Oh, there you are!" he said. I wasn't sure, but was hoping that he had seen someone else. It wasn't long until I found out who he had seen! As I went out of there, I didn't blat like a deer, I bellered like a wounded bear as I ran. He had already shot me three times before I could really get going.

It was a real fun game as long as you didn't get shot at a close range.

This John Conko was an outstanding athlete. He was a powerful, well-built Indian and he excelled in everything that he did like running, swimming, horseback riding, and all kinds of sports. He died at a young age from pneumonia while playing football in North or South Dakota.

On the Cliffs

In those days we did a lot of mountain climbing. One day I learned a good lesson while I was after a mountain goat above McDonald Lake.

I chased the goat I was after up and over several cliffs. One cliff I climbed over with just toe and finger holds as I went up the side and I finally lost the goat, or I couldn't go any farther. The goat must have been a better climber than I was. So, I started to retrace my steps but I couldn't remember exactly where I had come up. I hadn't paid attention to where I was going as I pursued the goat.

Those cliffs were a lot higher than I had realized. I started to get worried, looking down I couldn't see where the footholds and handholds were and there was no other way to get down, or up! And no one in the world knew where I was. I finally had to take a chance on where I thought I had come up, or stay up there. I decided to try, so I laid down on my stomach and eased my feet over the edge, feeling with my feet for a little bit of rock to catch the edge of my shoes. Then I tried for new handholds. Then, again trying to find or feel another place for a foot to try to claw into the rock, and then another hand. Finally, dripping with cold sweat, I managed to make it over the first cliff and had only two more to go. But they were not quite as bad as the first.

I was too young then to realize that I shouldn't be up there climbing without a rope, or that it was always harder to come down off of a cliff than it was to go up.

Near these same cliffs, it may have been on the same day, while walking through some shale rocks I saw a snake, or some kind of reptile. I have always been afraid of snakes.

I didn't see the head, but I saw about fourteen or sixteen inches of the snake. It was quite large and was a dark copper color and appeared to have a sharp, peaked back. I saw it going away from me, between the rocks. Then the snake, or it could have been another one, was coming toward me through the loose rocks. At that time I left that particular area in a hurry!

That was the only time I saw a snake like that. I talked to a lot of people, but no

Eneas Conko and his granddaughter, Jeanette Conko, in 1952.

one else has ever seen one and I still don't know if it was a snake.

Hunting in the Missions

Each year I would go into the mountains with the Indians to dig roots, prospect, hunt and fish. We also picked pine nuts from the limber pine. In those days the Indians killed game whenever they needed meat and many times I helped them get their fall supply. On a few occasions my friend, Thurman Trosper, and I went into the same area to get our winter meat for our families.

We hunted mainly in the Glacier area, which is some of the most remote country I have been in. It was a very rough area to get into with horses, but in those days the game was plentiful as no one else hunted in there.

In these early days we killed a lot of game with very big sets of horns from every species, but we never ever brought any of the horns out, and there were several that I would now very much like to have. In those days we never thought of bothering to bring them out, or having them mounted. It was the meat that was important.

Conko, A Good Shot

I hunted with Eneas Conko for a long time and in all the years I hunted with him, I never saw him miss a shot with his rifle.

One time he and I were hunting on foot near Island Lake, before there was a trail coming into that area from Glacier Lake. We had separated as we had seen fresh elk tracks and I went into a small canyon beyond where he was. I shot a mule deer and while cleaning my buck I heard Eneas shoot three shots.

After finishing my work, I went over to help Eneas, as I knew he would have something killed. When I got there, he had two cow elk killed just a few yards from each other. There was only one bullet hole in each cow, and as I had heard three shots, I asked him, "Did you miss a shot?"

He said, "No, the bull, he is laying up on the sidehill."

After cleaning out the elk, I told Eneas that my deer was not too big and maybe I could get it to camp alone. So he took my gun along with his and headed for camp.

I went back to the deer I had killed and managed to get it onto my back and started to camp with it. When I stopped to rest, I would look for a rock or log to set the deer on so I could get it onto my back again. I was about 150 yards from camp when a big grizzly bear came walking right across my pathway. With all that weight on my back my head was sort of down and I had been watching the ground as I walked. I must have looked up to see where I was going and when I saw the bear I froze in my tracks, but he just kept on going like he never saw me.

He went over a small ledge of rock and disappeared. It was getting quite late in the evening, and by the time I got to our camp, it was too dark to do anything about Eneas' meat. We were sure that bear would be on the meat, so we got up early the next morning and went to get it with the horses. We were very relieved to find the bear had not been there.

Around 1930 or 1931, I took a couple of friends, Harley Delff and Red Ingraham, on a short trip into the Crazy Horse. The evening before we left for home, we decided to bring some meat back with us so Delff and I went for a short hunt. We jumped two big mule deer bucks and one went one way, and the second the other way.

Delff said, "You take that one, and I'll take this one." We both fired at about the same time at running shots. Both of us connected, but I nearly missed mine. Conko had cautioned me that when making a fast shot with open sights on a gun, he always shot a little low on the animal.

When you first see your sights you have too coarse of a bead, which will cause you to shoot too high. I made a shot that I could never make again — as I pulled the trigger, that mule deer bounded up as they usually do when running, and my bullet broke all four of his legs in one shot. He went down in a heap. As he bounded, his four legs must have been in direct line with the bullet. In my years of hunting, I have had three of my hunters kill two animals in one shot, and a lot who made some fantastic shots, but I have never seen anyone accidently shoot four legs with one shot.

On the way home, as we were coming along the back side of Eagle Pass, one of our pack horses was killed when it slipped off the trail and rolled down over a cliff. We had to go down on foot and cut the pack off and then carry it back to the trail and load it onto our saddlehorses to get it home.

My Dad Getting Lost

About two weeks later, my dad and I, Eneas Conko, his wife Sofia and Mrs. Pierre, another full blood, went back into the same area to get our winter meat. When we reached the spot where a horse had been killed, we noticed a lot of grizzly sign.

We had gotten a very early start from home that morning, so it was still quite early when we got to our campsite. Sometime before, I had found a big outcropping of white quartz two or three miles away from our camp site and my dad wanted to see it. After making camp, we took a short cut on foot across country with no trail, through brush and over ledges and logs. My father was still a good hiker at that time and was doing well keeping up with me.

As we were coming along a little rock ledge, we discovered a good-sized hole back under a ledge and we went inside. The odor of grizzly bear was quite strong, and as we got deeper inside we found eight different big piles of leaves and grass that had been put in there by the bears very recently. Beside each pile of leaves there was a little pile of sticks about twelve to sixteen inches long. I still can't figure out what they were there for. Later, however, I told Conko that those bears must be going to have some stick games that winter!

My dad and I went on and looked at the little ridge of quartz for evidence of gold, but we found none in the quartz. On our way back to camp, Dad decided to go back just a little bit higher than the way we had come, and I thought I would swing down lower to try to find some game. I had taken the longer route and got back to camp just at dark and was surprised to find that Dad wasn't in yet. I went back in the direction that he should have been coming from to locate him and hollered but got no answer.

The night got very dark, so I turned back for camp, almost feeling my way. A cold, miserable wind started blowing too hard to hear a shot at any distance, and it was too dark to travel in the thick woods. All we could do was wait for daylight to come. At the break of day, Eneas and I both went out to look for Dad. I went in the direction I thought he should be in and Eneas went down the canyon. We were out about forty-five minutes when I heard Eneas shoot one shot. I was quite sure that he had found Dad, and he had.

When they got back into camp, my dad's face and hands were all scratched up. He said that he had spent part of the night up in a tree, as he thought sure he had heard something right near him. This was my father's first and only trip into the area, so it was confusing to him and he had gone up the wrong canyon. It was really my fault for leaving him by himself in a strange country so late in the evening.

The women gave him something to eat and he lay down for about an hour while Eneas and I caught and saddled the horses and packed up the camp. We then moved camp up past Loco Lake and up to a lake that is now called Cheff Lake.

The next morning we all three went hunting. I shot a good mule deer buck not too far from camp. I went back to get a horse to pack my buck in with, when I heard three shots way down in the bottom of Crazy Horse Creek. Shortly after I got my buck into camp, my father came into camp and a little later Eneas came in to tell us he had killed a bull and two cows way down on the creek bottom. It was going to storm, so we decided that maybe we should try to get the game back to camp that day.

The women immediately started to build the drying racks while we caught the horses and saddled up. We took off down the mountain which was very steep with no trails at all. We finally got to the game.

The Indians had a different way of packing their meat out than we do today, skinning it before they loaded it on the horses. By the time we had this done, it was getting late and starting to snow very hard, so it got dark fast. We started out of the dark canyon, walking and leading the horses back up the mountain. It got so dark that we couldn't see where to go, and we couldn't follow the horse tracks where we had come down. One of Eneas's horses, a stallion he called Web, was a very good horse. Eneas knew that if he was riding the horse, it would follow the same tracks back to camp, but he was not sure if the horse could carry him and the meat.

Eneas weighed about two hundred pounds and the big load proved to be just a little too much on the steep slope. That horse was sure trying, but fell a couple of times, so we had to stop for the night.

It snowed all night long. We built a fire at the base of a big, dead snag, and Conko and my dad sat by the fire all night. When I got sleepy, I laid down on the hair side of one of the bigger fresh hides and covered up with a smaller hide. I still had some learning to do; I went to sleep and when I finally woke up, I was lying in a pool of water. As it snowed, the flakes melted and ran off the smaller hide onto the bottom one, and down under me. I should have laid on the small skin and covered up with the big one so the water would have run off onto the ground.

I had just got out from under the hide when the snag came crashing down; the fire had burned the roots off the snag and over it went. It was a good thing that our horses were tied on the opposite side of where it fell.

As soon as day started to break, we headed for camp. It had snowed so much we couldn't see the horse tracks where we had come down the evening before, so Eneas just turned old Web, the stallion, loose and he followed his same tracks back to camp.

The two Indian ladies were sure glad to see us come into camp. They had the drying racks ready and had gathered a lot of the wood needed. It was a hard job to get enough wood with no pitch in it to the camp as we were quite high in elevation.

I was the worst meat cutter there, so I spent most of my time gathering enough wood to last through the day and night to come. Everyone was very busy all day, and it was long after dark before we had the last of the meat on the drying racks and were able to get to bed. My dad and I slept together, as we just had blankets.

At daybreak we brought in the horses and saddled them while the two women bagged up the meat. The parfleche bags made from elk hides were all filled with the Indians' belongings. Eneas and Sofia's packsaddles were ones that they had made out of a frame of elk horns covered with rawhide. Their horses were all packed, with the tepee going on last. Then everything was bound down with what we called a squaw hitch. At that time I used mostly sawbuck saddles, but I did use some Indian saddles for quite some time. I also used panniers made from rawhide and shaped sort of like a box.

We left Cheff Lake quite early in the morning, and, upon arriving at Summit Lake early, decided to camp there overnight. That afternoon we three went hunting again as we had room enough on our horses for a couple more deer or one more elk. My dad and Conko went down behind Frog Lake and Long Lake while I went up toward Elk Lake. When I was nearing Elk Divide, I saw a huge grizzly bear quite a ways ahead coming down the trail toward me with his head low. I knew he hadn't seen me so I ran about thirty yards away from the trail and hid behind a big tree.

I got my rifle in a good position to shoot while leaning again that tree, and watched the bear every step of the way as he came down the trail. I had been using my gun as a single-shot, so I had two more shells in my hand in case I needed them. In my mind I thought about what Phillip Pierre had told me once before about the grizzly bear: "If he don't make-em some trouble for us, we don't make-em trouble for him."

It was a very big bear, and as he came to where I had left the trail, he started to sniff my tracks. His hair came straight up on end and suddenly he looked at least twice as big — immense! I had my gun cocked with my finger on the trigger. He took several steps backwards, turned and walked briskly down over the hill.

I blew a sigh of relief, and, deciding that I had hunted far enough, went back to camp. An hour or so later, Eneas and Dad came back without having killed anything either. They told of how they had run into eight grizzlies working, digging roots in a slide area near Long Lake, so they also had decided not to hunt any further and returned to camp.

During the night it snowed again, and when we got up in the morning we found grizzly tracks of all sizes, and a packed trail they had made in the snow. Their trail went from the water's edge and around our camp, which was on the edge of the lake, to the water's edge on the other side of camp where it looked like they had gone back and forth all night long. Evidently they could smell the meat in our camp, but weren't brave enough to come and get it.

Many of these bears had been attracted into the area by the smell of the horse that had been killed two weeks before, just a quarter of a mile above our camp. When we left that morning there were grizzly tracks everywhere, but we never saw a one of them.

It was hard going for the horses as it was the second snow that fall, but as we crossed over the top of Eagle Pass at forenoon, with the fresh, new snow and the sun shining on our backs, it was beautiful. My dad never forgot his first and only trip into the Crazy Horse, and even though he got lost, he talked about it often.

Two Days On The Run

After my Dad and I told the story about finding the grizzly den, my brother Rex, Thurman Trosper, and his brother, Woodrow, all wanted to go back into the Crazy Horse to see the bear den. It was really too late in the season to go into that area, but the weather was nice so we decided to go.

We only got halfway there when a very bad snow storm came up, so we made camp at my old camp ground. By the next morning the snow was already up to our waists and the horses couldn't get anything to eat. It was impossible to get up to the grizzly den and also impossible to get back home over the trail we had come over on.

All we could do was go down the canyon with no trail for several miles, through brush and down timber, streams and bogs. The horses would bite off brush to eat as we fought our way down the canyon to the Glacier Lake Trail. We planned to take that trail, and then go by Glacier Sloughs where we usually tried to camp, thinking that the snow might be gone at that low level. From there we could go down into Swan Valley and then go north up to Jim Creek, where we would camp. There was always good horse feed there at Moore Meadows.

It took three days to get there. While we were camped at Jim Creek, we all went out hunting late in the afternoon. That evening my brother Rex got lost, and I looked for him until way late in the night. It was half snowing with rain coming down. About two miles from camp I heard him hollering, but I couldn't tell where he was. Each time I heard him, it sounded like he was in a different place. It was a new area to Rex, so he ended up staying out in the woods all night. He started a fire and kept himself quite warm, but the worst of it was that he was wearing my good, real heavy wool sweater, and he burned a big hole in the back of it! I kidded him about using my sweater to start his fire with.

From this spot on Jim Creek, we got home in one day by going over Piper Crow Creek Trail. This trail was not as high and rugged as Eagle Pass, and could be gotten over until quite late in the season. Three times over my career I got snowed in on Eagle Pass, and had to use this route to get out of the mountains.

One year when Thurman Trosper and my younger brother, Floyd, were with me, we were snowed in and had to use the same route to get out. After traveling in the deep snow all day long, we again camped at Glacier Sloughs. We had not yet killed any animals, and since our plans were to kill something to have meat to eat, we never took any along.

The evening when we got to our campsite, Thurman was sick and had the chills really bad. By the next morning he was no better and I was becoming concerned, so we kept him wrapped up good to keep him warm and I had my brother stay with him to keep the fire burning while I went out to see if I could kill something for food. I went a fair distance before I finally saw two deer, and I killed them both. It was all downhill, so they were not too hard to drag and as soon as I had the meat in camp I cut off a good portion, cut it up in chunks, and put it into a pot with a few vegetables that we had. By the next morning Thurman thought he would be able to ride, so we took off.

We had barely got started when all three of us got very bad cases of diarrhea from eating the fresh, uncooled meat. It was a bad time to learn such a lesson! We were on and off our horses every little ways, but we made it home in two days.

As A Young Teenager

As a young teenager I was just like any other young fellow; I started to notice that some girls were starting to be sort of attractive to me. One weekend a boy from Pablo, Harley Ingraham, came to stay the weekend with me. He was to be home on Sunday evening, so when that time came, we rode my gray horse to Pablo to his home by riding double. After getting him home, we staked my horse out in a good patch of grass and I stayed all night with him.

The next morning was a school day so I saddled my horse and right after breakfast I got onto my horse and started for Ronan to go to school. About a mile out of Pablo I slowed my good horse to a walk, as I saw five or six Pablo school kids coming out of a driveway. They happened to be all girls and I was sort of a bashful boy, but I did get nerve enough to say, "Good morning, Girls."

And do you know, the cute one in the middle of the group had nerve enough to say, "Yah, yah, yah, Smarty," and make a big face at me. If someone had told me that day that someday I would marry her, I would have said "No way, Jose!"

It wasn't too long after this, at the beginning of the next school year, that this same girl showed up in my class in the fifth grade. And wouldn't you know it, she sat in the seat right next to me. I soon found out that she was not as smarty as I thought she was, and for the rest of our years in school, we never sat more than one seat away from each other.

Every year the teachers always separated all the kids that had little love affairs, but through all our years in school the teachers never bothered us. When we entered our freshman year of high school, old Professor Polly had all the kids in the Assembly Room and gave us all a lecture. During his lecture he said before we got through high school, some would be rebellious, some would be good students, some of us would die. Then he looked right at Adelle and me where we were again sitting right near each other, and he said, "And some of you will end up in Matrimony." He was right in everything he told us.

After Adelle Rogers moved from Pablo to Ronan, I never ever had much interest in any of the other girls.

My Father Drinking

Before the 1928 Depression hit, the grain farmers and others were doing quite well making a living for their families, but nearly everyone that had borrowed money or owed money lost their land and their homes. Our father had been a hard working man and he always drank some, but about this time he got progressively worse when so many things started to go wrong.

My father was always a poor cow milker, so he left that up to my mother to do. We didn't have a cow barn. All the milking was done in an open corral; rain or snow, that was where the cows had to be milked. My mother was the official milker. She could out-milk anyone in the family by far. I used to try to out-milk her, but I never could.

The cows were milked for extra grocery money. The milk was separated from the cream which was taken to town and sold to be used for butter. The skimmed milk was fed to the calves and pigs. Several times my dad would pick up the cream check and spend it on whiskey.

After I married I could look back, and it makes me feel so bad that I didn't help as much as I could have. Few people knew he was an alcoholic because he made his own whiskey instead of buying it, before he got so bad. Many times I watched his still for him so it wouldn't get too hot, and would change the jugs when they were full. I just loved to sit with a spoon under the spout, let it fill and take it one spoon after another. I got to where I could hardly wait until he ran off another batch and I know I could have become an alcoholic very easily as I was beginning to want it all the time.

I thank our Good Lord that I had enough sense to realize what was happening to my Dad. And it is fortunate that, with ten boys and three girls in our family, and with whiskey available to all of us, none turned into alcoholics.

I finally made up my mind that I would not take anymore of it. One time when I was fourteen or fifteen years old, I had stayed all night with a friend whose older brothers had been in a lot of trouble for different things. When I came home the next night, I changed my clothes and went to clean out the horse barn. That was my job in the evening. I didn't see my dad come into the barn with the side chain off of an old tire chain. He was mad because I hadn't come home the night before.

He bent the chain double which made it about three and a half feet long and as I was bent over getting a shovel full of manure, he hit me across the back as hard as he could. The blow knocked me down and it sort of paralyzed me for a few seconds. As he was taking the second swing at me, I rolled over and caught him by the pant leg, and got him off balance. Then he tried to kick me, but I managed to get a hold of him and throw him to the ground.

The old barn only had a dirt floor and I managed to get him down with his face in the horse manure. I held him there for quite a while. He told me in French several times that if I would let him up he promised to leave me alone. Finally, I let him up and he went out the barn door. I went back to cleaning the barn. My mother and my older brother, Rex, saw him running from the tool shed to the barn with a pitchfork in his hand and they felt there was something wrong, and followed him. He came into the barn a second time like a mad man, which he was. I thought of trying to get out through the manure hole, but it was sort of high and too small to be able to get out of before he could get to me.

Again talking in French as he always did, he said, "You little S.O.B. This time I will kill you." I was trying to fend him off with the manure shovel when Rex came in through the door. As dad was trying to crowd me into the far corner of the barn, Rex got ahold of him and we disarmed him from the pitchfork.

He had been drinking heavily, and I believe he went and took a couple more drinks, and then passed out. When he was sober, he could be so good, and a lot of fun. Every fall we had gone deer hunting with him over by Fortine and Olney, and had a big time, but after that episode with the pitchfork, when he sobered up he cried and said that he would never take another drink.

I saw him stay sober for four or five months one time, but then someone would give him a drink or something would happen and away he would go again. Sometimes he would drink steady for three or four months at a time, and neglect his work. He would go for days without eating.

On other occasions, he would be just as jolly as could be and then all of a sudden he would turn and get mean and violent. Many times he threatened to kill Mom and all of the kids. And many times we boys took the guns apart so that they would not fire. Many, many times I would start to town horseback, and I would worry all the time that while I was gone he would kill the family. On two or three occasions I got halfway to town and turned around and went back home because the worry was too great when he was drinking heavily.

I think that this is why none of the family got to be alcoholics — we all saw too much of it. Our father, in his younger years, was hard-working, smart, and jolly for everyone to be around. What a shame that so many good men have ruined their lives and their family's lives. The younger kids in our family did not know our dad before he got to drinking so heavily, so they had no respect for him — so sad.

In 1936 or 1937 our mother could not take it any longer. She was at the end of her rope and with no way to make a living for her family, she left everything except their clothes, even the animals, and took her family to Detroit.

My father followed along to Detroit. When they left, everything was left behind including the machinery. There was not much left, and what was left was old, including a few horses, a few calves, a small band of sheep, and a big sow pig. The land belonged to Big Mary Mollman and someone leased the land.

With the help of a good-hearted real estate man, my mother was able to get a large house and started a home for old women. She was able to make a living for the rest of her family, and also Dad.

Adelle and Bud Cheff in 1950 upon the occasion of their 17th anniversary.

Part Three

MOVING AROUND A BIT

School Years

In my younger years in school I did quite a lot of fighting, but I can't remember ever picking a fight with anyone. Most of my fights were from sticking up for some other kid that I felt was being picked on by bigger and older kids.

I think I fought most of my fights for a German family that came to our school as they were just learning to talk English and kids made fun of them. I could still remember when I couldn't talk English either.

As a rule I got along quite well with most of the kids, I learned that I could take care of myself quite well.

My mother made all the girls their dresses and also made over some of our clothes from things that had been given to us. Consequently, I had to wear made over suits that sometimes didn't fit me too well. One day at school I overheard some of the girls talking about me always wearing made-over clothes and that made me feel really bad — and from then on I always felt self-conscious of my clothes.

I preferred wearing overalls or jeans and a sweater instead of a jacket, but my mother thought we should wear better clothes and wanted to see her boys with white shirts and ties. I always wanted a cowboy hat and jeans, which she hated to see me wear; she absolutely didn't want me to be a cowboy. I guess I was the odd ball of the family.

In all my years in school, all of the boys that I associated with were all of the tougher type of boys — not troublesome or problem kids but we would fight or could fight if we had to. I don't think there was anyone in our group that was not respected in our town or community.

We all had lots of fun but we never ever damaged or stole anything except apples, to eat, off of people's trees. But one time seven or eight of us did borrow a bicycle apiece without permission from different kids in town that owned one. None of us had ever had a bike.

We sneaked out of town to the northeast in the dark on a bicycle ride. About four miles out of town one of the boys went off the road into a rock pile while going down a hill quite fast. He bent the bike he was on bad enough that it couldn't be ridden, so we took turns pushing it all the way back to town and into the yard from where we'd taken it. Then we returned all the other bikes to the rightful owners.

Most of the bike owners did not know that their bikes had been used, but the poor girl who owned the bent bike discovered it the next morning. We were soon all found out and our parents had to dig down and each put $5.00 towards buying the girl a new bike.

All of us tried the taste of moonshine and we tried chewing and smoking just like most normal kids, trying to be smart and big. I was starting to get addicted to Copenhagen. My Dad had Dr. Resner put something into a new can of Copenhagen, and gave it to one of my friends to give me a chew. As we got out of school, as usual we took a chew and my friend handed me the new, open can. I took a big pinch, then got onto the school bus. We weren't very far out of town when that old school bus started to go around and around.

The bus door was in the back and I think the other kids thought I was crazy, but I just made it to the door on my hands and knees before I started heaving. I think I heaved all of the eight miles home. When I got off the bus I fell flat down and managed to crawl off to the edge of the road, and laid there for a long time before I could get on my feet to go home.

This was a quick cure for a one-can-a-day tobacco chewer. To this day the smell of snoose makes me sick right away.

A little later I started smoking with the other boys and I was rolling my own and getting just as addicted to cigarettes.

One time most of our gang went swimming just northwest of the cemetery in the ditch at a concrete drop. We all decided we were going to quit smoking, so we threw our tobacco into the water and let it float away down the ditch. A week or so went by, and all of them were starting to smoke again, except me and one other boy, and after about a year or so he also started again. I was the only one that never smoked another cigarette.

About half of my old friends ended up as alcoholics, and most of them are dead today. What a shame. We were all athletic and were on the ball and track teams, and were all good fellows. Some died quite young.

In my younger years when I was in school, there was a livery barn where they used to rent horse teams and saddlehorses — at one time there were three of this type of barns in town. The one nearest the school house just across the road was a fun place to play in, especially in the large hay loft. It was where the Ford garage is now.

The blacksmith shop was south, just across the street from the schoolhouse and it was fascinating to go and watch the blacksmiths at work. I was there at every opportunity. Ernest Landquist and Al Needum and his father were the smiths that I watched heating and pounding the iron into forms for something.

Next to this shop was Lemire Brothers store. Then along the school yard fence was a hitch-rail, long enough for several teams and lots of saddle horses. In the spring of the year I often rode a horse to school and at recess and lunch time I would pull grass to feed my horse. Usually there were other kids that were ready to help me.

During these early years, each of the stores had a large hitch-rail so that all their customers had a place to tie their teams and wagons, and saddlehorses. There was only a boardwalk on Main Street then, with a ring for the horses to be tied to.

When I was a boy I saw a lot of runaways as the horses were scared to death of cars. When a car came to town some of the horses would start snorting and some would pull back, quite often breaking their lead rope. Away they would go with the empty wagon! Sometimes teams would go all the way home without wrecking and on other occasions someone on the road would see them coming and get them stopped. Or someone with a saddle horse might overtake them and stop them.

During the winter-time the people had a lot of country dances. My father played the fiddle for most of them. When the snow was deep in mid-winter, we often went by team and sleigh for many miles. We would haul hay to feed the horses, and the sleigh box was filled with as much straw as was needed to sit in with a bunch of blankets to cover up with. People usually danced until daybreak.

Death of Joe and Mary Woodcock
One day a truck from the Charlo area brought a load of dead pigs and dumped them out just below the canal right where Grant's buildings are today. At that time no one lived nearer to the spot than we did.

The next evening as we boys and dad came down from the area we were logging, Mary Woodcock was at the pile of dead pigs with her horse and buggy. She already had her buggy loaded up with all the pigs that she could get on it and she had some tied on so that they wouldn't fall off.

We stopped our team and wagon and my Dad tried to convince her not to take those pigs as they must have died from some kind of a disease. He had heard that there was hog cholera in valley and some of the pigs had turned blue, and were bloated up. Dad told her that she would get sick!

She said, "Good Cachon" and refused to listen to the advice — she took that buggy load of pigs home with her. A few days later we learned that Mary and her son Joe were both dead. Joe was only two or three years older than I was and we had played together a lot when we were boys.

Phillip Pierre
Phillip Pierre used to come to our place quite often and tell us a lot of stories that had happened. I have forgotten most of what he told us, and I feel bad about that. But I do remember the story he told about one time that he, Eneas Conko, and Baptiste Bonapart rode horseback to Missoula.

In those days the Indians had a horse trail at the top of Evaro Hill that went through a little canyon that lies east of Highway 93. This trail came out quite close to Missoula, which saved them quite a distance of riding.

Their purpose in going to Missoula was to get some whiskey to bring back to the Reservation. They managed to buy what whiskey they wanted, and had it tied on their saddlehorses ready to go home, except for Phillip's jug. I will try to tell this story like Pierre told it:

"Eneas, Baptiste and me, we look to my jug. She looks like it good. We taken off top. She smellem some good. Each one us we takem one drinkem. Each we tryen some one more drinkum. Eneas, Baptiste, me lil bit we feelum some good. We like it to look at it, the town. I put it, my lil rope on mine jug. I can carry it good, um. We walk one more, some times we drinkum my jug. Dat town, she gotum lot some people."

My mother, my three sisters, and my sister-in-law were all there listening to him and in those days, no one said anything off color in front of any of the ladies.

He said, "One big one policeman, he say it us. 'What you Injuns thinkum can you do!' He say, 'I gon takum you to da jail.' I telum I don't like it to go to the jail. Dat big one policeman ketchum me, I give it, my jug, to Eneas and Baptiste, and they run away with mine jug. I start it to fightem dat big one policeman. I can no fighten so good, he's too big for me he's too strong one, he try to tro down me. I tinkum maybe he'es gittum me. Wit my two hands I grab on I ketchum by the crotch, I tro heem right down. Wen he holler like one big bull I run away. Eneas and Baptiste dey gotten my horse already, we can go. We gotten some good one horses. Dae can't kechem us. I getem on my horse. Now we can runum over dem policemans. We ridum fast our horses right trew dis town to da river. We turnem around our horses. We come back fast! I holdum my jug high. Tree of us, we holler our Injun holler. Everybody day run away from us. We gon go home dis time. Dem policemans dey can't no ketchem us no some more."

Mrs. Brush In The Canal

One late afternoon from our house we could hear a woman screaming like she was scared to death. Some of us ran up about a quarter of a mile to the bridge that went across the big ditch.

Mrs. Brush lived about a quarter mile from this bridge and on this particular day she had driven their little Model T Ford pickup to town. As she came home from town and came up over the ditch bank onto the bridge, she found that Louie Mollman had closed the big pole gate at the far end of the bridge.

When Mrs. Brush came onto the bridge and saw that the gate was closed, she must have gotten scared and excited and forgot how to stop the Model T pickup. She turned it to the left, right off the middle of the bridge — and into the canal she went.

By the time we got up to the bridge, her voice was started to get sort of squeaky, she had yelled so much, and it was easy to see why.

Their open-top pickup didn't have a cab on it and when we got there she was standing on the seat. The canal was plumb full of water and all that was out of the water was the top half of the back of the seat, and half of the windshield.

We had to take some rails off of Louie's rail fence and put one end of them on the edge of the bank and the other end on her pickup. She then crawled out on her hands and knees and she was just about petrified; she may not have been able to swim.

Problems Of My Own In Crossing The Creek

In my later years of school I was active in sports and also busy trying to keep my eyes on Adelle, so quite often I stayed the night with some of my friends, and sometimes I would just sleep in the schoolhouse. But most of the time I would ride the school bus home.

I would hurry to get my chores done and then catch a horse, grab something to eat, and jump on my horse and head back to town for a one-hour ride of eight miles. Our basketball practice was at seven in the evening and after practice I would get on my horse and head for home.

About this time the Rogers family moved to a place about one and a half miles from town on the same route that I traveled. Adelle played girl's basketball and practiced on opposite nights that the boys did, so on her practice nights I saddled a horse and went in again. She usually walked in to practice, but after she was done, we would ride my horse double back to her place. I would let her off and kiss her goodnight, and then I would ride on home.

At all the school functions or shows, or whatever went on, the only way I had to get to town was to walk or go horseback. I had a well-traveled trail through the woods to where I came out onto the road one mile south of town. Along this eight-mile trail I had different stretches of the trail that I always galloped; then I would walk my horse for a distance, and then I would gallop again.

All of the horses that I rode got to doing this without being urged on. They would start to gallop on their own, and stop on their own. When I was tired and sleepy at night I got to where I could sleep while my horse was walking. Then as he started to gallop, I would wake up until we got to the next walking place.

Rain, snow or cold, nothing stopped me from going to town. Many times it was thirty below zero and still I went, but I wore a long overcoat, a wool scarf and a pair of white Angora wool chaps that really belonged to my older brother, Rex. He seldom used them. My overcoat was loose enough so that when Adelle was with me I could wrap her right inside with me.

One night when I was about fifteen or sixteen years old, I was riding Babe, a frisky mare that had done a lot of bucking in her younger years. She was the great, great, great and maybe greater, grandmother of a lot of the better horses still on the ranch. This dark night I was thirsty so when I came to South Crow Creek that I stopped my horse and got off. I laid on my belly and got a good drink of water. The creek bank had quite a slope to it, but instead of turning my horse around to get on from the higher ground, I tried to get on from the lower side.

I was active, but not enough. I had gotten my foot into the stirrup and had to jump in the dark to catch the saddlehorn. Well, I missed catching the saddlehorn. My other foot went out from under me and I fell. It scared Babe, and away she went, dragging me through the creek, which had a lot of water in it. The last thing I remembered was grabbing the horse's tail and flipping myself over. At some point I must have come loose. When I woke up, it took me quite a while to get oriented enough to figure which way to go. I had to walk about a mile to our gate, where Babe was waiting for me. I took her through the gate and to a big log, where I managed to get back on and finish the ride home. I was lucky — I had a lot of bruises but no broken bones.

Crossing Crow Creek

A year or so later I was riding a horse I called Percy, one of the best horses I ever straddled and an offspring of Babe. It was a very dark and rainy night and I could see nothing as I approached North Crow Creek, where I had previously chopped a trail for about a 100 yards through real thick brush on both sides of the creek channel.

When I rode down the hill to the bottom, I should have been about fifty yards or so from the creek channel but I could hear my horse's feet in water. He didn't hesitate one bit, but kept right on going.

Soon my feet were in the water, but I didn't realize quickly enough what had happened. We were out in the main current. By then I had crawled to the top of my saddle and my horse was swimming. The current kept washing him against the brush on the side of the trail. When we hit the main channel, the water was boiling down and even in the dark I could tell we were being washed downstream.

I was getting very nervous because I knew that there was a barbed wire fence and an old railroad trestle just a short ways downstream. I felt Percy turn and start to swim upstream, against the current. My weight on his back kept him submerged quite deep and made it difficult for him to swim. I wouldn't get off because I couldn't see to get a hold of a stirrup, so that I could swim with him, so I just hung on for dear life.

He finally got back to the pathway, and then to where he could get his footing. Oh, what a good feeling to get out of there! If he had not been strong enough to swim against the current, we may both have lost our lives.

We were not far up the trail when Percy was ready to go again, to get himself warmed up, but what a cold ride we had for the last five miles!

The high water was due to the fact that it was in the spring of the year, and the reservoir was filled up. All of the water from the creeks and canals were turned down Crow Creek.

I went back in the daylight by a different route, and was scared all over again. The water was over the bridge and all the low land was covered with water. It was astonishing to think I had gone through that the night before! And I believe I would have drowned if I had been on any other horse than Percy, except maybe his mother.

Tacks Under My Saddle

I always alternated the horses that I rode to let them have a rest, but I did ride Percy more often because he was such a good horse.

Every time I rode to town, as I was leaving, I would untie him and get on. His head would be high, and his tail would be straight out, and he would let out a loud snort, loud enough that you could hear him for a long way. Sometimes he would snort several times before getting out of town — he had the looks and action of a real wild horse.

Then one spring day I rode him to school and tied him to the hitch-rail just outside of the school yard. That evening after school, I got on my horse to go home and he acted very odd and never gave his usual snort. And he would not gallop. He stopped and squirmed several times and I got off and led him a lot of the way. Finally, we got home and I unsaddled him. To my surprise, a Bull Durum tobacco sack filled with tacks fell to the ground. My horse had a hole chewed into his back bone, nearly as big as my fist.

I felt so bad that I had not suspected that some thoughtless idiots would have done such a thing. Someone thought they would see me get bucked off and instead they had ruined a good horse. There was no more riding for him that season.

After he healed up, I had to cut a hole in my pad to protect that spot. I tried every way I could to find out who had done it, but I never did. And maybe it was a good thing I didn't as someone would have gotten hurt. In fact, it's such a sore point with me that if someone today told me they were the one who put tacks under my saddle, I would still hit them right in the nose!

Chasing Horses

One day an Indian neighbor, Louie Hammer, asked me if I would watch for his little band of horses, which were missing, and if I saw them if I would run them up to his place. I told him I had seen them quite often on my way to and from town.

This particular day I was riding a little bay horse that liked to run and to chase horses, a hard horse to hold, or to slow down. I found the horses and shortly after starting the band towards Louie's, I gave my horse a jerk on the reins. The bit broke and came right up to the top of his neck, which left him free to run as fast and anywhere that he wanted to go.

He immediately caught up with the band of horses and they all started leaving the band, one or two at a time. In all my life, I have never jumped off of a bucking or running horse, and now I was going at too great a speed to think of jumping off and I surely didn't want to lose my saddle.

There was a lot of big pine stumps along the road left from the logging a few years before. All of the horses had peeled out of the bunch until there was only one horse left, and that horse was doing his very best to get away from me and my crazy horse. Many times I had to raise my feet to go over a stump without hitting it, and the horse was turning so short and leaning so much that my feet would touch the ground — and all the while I was trying to get my lariat out and still stay on the horse's back. I finally got a loop around his neck and started leaning back onto the rope, choking him down. He didn't want to quit, but he started to stagger and fall when I jumped off of him.

When I finally got him stopped he was almost white with lather. We both stood there for quite a while; I was puffing almost as bad as he was. My hands and face were all scratched and I had a lot of bruises from hitting limbs and little trees.

The outcome of all that was that I wasn't able to get Louie's horses in that day, though I did a day or so later.

Don't Ride on Sunday

During our school years, I often brought several horses into town for some of the kids that didn't have a horse when we went on school picnics and other outings. A Sunday horseback ride was planned and on Saturday evening I brought a few horses into town. I staked them out in a vacant lot where there was a lot of grass and on Sunday morning everyone gathered in the east part of town.

Adelle's dad was quite strict with her and he permitted no horseback riding on Sunday, but she was going to break her father's rule that day. Now there was a runaway bay horse in the bunch I had brought in and I had planned for one of the boys to ride him, but when Adelle saw that pretty bay horse, that was the one she wanted. I tried my best to talk her out of riding the bay; I told her that he would run away with her. She said he would not, that she could handle him. I was uneasy when she took that horse, but decided maybe she could hold him. And I was riding a bronc that I was breaking to ride.

As we were leaving town and approached the Cemetery Road, she saw a car that looked like her dad's. She kicked her horse and away she went on the fastest ride she ever had. My bronc didn't know what it was to really run yet, so I couldn't get him to go fast enough to catch her. Junior Bell had a race horse, so he said, but he was unable to gain on her either.

I got really worried about her because at that time there were no more fences after you got a mile and a half east of town and Louie Michelle and Old Patchee, two Indians, had three or four bands of horses running loose in the woods in that area. If the bay horse with Adelle on him were to run into one of those bands there was no telling what would happen.

Luckily, as she approached the end of the lane, two young fellows, Tip Leighton and Bob Sands, walked onto the lane from an old road. They scared the horse, and he finally stopped. Adelle sure was glad to get off that horse, and was thinking maybe her dad was right, she shouldn't ride on Sunday.

Professor Polly

During all my years in school we had the same professor. After all or any of the school functions, if there was any cake, candy or goodies, he would take them upstairs and lock them up in his office. He also locked the basketballs there.

On weekends we often gathered and sneaked into the schoolhouse where we played ball. Some of us would make sure, beforehand, that one or two windows in the building were not locked. Sometimes the unlocked window would be on the second floor so we kept a pole hidden in the weeds away from the building. We would get our pole, lean it up to the window and one of us would climb the pole, go through the window, go down and open the door from the inside. Then all the rest of us would sneak in.

Old Professor Polly caught us playing ball there several times when we were not supposed to be there.

We usually tried to keep a ball hidden somewhere in the school house. Once in a while we didn't have a ball and would have to get one from his office on the third or top story of the building. If it was after a school function, we also were certain that we needed some of those goodies that he had locked in his office. Now there was a manhole in the ceiling that was used to get to the top of the schoolhouse and I would take my lariat rope and one or two of the boys would help me onto their shoulders. I would open the trap door and crawl up onto the roof of the schoolhouse and usually one of the other boys came up with me.

The school bell sat on a frame at the edge of the roof and we would tie my lariat rope to the bell base. We had to be careful that we didn't ring the bell by pulling on the wrong rope. I would then take hold of my rope and let myself down over the edge of the roof and down to Professor Polly's window so I could go into his office. The other boy would take my rope off and go back down through the trap door and close it.

The door to the office had an inside night lock on it and I would just turn the knob on the night latch and the door was open. None of the other boys had the nerve to let themselves over the edge of the roof at that height, so I always had that job.

We would take one of the several balls that he had in there and if there were goodies that had been taken from our school functions we would take some of them as we rationalized that they rightfully belonged to the kids anyway.

We were careful not to bother anything else. Then we would push the door shut and it was locked again.

Professor Polly never did find out how we got in there, or if he ever knew, he never did lock his window. It was the highest one in the schoolhouse and every day he would open that window to throw his chewing tobacco cud out the window. He never suspected that anyone was getting through that high window into the building.

My Girl Friend

In my eyes, Adelle was the prettiest girl in our school. She was a friend to nearly all of the girls and was highly respected by all of the kids, both boys and girls. I think a lot of the boys would have liked to have her for their girl friend, but nearly everyone knew she was mine, even though I didn't have anything to offer her.

I didn't have a car, or money; all I had at the time was a saddlehorse. But as the years went by, I continually got more attached to her. Adelle's dad was quite strict with her, and I am sure he didn't want his lovely daughter to get tangled up with someone as poor as I was. However, nearly everyone else was short of money then, too, and although I was poor I had a lot of friends most people seemed to respect me.

In Love

By 1933 we were together at every possible opportunity, and wanted to be together always; even though we were kids, getting married kept entering our minds. So, after talking it over with our friends, Grace and Alton Ingraham, we decided to elope.

At the time I and three of my friends were working for a man named Bruer, thinning sugar beets by the acre for a price per acre I don't remember out west of Pablo, and camping in an old granary that was on the place. Bruer milked quite a few cows and told us he would give us all the milk and eggs that we needed if we helped with the milking.

When milking time came, both Mr. and Mrs. Bruer brought out all the buckets and milk cans and set them down in a row right behind the cows. When the first bucket of milk was milked and set down, about ten or fifteen cats came running and all got around and up onto the bucket to lap up milk. I ran and started to chase them away but Mr. Bruer informed me that I was to leave them alone, as they needed their share of the milk, and got the first chance. So the cats would line up around the bucket, and were left alone until all had their fill.

The cows had been on green grass and it seemed like every cow had to take a turn at letting fly. That green, soft manure would fly onto and into the buckets. We ate a lot of eggs that summer, but all four of us lost our appetite for milk. And for a long time it was hard for me to eat store-bought cheese or milk.

Getting Married

On June the 10th, 1933, I borrowed the old Model T sedan from my folks. I had already told my mother some time before that Adelle and I were going to get married and I drove into town and went to Adelle's house to get her. She had on a beautiful long green dress. We then picked up our best friends, Grace and Alton Ingraham, and because I would not get any money for my beet work for another week, so Alton loaned me $2.50 to buy my marriage license.

We drove to Polson, but the courthouse was closed because it was late in the day. So, we found out where Jimmy Harbert, the Clerk of Court lived, and drove up to his house, and told him we wanted to get a marriage license awful bad. Such a nice little man! He agreed to ride down with us and help us. We all went out to get into the car, but it wouldn't start. We cranked and cranked, but it still would not start. So Jimmy said, "Lets all get into my car."

He took us down to the courthouse, unlocked the door, and led us up to his office. He got out the marriage license, and asked me my age. I started to say 21, but before I could finish, he wrote down 21 or bust. Then, not looking at Adelle, he said, "And I presume you are eighteen." Then he asked us who was going to marry us. Well, we didn't know, so he said, "I know a very nice Methodist minister that might do the job. Let me call him." After he completed the call, he told us that Pastor Smith would be there in a few minutes.

In a short time, the minister was there and we were married there in the courthouse just before the clock struck 12 midnight. Then Jimmy Harbert drove us all to the top of Polson hill where we could look over the town and the city lights. He gave us a lecture all the way back, and told Adelle that if I ever abused her to let him know. Can you imagine someone today doing such a thing as opening the courthouse in the middle of the night? He was a smart man, and knew both of our parents; he also knew that we were two scared kids.

After he let us out at his house, our old Model T started right up. We drove down to an all-night restaurant and Grace and Alton treated all of us to a dish of ice cream. Adelle was so nervous she couldn't finish hers, so I ate it — and I've eaten her leftovers ever since. Adelle went home that night, and I took the car back to my folks.

The next day Adelle gathered part of her clothes, put them into a bag and hiked across the field to Ed Piedalue's house where Grace Ingraham was working. That night we went to Grace and Alton's place in Pablo. Alton was away someplace, working. They only had one bed, so Adelle and I slept in it with Grace.

The next morning we went over to Adelle's grandparents just a few blocks away and told them what we had done. Adelle's grandmother told her not to feel bad, others in the family had done the same thing. They were such a nice old couple, and insisted that we stay with them until we could decide what we were going to do. We just loved that old couple!

Went To See Her Folks

When Adelle's folks found out that we had gotten married, Adelle's dad raved around for a couple of days but her mother came up to see Adelle, and brought a couple of her blankets to give us. She also brought more of Adelle's clothes.

We had been married three or four days when Adelle's brother Jess (Junior), and Harley Ingraham came to the house, asking for me to come out. We went across the street behind a long, low building.

Their intentions were to beat me up, but neither one would confront me by himself. I suspected that they were up to something, and kept my back to the building so I wouldn't get hit from behind. They finally told me what their intentions were, but ended with both shaking my hand and wishing me luck.

We were married about two weeks before we got enough nerve to go to see her folks. When we got there, her dad said, "I should kick you both in the seat!" But he accepted us both and after that we got along fine through all of their lives.

I Went to Work For Tom Moore

Then I went to work for Adelle's uncle, Tom Moore. I got one dollar a day, and worked long days.

My first morning there he gave me a team of horses and had me hook them up to a manure spreader. We drove around behind the barn, and I never, ever, saw such a mountain of manure. He told me that he would like for me to start loading and hauling this manure out onto his field. He gave me a manure fork and left to go to work on his road contract.

I started to pitching manure into that spreader, but it seemed to me that I was not progressing very fast, so I went into his big horse barn where I found a big beet fork with the knobs all worn off the tines and I traded forks. I was young and strong and back I went to the manure pile and tore into the pile, which was so huge it looked as if there never had been any manure hauled out of there.

With the old beet fork, it didn't take me very long to get a good, big load on the wagon. Then I drove the team to the field and started spreading the manure. This was kind of fun for me because at home when we hauled manure we had to also pitch it off, and here all I had to do was to pull the lever to engage the spreader. In a short distance the manure would be all out, and I would go back for another load.

When I started on that pile, I thought to myself, "I will be here from now on. But, to my surprise, when quitting time came the second evening I was out in the field dumping the last load, and that pile was gone. Tom couldn't believe it, and I couldn't either, but it was so. Then he put me to work driving three horses on a fresno while the highway was being rebuilt. Uncle Tom had the contract to do the road from Ronan to north of Pablo and the work was all done with horses.

I Build A Cabin

In August of that first year, Harry Byrd offered to let us build a log cabin just across the road from Adelle's folks. We decided to take him up on his offer and we stayed with her folks while I built the log cabin.

I used Harry's team and wagon, went up into the woods right where the Woodcock Addition is now, and cut the logs with a crosscut saw. Harry helped me haul the logs on his wagon. Then I pealed them and a man who lived with my folks, Mr. Forton, came to help me build the cabin — and my Dad also helped a couple of days. It only took us a few days to erect it and then Adelle and I moved into our new home.

We both had a good feeling to have a house to ourselves. Adelle's folks were real good to us and many times Adelle's mother would cook their supper, then send part of it over for us.

Adelle's dad was a painter and I helped him paint a few houses. Times were very tough then and when people didn't have money to pay for his painting he would trade his work for anything he could get.

He gave us a wood range stove and a dining room table, and ten beautiful hens and a rooster. Subsequently, Adelle's two older brothers would sneak their rooster to our house under their coats, and let him fight our rooster and Adelle would get mad at them.

Her dad had painted some buildings and took a Jersey milk cow that was going to have a calf for part of the pay; he said if it was a heifer we could have it. One morning as he drove by he called to Adelle and said, "It's a girl." So we had a beautiful little Jersey cow that turned out to be the best cow that we ever owned. Nearly everybody that saw her wanted to buy her.

Splitting Posts For Joe Piedalue

One day a neighbor, Joe Piedalue, got ahold of me and asked if I wanted a job splitting some fence posts. I don't remember his offer for each post, but he had a big pile of dry cedar all cut to post length.

The next morning I took my wedge, mall, and axe and started to split the posts. Joe was gone somewhere for the day. These logs, being dry for a year, split very nice after I used my wedge to split them in two pieces. I had a post with nearly every whack of my mall — and the work was right up my alley as I had made a lot of posts with my dad.

Now Joe was a good guy, but sure liked to squeeze his pennies and when he got home that evening I had his posts all split and neatly piled for him. Joe, who was French, spoke in broken English, saying, "I can't pay you that kind of money." He thought it would take me three or four days to do the job, but he did pay me as agreed.

Topping Beets for Rex and Earl

The fall of 1933 was the wettest fall I can remember. During the month of October, I went to work for my brother, Rex, and brother-in-law, Earl Franks. They were growing sugar beets one mile south and one and one half miles west of Ronan and my job was to top the beets.

The rows were lifted with a team of horses pulling a lifter that went under the row of beets and brought them to the top of the ground. The toppers went along behind the lifter, each with a big, fourteen-inch knife with a hook on the end, shaped like a big eagle beak. We would reach down with the hook on the end of the beet knife, pull the beet up, chop the top off and throw it into a pile. Then another person would throw the beets onto the beet wagons with a beet fork.

The wagons had four-horse teams on them and we got so much rain every day that the wagons were miring down, and getting stuck all the time.

Viola Mae was Born

On November 14th, Adelle started to have labor pains late in the afternoon and I ran one and a half miles to town to get the doctor. Adelle had not been to see the doctor while she carried the baby.

The night was so foggy we could hardly see the road as the doctor and I drove back to our place. I stood on the running board and would tell Dr. French when he was too close to the ditch; finally, we got to our cabin.

Adelle's mother and Mrs. Harry Byrd were there. Adelle was all night trying to have the baby and, along in the morning, the doctor finally had to take it with instruments. It was a good thing that we were not out where we couldn't get to a doctor because she would not have been able to deliver by herself.

Our daughter was born November 15, 1933. The next morning Adelle's dad went to Pablo and got Eva Minster, who was a nurse, to come and take care of Adelle for a few days. Grace Ingraham came with her baby son, Gale, and stayed until Adelle could get up.

We were so proud of our little baby girl, Viola Mae. Every Saturday night we would take her in our arms and walk into town, mostly just to show her off. That winter the roads got very icy, so we would put our baby between us, and sing and dance all the way to town on the ice.

Moving From Byrd's

When we built that log cabin we were led to believe that we could live there as long as we wanted. Well, we were there about ten months when we were told that Harry had a sister and brother-in-law coming out from Missouri and they needed the cabin for them to live in, so we moved to an old house east of there, about one and a half miles away. Part of the windows were out and we had to nail tin over the many holes in the floor.

About the time we moved there, the Geological Aerial Mapping surveyors came into the valley to do some re-mapping. They went to the Indian Agency to find an Indian guide to take them onto the peaks; the Indian Department sent them to me. I was not a guide at that time, but I did get the job. This was not a very long job, but every little bit helped.

Most of the time I had only one other man with me, a young, active fellow. We climbed several of the peaks in the area and on each peak we would build a rock monument by piling the rocks and then wrapping them with white muslin.

On several occasions I packed a thirty-pound instrument on my back, which made quite a load along with the other equipment, and it was quite a job to make good time. We always came back the same day, and sometimes left at four in the morning and wouldn't get back until late at night. It was a fun job, as I always liked to climb in the mountains.

The surveyor stayed with us and one day while we were gone, Adelle put Viola Mae in her little wagon and pulled her to her folks place to get a rooster which she killed and cooked so she could have a good chicken dinner for us that night.

This fellow was an ambitious guy and a good climber. We hiked to the top of the main peak on McDonald in several hours, less time than anyone before us according to information in the bottle there. While picking up rocks to build our monument, we saw a bunch of Ptarmigan feeding. The note in the bottle described another climber seeing them some time before we were there, and this was the only time I saw Ptarmigan in this area.

We also put up four-way flags that were about ten feet high on several of the section corners out in the valley.

We Moved to Grandpa's

Adelle's grandmother died and her grandpa was crippled and alone so we moved back in with him, and Adelle took care of him while we were there. That winter I went to work on my first construction job, working for Poston Brothers while they built the new highway through the Big Draw running from Elmo to Hot Springs.

On my first morning, I was put on a dump truck. They didn't ask me if I had ever driven one, and I had not. I was told to go out to the gravel pit and I got the truck started and managed to get out of the yard and onto the main road, but then the truck stopped and wouldn't go. The boss came along, asking me what was the matter. I said "It just doesn't want to go."

He got out and opened my door, looking in at the controls. "Take that damn emergency brake off," he said, "and maybe it will go!" I did, and it went. I was on that truck for some time, and one day they asked me if I would like to go onto the service truck. I told them I would like to try it. I hauled fuel and greased all the heavy equipment.

It was a job that helped me learn a lot about equipment. Sometimes I had to start some of the equipment and move it to different positions, so I could get to the different parts to do the work on them. And sometimes I would help with repair jobs, and it was good experience for me, working on caterpillars.

We didn't have a car yet, so I had to hitch a ride to and from the job on weekends. During the week, we all stayed in the road camp where they fed and housed us in bunkhouses. One evening I didn't have anyone to ride home with so the boss let me off half an hour early so I could run about four or five miles to try to catch the passenger bus on Highway 93. I ran all the way and got about 100 yards from the highway when the bus went by. Disappointed, I started to walk home from near Elmo but I caught a ride into Polson, and not far out of town I caught another ride to our home in Pablo.

Back To Work For Tom Moore

After that job was finished, Tom Moore, Adelle's uncle wanted me to came back and work for him again. I walked to work down the railroad track for some time and then they fixed up a little house on their place for us to live in. We moved down there and they paid us $35.00 a month and gave us our milk, cream and eggs.

One cold winter morning, Uncle Tom couldn't get his old truck, a square-cabbed International (about a 1922 model) started. He hooked up his big team of horses to the sleigh with a hay rack on it, but one of these big horses was quite skittish. Tom got his wife, Adelle's Aunt Grace, to come with him to drive the team hooked to the bobsled and pull the old truck to start it.

As they came out into the hay field with Grace driving the team and Tom in the truck trying to start it, the truck backfired with a couple of real loud pops, like gunfire. The big team spooked and took off, and Aunt Grace, who was a little woman, couldn't get them stopped. They jerked her hands back and forth over the front of the hay rack, which peeled all the skin off her knuckles. Tom jumped out of the truck to try to get up to help her stop the team of horses, but when he let go of the steering wheel the truck started to whip back and forth; it knocked him down and nearly ran over him.

The team ran through the herd of cattle. A big, mean bull held his ground, so that powerful team of horses ran right into the bull, knocking him down and running right over the top of him, followed by the sled. Dragging the sled, the bull and the truck was a little too much for that big team, and they finally had to stop. By the time I got out there, the team of horses were standing still and trembling. Oh, what a picture it would have been if someone had come by with a movie camera!

Finally, we got the cows into the corral. The old bull seemed to have calmed down, and as we sorted the cows, I forgot about him. All at once, Tom hollered at me to look out. Out of the corner of my eye, I saw that old bull coming. We were in a good, high, solid corral, and I made it to the fence, jumping and pulling myself to the top just as the bull put his big, hard head right through the fence, right under my feet.

Another time that same bull hit Tom's horse under his belly, throwing both of them onto his back. Tom fell off one side, the horse off the other. Uncle Tom's dog grabbed the bull's tail, keeping him off Tom until he could get on his feet.

Aunt Grace was a terrific cook, the best I ever knew. One day when we were there for dinner, and Viola Mae was still small, she disappeared outside the house. From the window inside, Adelle and Aunt Grace saw her outside the yard, in where the cattle were. The big, mean bull was laying out there, chewing his cud and Viola Mae was about three or four feet from his head. Adelle screamed for us.

I didn't take time to go through the gate; Adelle still tells about how I went over that fence without touching it, snatching up Viola Mae. The bull didn't even quit chewing his cud.

Aunt Grace had been complaining that something had been getting into her chicken house and breaking her eggs. We were sure it couldn't have been Viola Mae because the latch to the door was higher than she could reach and one day Aunt Grace glanced down to the chicken house just in time to see Viola Mae's little bottom disappearing through a twelve-by-twelve inch hole that was cut out for the chickens to go in and out. Her fun was stopped, but Aunt Grace and everyone else loved her in spite of her egg breaking.

Hunting At The Kelly Ranch
In the fall of this year, Adelle and I took a few days off to go hunting. We went with my sister Bernida and her husband, Herman, and my brother Floyd. We went in Bernida and Herman's car to a spot west of Kalispell near McGregor Lake and stopped at the Kelly Ranch to ask about the hunting as this was a new area to us.

The people were very friendly, letting us stay in a little cabin that they had at no charge. We all liked each other, and we stayed there for a couple of days while we hunted, getting some deer. The people's name was Miller, and they were the overseers for the Kelly Ranch.

We Bought Our First Car
After we got back home, Alton Ingraham took me to Missoula in his car to help me shop for a car. He knew a little more about them than I did. At the H.O. Bell Ford, we found a 1928 Ford coup that sounded good. It had a rumble seat in the back end.

It took all the money I had to buy it, $125.00, but it was our first car and we were quite proud of it. It was secondhand, but it was a good little car though it did burn out a condenser once in a while (at the time, a condenser cost only cost about 35 cents).

Going To Work At The Kelly Ranch

Later that fall the Miller's from the Kelly Ranch drove down and wanted us to go to work for them. They would pay me $45.00 a month. We debated, but decided to go there. That represented a $10.00 a month raise and it was quite a bit at that time. We went there in mid-winter and the snow there was still real deep.

They ran whitefaced cattle and had about fifty registered Percheron horses, but had only one team that was broke, plus one saddlehorse. The rest were wild and not even halter broke.

They had three big registered stallions, but only one was broke to lead, and everyone on the place was scared to death of the two that were not halter broke. To get them to water, they would just open the pens and let them go on their own. The guys were afraid to get in the pens, as the stallions would take after them.

One of the first things I did was to catch both these horses. They were four or five years old and had never had a rope on them and weighed about 1,600 pounds apiece. When I caught them, they squealed and bellered but I finally got a halter on them and tied them up. The first couple of days every time I got close to them they would start to squeal and beller, but in three or four days I was leading them all over the place.

While I was there, I broke all the big horses to work and all the saddlehorses on the place to ride. In the spring of the year, after the cattle were turned out on the range, the ticks got very bad; in fact, I've never, ever seen them like that. We had

Viola Mae and Bud (by fence) at Kelly Ranch in 1936.

to ride every day, so it was a good time to break the new saddlehorses though we constantly got ticks on them and ourselves.

The ticks got on the cattle in gobs. They would gather anywhere along the spine in bunches, sometimes on top of each other. If they gathered behind the head, it didn't take too many, like a spot about as big as a silver dollar, and the cows would go down. They were kind of paralyzed, and a cow could not move a muscle. We would get off our horses, take out our pocket knife and cut the ticks off next to the skin. We also carried a little bottle of iodine with us, and would put some on the spots where we cut the ticks off. Within a few minutes, the cow would be on her feet and going again as if nothing had been wrong.

We cut ticks off of a lot of cows that spring; the first and only time I had to do this.

Bear at Kelly Ranch

In the middle of June the Kelly Ranch was beautiful. The meadow was several hundred acres and always had deer playing through it. And wherever I went, I had a friend with me by the name of Bum, a good cow dog.

When I was a boy, I used to see this kind of dog quite often. He was a big, black dog with sort of long and bushy fur, a brown spot over each eye and a short tail. He was not too pretty, but he was a real good dog. He was a coyote killer, and killed nearly every coyote that came out into that big meadow. All we had to do when we saw a coyote was say, "Coyote!" and old Bum would start jumping up and down to try to see it. And away he would go!

He was smart enough to approach them from the timbered side of the meadow so they couldn't get into the timber. Quite often the big, older coyotes would turn on him to fight. Old bum wouldn't even slow down; he would hit them hard and send them a rolling. Then he would be right on top of them. I rode out there several times just to see how he killed them, but each time they were dead by the time I got there. What a dog!

The ranch had an earth-filled dam and reservoir to catch the snow and spring runoff, and hold it for irrigation water during the summer. I had been riding up there horseback and had been cleaning the trash out of the ditch that led down into the meadow when old Bum started to bark a short ways away, so I went up there. He had a porcupine up in a little tree so I found a good stick and killed it. He was smart enough not to bite it, so I think he had gotten one before.

Well, the next day the boss told me to take my gun along and if I saw a nice young buck on the way back, to bring one in for the ranch. I rode up into the canyon to where I had stopped working on the ditch the day before and I stopped and tied my horse at a spot that needed some cleaning.

I had only been there for a few minutes when old Bum started to bark and I started up to kill another porcupine. I was just bending over to pick up a good stick when I heard something behind me. I looked up and here came a huge big black bear, right at me. I took off running and yelled for the dog at the same time I ran around a big clump of bushes. With every step I took, the bear was blowing and grunting right in the seat of my britches. When Bum got there he grabbed it from the back end and the bear turned and started fighting the dog. I ran on to my horse and grabbed my old 30-30. I was so nervous I took a quick shot at the bear, and it turned and went up the canyon.

I called Bum off, but then I found that there was blood. It was kind of hard to follow the bear's trail, so I let Bum do the trailing. I followed him on my horse, but he was quite a ways ahead of me when I heard him start barking. When I finally got there, the bear was laying under a big tree and was dead. From its claw marks, I could see it had climbed up the tree a ways and then had fallen out, probably from losing so much blood.

The bear was a female, and by looking at her teats I could tell that she had cubs. I felt terrible to think I had shot a momma bear. My bullet had hit her in the neck, and cut one of the main arteries, causing her to bleed to death.

While I was skinning her, I heard something up in the tree, and looked up to see her three babies. I could have cried. I think that the momma bear had left her babies alone while she went to feed that morning. Bum probably got after her babies, and when she heard him barking, she came back to protect her cubs When she got to me, she probably thought I was the one after her cubs, so she took after me. Then, when the dog came to help me, the cubs took off, going farther up the mountain.

After she left me she probably followed her young, up into the tree, where she fell out dead. A few days later, one of our neighbors wanted to try to get the cubs so we went back to that spot, but her cubs had eaten their mother completely up, and were gone.

We Have Company

One Friday night, some of our friends came from Ronan to see us while we lived at the Kelly Ranch. We were sound asleep and woke up during the middle of the night to find some people crawling through one of the low, open windows. It was

Bud's brother, Floyd, brought the folks up in his new Chevrolet truck to visit Bud and Adelle at the Kelly Ranch, where Bud was working, in 1936.

dark when they got there, and they didn't know where the door was so, spotting an open window, they all came through it.

That same weekend my side of the family also came to see us, bringing extra friends with them. My brother, Floyd, had a new one and a half ton truck with a grain box on the back of it and since the weather was real nice, they had put some benches in the grain box and all piled into it. I don't remember how many people, but there were lots of them and everyone had a big time.

On their way home that Sunday afternoon, some of my younger brothers almost killed our brother-in-law, Herman Byrd. The whole gang was eating marshmallows, acting crazy and feeding each other. Herman was eating them fast, so they started shoving them into his mouth while someone held him down — a group of kids, not realizing what they were doing! Poor Herman was unable to say anything or stop them, and started to pass out. Thank goodness, a long string of marshmallows came back up and even out through his nose, a lucky thing, or he would have choked to death.

Me and Viola Mae in Missoula

When Viola Mae was about two years old, we went to a funeral for one of Adelle's cousins in Missoula.

We rode to Missoula with Uncle Tom, Aunt Grace and Uncle Harry Moore. We all ate at a restaurant, then we did some shopping. Adelle and I were about four or five blocks from the car when Viola Mae got a real bad case of the runs. I was carrying her in my arms when it happened, and it went all over the front of my suit.

She had on little silk panties which didn't hold anything, so I cupped my hand under her little bottom. I tried to hand her to Adelle, but she refused to take her, so I headed for the car. I was trying to hold Viola Mae away from me, with the potty dribbling down between my fingers. And Adelle was coming along behind, pretending she didn't know who I was.

Wouldn't you know it, I met several people that I knew on that street and as I approached the last block, I was stepping high and fast. Uncle Harry was standing by the car, and when he spotted me he started to laugh. The closer I came, the harder he laughed; the poor guy laughed so hard he had to sit down on the edge of the sidewalk.

I don't know why there had to be so many people on that street just then. Everyone that I met shied out around me, and everyone had to start laughing. And my good suit was a mess and I wondered how could one little girl do so much!

We Have a Son

Adelle was pregnant with our second child while we were at the Kelly Ranch. Later along, in August, she decided to go stay with my folks until time for the baby. I stayed and worked until her due time in September. We decided not to go back after that, and moved back in with Adelle's granddad after the baby was born on September 8th, in my folks log house on the Mollman place. My sister, Bernida, arrived from the eastern part of Montana just before the baby came.

When "Buddy," Vern Edmond Jr., was born, Mary Katherine, an old Indian lady, brought Adelle a little sack of dried meat for a gift. At the time two of Adelle's uncles from Ohio were there and Mary gave them each a piece of the dried meat. Bert ate it, enjoying it, but Bill looked at Mary Katherine's dress and her hand that didn't appear too clean. When he thought no one was looking, he turned around and spit the meat out into his hand.

Kerr Dam

I thought that I would try to go to work on Kerr Dam. I was told that a person had to be there real early to get in the hiring line that filed past the hiring window every morning and when I got there, already there were about 75 or 100 men in line. I went there every morning for a week or more and it was the same thing every day. Each day only three or four men in the line would be hired. and there were men from all parts of the country trying to get work here. There were no jobs anywhere to be gotten.

I was about to give up when one morning a man came and took me by the arm, and led me out of the long line of men. He took me into the office and asked me what I could do, or if I had a trade. I said no, but I was willing to try anything. They gave me a badge with a number on it to pin on the front of my shirt and then they took me and four other men to the dam site.

They showed us a ladder that was fastened onto the side of a cliff, which went straight up for about 200 feet. They told us our boss would be up on top, where he would show us what to do. I was the third man on the ladder, but when we got about one-third of the way up the man above me looked back down.

He said, "You'll have to go back down, I just can't go any higher." So, we had to go down and let him off; he just couldn't take the height. We started back up and got a little over half way, and the guy behind me said he didn't think he could make it either. I told him, "Oh yes you can. Don't look down, just keep right on climbing." When we got to the top, he let out a big sigh of relief and said it just felt to him like someone was trying to pull him off that ladder.

We met our boss and were each given a pick and shovel and told to clean the dirt all off of this cliff, right down to bare rock. This would be where they were going to start drilling the rock to cut the keyway out for the dam. I worked on this muck stick, as they called a shovel, for a week or so, and then one day old Pete Freeland, the tunnel superintendent, came by and told me he needed me down in the diversion tunnel.

This was only a pilot tunnel about eight or ten feet in diameter. They had a track and little mine cars in there and we worked in pairs; two of us would load a car as fast as we could shovel, and then take it out to dump it. Another crew of two men loaded their car as fast as they could. After this tunnel was drilled through the mountain, they enlarged it enough so all the water that was in the river could flow through it while the dam was being built.

Next I worked on one of the two power tunnels which were dug on about a forty-five degree pitch from the top of the dam down to the power house. I got to drill with water liners and jackhammers while I was working there. Then they put me to work as a signal man for a hoist that let the big dump truck down into the tunnel where it was filled with loads of rock.

When the truck was full, it was pulled back out. It was not possible for them to run the truck motors because the gas fumes would get to the men. The operator of the hoist was on the outside of the tunnel where he couldn't see and I was down on the inside. I had an electric cord with a button box on the end; when I pushed the button, a light flashed on the operator's control panel. One push on the button meant stop. Two buttons meant hoist up, and three meant come down. If we wanted it to go up or down at a faster speed, we repeated the signal. Then the operator would speed up the cable hoist.

Slide

After I was done with that part of the job, I was sent down to work in the keyway on the far side of the river. This is where the big slide was. When I first went in there to work, I was afraid because right over us was a big triangle-shaped part of the mountain, about 100 feet in diameter with natural seams all around it. I mentioned to some of the other workers that I didn't like the looks of it. But the rest of the crew didn't seem to be concerned about it, so why should I be? I would tell myself that it was safe, but it looked to me like it was just setting there, several hundred tons of it, waiting to come down.

I was working on the midnight shift, called the graveyard shift, from twelve to eight in the morning, drilling and blowing the rock out of the keyway where the dam would be placed. The crew just before us had finished blasting out their holes before we came onto our shift and we all went in and started to get ready so we could drill with our jackhammers.

Another man and I were the farthest up the mountain and nearly against a ledge of rock that was fifteen or twenty feet high. Louie Vanderburg, one of our men had just left us to go out to the toilet, and a young man by the name of McNeily, our waterboy, was bringing us our drinking water. All of a sudden I heard a roar.

"For God's sake, run," I yelled. I knew what was coming! I stayed as close to the wall as I possibly could, and still run. Many, many tons of rock started to pour over our heads, but the little ledge protected us, causing the rock to fly over the top of us.

Young McNeily was quite a ways ahead of me as we got to the outside part of the main slide. We were running along on a ledge that was flat and about thirty feet wide when some rocks came down ahead of me and hit McNeily, knocking him off the ledge. I could see him moving a little as I went by him. I had to run to the end of this ledge and then I went down around and ran back to pick him up.

I started to carry him out when three or four fellows from another crew came running to help me. More rocks came down and broke both legs of one of the men and crippled one of the others. The nice young man, McNeily, lived for about two days then died.

After waiting a while for rocks to stop tumbling down, a few of us went back in there. We only found one body — that of Henry Couture. He was flat like a giant roller rolled over him. We just scraped him off the rocks and put him in a blanket; we knew it was him by his badge number on his overalls.

While looking for others, three or four times I thought I heard a man's voice and I told some of the other men, but they said, "Maybe." I thought maybe I just imagined that I heard it, as I was so nervous.

I came out real fortunate with only a few cuts and scratches. We then went up to the top of the cliffs and drove steel pegs along the edge of the cliffs, then hung long ropes from each peg. We used boatswain slings to hang from the ropes while we barred the rocks loose. It took two days and two nights to do it.

Early the morning of the slide, my brother, Rex, showed up way before time for him to go to work. He had known that I was in that crew and the radio had announced that everyone had been killed. When he saw me I got a big hug. Then, when I got home from work, some friends of ours, Lena and Beal Ingraham, had just come to our house to be with Adelle as she got the news that all of that crew of men were killed.

When going back to work that night I sat in my car for quite a long time before I could make myself walk down into that canyon to go to work. It was an awful feeling to know that all those men were killed — and still, a good feeling that the Lord spared my life, along with Louie Vanderburg, the one that had left to go to the bathroom.

On the third night when we went to work, the high scaling was done so we went in to start uncovering and find the bodies. Already the smell was real bad and while I helped with the digging, I didn't want to be the one to find the bodies. As I was digging in one spot, the smell was real bad; I pulled my shovel out, and the end of my shovel was covered with brains. I just had to walk away and tell the others that there was a man under there.

The man who had been working with me at the time of the slide, Jack Anderson, was also killed. We found him all in one piece, still standing up with his shovel in his hands. He had backed up against the rock ledge and the rock had poured over the top of him and as it piled up in front of him and then came back and had pinned him there. I felt so bad when we found him as he only had a few cuts on his legs and I still believe, to this day, that I did hear him when we were first looking for them. I feel that had we known, we could have saved his life.

Another crew was formed and we began working on the opposite side of the canyon. We were working here for a few nights when, one night, someone found a great big bull snake that was partly dead from being blasted when the crew before us set off those shots. Well, I don't like snakes and I am also afraid of them — I just can't help it. This snake was three or four feet long, maybe longer, and about four inches in diameter. Some of the guys were fooling around with that darned snake, so I went down below them a ways to work.

I didn't know it, but the boss told this guy not to throw that snake on him so they decided to throw it at me. Well, I had my back to them when all at once that snake hit me in the back of the neck and came around both sides of my neck, pulling me right down on my face. It scared me so bad and also made me so mad that when I finally got to my feet I looked up to see who had thrown it.

I could tell right away who it was and I didn't even notice how big and husky he was, nor did I care. When I got close by he started to run and I caught him by the back of the neck. As he tried to get up and over a little ledge, which he didn't get over, I jerked him over backwards into the rocks and started beating on him. It was a good thing others pulled me off of him because I was berserk enough that I was trying to get a hold of a rock to work on him with. The boss sent him in to get his time because he had already warned him not to throw the snake.

One day the superintendent came along and asked me how I would like to go oiling on a diesel-powered one and a half yard shovel. He told me that it would be a job that would last longer, with the same pay, so I went to work as an oiler. Clifford Artist was the operator and we got along real well, and worked on several different machines. This was good experience for me.

One time Cliff and I were sent down below the powerhouse to dig a ditch for a pipeline up through the bank of a little hill. For some distance the banks on each side of the ditch were from six to ten feet high. We had a small one-half-yard steam shovel that had been converted to air and we finished the ditch just at quitting time in the evening. Then a crew of all Indians were brought in to lay in the pipes and while they were all in there laying pipe, one of the sides caved in and buried them with dirt. Several of them lost their lives before they could uncover them.

I knew several of them, one very well, Paul Enemie. He had been a neighbor and had worked for my parents several times, putting up hay and helping at harvest time.

I had worked on this dam for some time before I found out how I had really gotten this job. Adelle, the wise little gal, wrote a letter to the project engineer, telling him how hard I had been trying to get on there, and also how badly we needed the work. If it hadn't been for her, I may never have gotten a job there. I continued to operate until the dam was completed. Then my superintendent wanted me to go to the Panama Canal on another job with him. It sure did sound tempting, but I stayed in Montana.

We Moved to the Plant Place

After the dam was done, there was no work or jobs anywhere. I could have went back to work for Tom Moore again, but we decided to lease eighty acres that belonged to Tony Plant. He lived in Arlee at the time and his land was just above the ditch, east of Godfrey Johnson's place. My son Buddy now owns both places and that piece of land joins son Buck's place on the south.

My folks had left shortly before to move to Detroit and if I could have leased that eighty acres sooner, I could have taken all of my folks equipment, tools, harnesses, a few cows, sheep, calves, and a sow. That would have given me a good start, but someone else had taken it all over except three or four horses, which I did get.

We moved onto Tony's place during the winter, which was beautiful and open, and we didn't have very much to move, because we didn't own much.

By then the Model A ford was starting to get a few aches and pains, so we traded it off for a 1937 Chevy sedan — a knee-action front end instead of springs.

During the month of February, I borrowed an old, broke mare from Charlie Brush, one of our neighbors and hooked up my saddlehorse and another unbroken horse with her to a one-bottom sulky plow. I worked the unbroken horse for half a day and then I would put a different horse in. I did this for three or four days and then, finally, got more harness together and a two-bottom gang plow and hooked up six horses.

I made quite a few crooked furrows for a while and when the horses tried to run away I would just sink the plow in a little deeper. I finally got them all to working all right and I returned the old mare to Charlie. I plowed all of the ground that needed to be plowed during the month of February and seeded it down real early. When we moved into this place, it had an old log house in which we had to patch some holes in the floor with tin can lids, and a barn with dove-tailed corners.

We did have a nice stream coming right past the end of the house, so we built a little spring house right over the stream. We made a trough out of wood with compartments in it and had the water running through it; this way we could raise the level of the water so we could keep our milk and cream in the cold water.

We managed to acquire a few more cows, and I was milking some of them. We separated the milk and fed the skim milk to the calves and pigs; the cream was taken to town and sold at the creamery to provide us grocery money.

That summer a friend of mine, older by a few years, was going to go to Washington by covered wagon and he sold me six horses and two colts for $10.00. Two of them were cripples, but were still good brood mares.

I don't remember where I got the ten dollars as it was hard to find at that time, but that gave me quite a few horses. At that time none of the land in the woods was fenced, so I could just let the horses run loose.

Putting Up Hay on the Plant Place

The Plant place that we were on was good producing land, and we always had good crops and good hay. Below our house we kept about 20 acres for pasture and I always kept it well irrigated, so it was nice and green all summer.

I ran irrigation ditches all over the place. I made the elevation of the ditches by using a good straight board one inch by six inches by sixteen feet long and nailed a leg on each end of the board with the front leg one inch longer than the back leg. I then put my carpenter level on the board and kept moving the board ahead and, placing the back leg where the front leg was, moving the front leg up or down with the contour of the ground until it showed level. Then I drove a wooden stake at every point where the ditch would make a bend. Finally, I took my team of horses and hooked on to the walking plow, and plowed out the ditches.

When haying time came I had a horse-drawn mowing machine and an old dump rake. I would mow down the hay and then, when it was dry enough, I would rake it up in windrows. When I was done raking, I straddled the team over the windrow and went up and down each one, putting the hay in bunches.

Adelle helped me shock it with a pitchfork and we piled it up in neat little piles so that if it rained it would not get very wet.

I made a stacker by fastening a good stout pole up on a big pine tree with a cable and pulley on the end. We used the team and wagon with a hay net in the bottom of the wagon hayrack. Adelle and the kids went along on the wagon to the field and we let the kids play in the field, or along the little creek, while Adelle and I pitched the hay onto the wagon.

When the wagon got quite a lot of hay on it, I had Adelle get up onto the load and tramp it down so we could get a good, big load. She always liked that job with her short legs up in that loose hay! Often, when I threw hay up, it happened to land on her.

When we had a load, I would push the kids up onto the top of the load and then get up myself, taking it to the hay stack near the barn. I unhooked the team from the wagon and hooked them onto the hoist cable. Then, as the hay was hoisted over the stack, Adelle would pull the trip rope and drop the hay onto the stack. Then she could get a little rest while I went up and stacked the hay — but then, out we would go for the next load.

Adelle's Strawberry Patch

We always had a big garden and a big raspberry patch. On our second year on the Plant place, we put in a big strawberry patch and Adelle was doing all the care of them and thought she was going to sell a lot of strawberries.

On one occasion, when she was pregnant with our son, Kenny, she had been weeding the berry patch by crawling on her hands and knees with her belly almost dragging on the ground. She worked hard and was excited when the berries started to ripen and looked so pretty!

But one night, Landquist's cattle (he was our neighbor) knocked the fence down and about fifty head of cattle tore her strawberry patch to pieces. I felt so sorry for her and she had a good cry over the hard work she'd lost.

Our Son Kenny

That baby was born August 22, 1939, in our log cabin on the Plant place. I was alone with Adelle when the time came and I sent my brother, Louie, to get my sister.

Bernida came and cut the cord. Then Dr. Brooke came after that, and he cut the cord again because it was too long. We named our new son Kenneth Ray (the Ray was for my brother).

I Worked on W.P.A

While we were on this place I got a job on the WPA — the Works Program Administration formed by the government, all over the U.S. to stimulate employment. Each county had the program that included work on county roads, parks, schools, refuges, and many other things.

I worked on roads for the Fish and Wildlife and on the golf course in Polson, making $44.00 per month. I would go to work on a certain day of the month, work for two weeks, and then I would be off about two weeks. I helped plant all of the trees on the Polson Golf Course.

We got the trees, which were about four to six feet tall at the time we dug them in midwinter, northeast of Pablo. We got them by carefully digging a trench around each tree about 5 feet in diameter, leaving a lot of dirt on the roots. Then we lifted the trees with the cone of dirt, wrapped them in burlap and let them freeze. Then we gathered them and hauled them to Polson and planted them at the golf course; every tree that we transplanted there survived and they're huge today, more than fifty years later. I think we planted those trees in 1938 or 1939.

Climbing The Peaks In The Missions

About this same time, in the later part of August, Jack Romer, who was the son of the wealthy lady that had just finished building a new home nearby on Post Creek, hired me to guide him on a backpacking expedition. We were to climb all of the major peaks in the Mission Range, from Mt. Harding south to Gray Wolf Peak.

We left our ranch early in the morning to ride horseback as far as Summit Lake, with one pack horse for our packs. My wife, Adelle, and Dorothy Allard, a neighbor lady, went along with us to bring the horses back to the ranch.

Jack and I would go from there on foot. I was reluctant to do so, but I was riding a horse that belonged to a friend of ours. The horse needed a lot of hard riding as he had been giving them trouble, and the man insisted I ride him.

After reaching Summit Lake we had our lunch and the girls started back down off of the mountains with the horses for the ranch. Adelle went in the lead, riding and leading the pack horse, and Dorothy came along behind, hazing the loose saddle horses, including the one that belonged to my friend.

The girls got back down to the big cliffs on McDonald Trail that are several hundred feet high okay, but then things got bad. When this trail was built a few years before, a few switchbacks were blasted in the face of the cliff. Dorothy later told me that when this crazy horse got to the edge of the cliff that, instead of going down the trail, it went to the very edge, pawed a couple times and then laid down and let itself roll down over the cliff.

Dorothy started to scream for Adelle, as she knew that Adelle was directly below where this horse went tumbling, end over end, down over the cliff. And there were so many rocks and dust raised up that Dorothy couldn't see what was happening.

The horse came tumbling down, almost on top of Adelle, but did hit onto the trail just in front of her feet, and then it bounced on down the cliff, rocks flying everywhere. Had Adelle been another step further down the trail, she would have been hit.

After seeing what happened, the rest of the horses came down just like soldiers, but the girls then had to go down and find that horse — all the while praying that it would be dead, as they had no way to kill it, if it were badly injured. But, after rolling for a quarter of a mile, it was very dead. They managed to get the saddle off, but it was not worth bringing home, it was so broke up.

When Jack and I were ready to climb McDonald Peak, which is the highest peak in this range of mountains, we made our camp a short ways below Ice Flow Lake. While we were there, a large part of the glacier broke off and fell into the lake, causing the water to come up onto the shores of the lake, and sending a big surge of water down the creek.

Early the next morning we started to climb the peak. We didn't see any grizzly at all on our way up, but on our way down off the peak, we saw one old sow and four cubs going over the east ridge. Earlier we had seen a lot of sign in a meadow that we always called Grizzly Basin, where we could hardly get through the meadow without stepping on bear piles.

Before we got back to our camp, it started to look like it was going to storm and about dark that evening, it turned cold and started to snow very hard. At daybreak the next morning when we got up, it was still snowing. A little later we heard a little bit of mumbling sounds and, upon looking out of our little tent (one made out of airplane silk), about thirty yards in front of us was a big grizzly briskly going by. Jack quickly grabbed his .45 caliber six-shooter and also his camera. He handed me his gun, the only gun we had with us, and started taking pictures, but it was still snowing.

After the first bear went by, two more came along and it seemed as though they were going to simply pass us by, which they did. In those few minutes nine grizzlies had gone by our tent with not one of them bothering to even look toward us. They must not have been able to smell us, or didn't care, and I think they were all concentrating on moving down to a lower elevation out of the snow.

As it ended up, none of Jack's pictures turned out because it was snowing so hard. By that afternoon the sun was out again and we never saw another grizzly on the rest of our trip, confirming the notion that you only see the grizzly when you least expect them.

In later years my sons and a daughter-in-law got to see some bears at close range in this same area. They heard one bellering that must have fallen into one of the many cracks in the glacier, but were unable to locate it. This area was once known for its many bears, but there are not so many any more.

Building Our Cabin On The Plant Place

The first year we spent on this place, I built a root cellar for our fruit and vegetables and an icehouse to store our ice in during the summer months.

When winter came and I had all my farm work done, I went up Suzanne Creek and cut a set of house logs to build a new house. I cut the trees down with my crosscut saw, and then skidded them down the mountain with my team of horses. I then peeled the logs and proceeded to put up a new house.

Adelle had become anxious to get out of the old house because we had discovered that it was infested with bedbugs. In those days, nearly every old house in this valley had bedbugs in them.

The Cheff family poses, in 1942, in front of the cabin they built on their property. From left in photo are Adelle's brother, Billy, Adelle and Kenny, Adelle's brother Bob, Bud, Viola Mae and Buddy.

Cut Wrist

I had our new building nearly done and was chopping one day on a board with my razor-sharp axe when Adelle came out in front of me with only a short smock on. She was real big with Kenny at the time, and when I saw her I started to laugh at her cute performance. Just then, my axe handle caught on the edge of the board, and the axe went sideways, right into the wrist of the hand that I was using to hold the board. Blood spurted up to the ceiling.

Adelle grabbed a sheet and wrapped it around my wrist and we got into the car and went to the doctor. I didn't know how much I was bleeding and I should have just held pressure on the artery, but we were a couple of dumb kids and didn't know any better.

When we got to the doctor's office, the bottom of the car was full of blood. I managed to stagger into the office and as I was going in, an older lady was walking along the street. She gave Adelle a dirty look for not getting out of the car and helping me, but poor Adelle only had that short smock on, and was covered with blood besides. She was afraid to get out of the car.

We got there just in time as I had already lost too much blood. I still carry the big scar on my wrist.

A week or so later the cut was healing well. I was just starting to break a young mare we called Babe, who was bad to buck, and I wanted to get her bred to Ed Crawford's stallion, since she was in heat. I decided to take her to Ed's, which was only three miles away. My arm in the sling and Adelle said to me, "You are not going to ride that horse!" I told her no, I would just walk and lead her.

Well, I did lead her and walked through the two gates that had to be opened. Then, when I got down over the ditch bank and out of sight from our house and in the lane that was a half mile long, I decided I would ride. I managed to get onto Babe with one hand.

She wanted to buck, but I kept her from bucking all the way down that lane. But when I got to the end of the lane, there was no fence on one side of the road and Babe took off, then lit into bucking right through the trees. I finally got her stopped, and went on, put her with the stallion and bred her, and then I rode her home.

By the time I got home, my hand and arm were swollen quite bad. I didn't go to the doctor for a couple of days, and by then my hand and arm had turned black and were giving me a lot of pain. The cut didn't break open, but the artery broke loose, and was bleeding internally. The doctor cut my arm open again with a knife that still had blood on it from someone else, retied the artery and then scraped as much of the old blood out as he could.

Then I got infection, and nearly lost my arm.

The whole episode ended up being my own fault, as I should have listened to Adelle and not gotten on that horse and, after I did, I should have gone right in to the doctor as soon as I hurt it again.

Viola Mae and I Huckleberry Picking

Early one morning I was going to go pick huckleberries and Viola Mae wanted to go with me. She was only about four or five years old, so I put her behind me on the horse and we went up high in Suzanne Canyon. We followed an old trail that I had cut into that area several years before.

When we got to my favorite patch, I tied our black horse up to a tree. We called her Skoconut, a name my dad had given her as a colt. Viola Mae and I hiked about 200 yards farther up the mountain to pick the berries, but she got tired that I laid her down on a little blanket to let her take a nap. Before leaving her to go on picking berries, I told her, "If you wake up you stay right here. Don't leave, or go any place. I will be right up the hill here, not very far."

I left her and started picking. The farther up the hill I went, the better the berries were, so I kept on going up the hill and out of sight of Viola Mae. When I finally got my bucket full of berries I was quite a distance up the mountain, and I realized I had been gone for quite a while, so I rushed back down to where I'd left her.

When I got back to her, Viola was still sitting on her blanket and she told me, "The horse, Skoconut, came up here, and she laid down and rolled around, then went a little ways and laid down again. She went up that way. But the saddle was not on her, and I couldn't see her tail! She sure did look funny."

We walked up about 20 yards to see where the horse had been rolling, but I knew that the horse had not gotten loose, and she wouldn't have come up to where we were if she had. It was very plain to see that a very large bear had been there, and had been rolling in the grass and bushes. I made sure that I kept Viola Mae right with me the rest of the day.

No Money, But Fun

In those days we didn't have any money and no one else had any either, but we still had a lot of fun. We had no electricity and used kerosene lamps instead, and we carried water from the streams because we had none in the house. We had a two-seater outhouse and whoever had to go at night used the chamber pot.

One cold winter morning it was real icy outside and Adelle was breezing right along, going out to the outhouse to dump the pot, when all of a sudden she hit an icy spot and her feet went out from under her.

That old pot flew up into the air and its contents came down all over her. She got back onto her feet, screaming loud enough to wake up the whole neighborhood, and ran for the creek — one time she didn't mind that cold water.

Four in a Bed

We have told our children and grandchildren about sleeping four in a bed during the Depression of the Thirties and they find it hard to believe. One time my sister, Bernida, and her husband, Herman, came to stay. Adelle and Bernida both had little babies. We only had one double bed, so when bed-time came we all piled in.

Adelle and Bernida had the babies on their stomachs and Herman was on one side with me on the other. There were no queen or king sized beds then, at least for us common folks, and we were pretty crowded.

Another time we did the same thing with my brother, Floyd, and his wife, and also with good friends Grace and Alton Ingraham.

Our kids asked, "Why all in one bed?" Well, one bed was all we had. Then they asked why we didn't make a bed on the floor. That was easy to answer — we only had enough blankets for one bed. People nowadays can't understand this.

The Happy Dozen

We had a friend, Dorothy Allard, who lived with her husband about a half mile from us. She and Adelle were quite near the same age, and they both belonged to the same club called the Happy Dozen; the rest of the ladies in the group lived in town.

These ladies were really a happy dozen, but I think there was more than one dozen of them. They were all good, clean, happy people and I think a big share of their business was planning parties, and most of the time the men were all included.

It seemed that most of the parties were held either at our place or at Allards. The pasture below our house was almost like a lawn all summer long as I kept it irrigated so it was always green. We played baseball and softball games there, as well as croquet and other games.

We even went on overnight trips up to Mollman Lakes. It seemed like every week there was something going on.

We had house parties of all kinds where we played different types of games and card parties and we went together as a group to dances all over the valley. No one had much money, but we all had a lot of good, clean fun; none of the women did any drinking and only three or four of the men drank anything.

One time a party was held at Allards, who lived in the house my folks had built and in which I had been raised, on a very, very foggy night. One couple had their parents' car and brought some of the others with them, but on their way home early the next morning it was so foggy that, when they came to Highway 93, they didn't see the highway and drove straight across it, smacking into a telephone pole.

They were not going fast, so no one was hurt badly, but the car was smashed in and the women in the Happy Dozen planned a box social at the Parish Hall to pay for fixing the car. Now this was a dance where all the women brought a fancy box lunch and at midnight the lunch boxes were auctioned off with the man who was the highest bidder on a specific box lunch having to eat the lunch with the woman who made it. The ladies made plenty of money to repair the car and I recall that Joe Piedalue won the bid for Adelle's box lunch; I simply didn't have enough money to outbid for it.

In those days everybody seemed to be willing to help those that were less fortunate. I've always felt that if we had potatoes and gravy, bread, meat and fruit — what else did we really need? During the Depression, all the people that could raised a garden, and if they could, they would also have a cow for their milk. We always had a big garden, cows, pigs, a few chickens and a big berry patch. Every year we went up in the mountains and picked huckleberries and Adelle canned a couple of hundred quarts of fruit and jelly, with the canned goods, the fruit and the vegetables being stored over the winter in the root cellar.

One fall Adelle had bought several boxes of peaches and had them ready to can, but when she went out on the porch to start bringing them into the kitchen over half of them were gone. She couldn't figure out where they could have gone, but about three weeks later she discovered most of her missing peaches rotting in an old barrel along side of the yard. It didn't take her long to figure out that our son, Bucky, who was about three or four years old, and his two cousins, Mark and Jim, who were just a little bit older, had carried them to the barrel one or two at a time, and thrown them into the barrel, which was higher than their heads. They must have been three busy little boys for quite a while.

We got honey from wild bee trees. One time I found a big tree, which had fallen down, with a bee hive in it right on the spot where our son, Buck, and his wife Cheryl's house is now.

Adelle and the kids went with me to get the honey. We took our washtubs, wash boiler and all the buckets we had. And I took my crosscut saw, axe , maul and wedge, loaded everything into the old wagon, hooked up the team and went over to the spot where the tree was laying; I found, upon cutting into the tree, the largest beehive I have ever seen.

We filled every container we had, and still left some behind. Then Adelle had a big job to separate all that honey from the comb, but we had honey for a long, long time.

Food We Bought

When it came time to buy food, we first bought the necessary things like flour, sugar, yeast, baking powder, salt, pepper, spices, dry beans if we hadn't raised enough, oatmeal, and cornmeal, lard if we didn't have our own, cocoa, vanilla and rice. We seldom bought anything in cans, or fresh vegetables or fruit. We would buy penny bars of candy for each member of the family.

We had to buy coal oil or kerosene for our lamps and, of course, gasoline for the car. I remember we paid 12 cents a gallon, and sometimes even less than that for gas.

Every fall I would go hunting some place to get our winter's supply of meat and we always canned a lot of the meat because we had no refrigeration until later years. Then a locker plant was put up in town, and people rented a box to freeze and keep their meat.

We made ice cream in our hand-cranked freezer nearly every Sunday, and often during the week. If we knew someone was coming to visit, we would make ice cream and Adelle would bake a cake.

Putting Up Ice

I built an ice house on the Plant place and I also built one on our old place. We would go to Kicking Horse Reservoir just below where the water flows into it to get good, clean, clear ice. I always liked to get it about the last of January or the first of February because I could haul the blocks of ice on my bobsled. This sled was low and easier to load, and there was less chance of cracking the ice with the long runners.

I liked to make my blocks about twenty-four by 16 inches, but it depended on how thick the ice was. I would take two boards, each about one by ten inches wide and sixteen feet long and use them like a carpenter square, making twenty-four-inch marks the length of one board, and sixteen-inch marks on the other. Then I drove a little nail near each end of the boards so the nails would stick in the ice to keep the boards from slipping around on the ice.

Once on the ice, I shoveled off all the snow and then marked out the blocks by putting my ice saw with the teeth down, and dragging it back and forth along the side of my boards for a straight edge. If I wanted, I could stand on my board and saw alongside of it.

It was important to try to saw each block the same, keeping them as straight as possible. Then, when they were put in the ice house, they would fit together better.

I usually tried to place them in the ice house the same way that they came out of the water.

If we had good sledding snow, I would be able to haul a bigger load than I could on a wagon. Then I would haul sawdust from some of the old sawmills with my team and sled.

I would put about fourteen inches of sawdust on the bottom of the icehouse, then put in a layer of ice. I tried to pack all the cracks between the ice full of snow. Then I put a thin layer of snow, about one inch thick, between each layer of ice. The fewer air holes left between the blocks of ice, the longer the ice would keep. After the ice was all in, I would pack the sides and top with about fourteen inches of sawdust.

During the hot summer, we tried to repack the sawdust tight around the ice and it was a nice place for the kids to play in the hot summer, and as long as they didn't uncover the ice I didn't mind. Sometimes, however, they uncovered it and cooled their feet on it, and that we did mind.

One beautiful February day, Adelle and I went after some ice. The sun was out so nice and warm, reflecting off the ice, and we got all the blocks pulled out of the water with the ice tongs and got it loaded. Then, Adelle tried her best to talk me into going swimming with her in that beautiful water. When she was younger, Adelle loved to swim and so did I, but I knew what it would have felt like to jump off the ice into that water, so I wouldn't go in.

Another winter, when Buddy, our oldest son was about six or seven years old, we had an open winter, with very little snow. I wanted to put up my ice but kept waiting to get a good sledding snow, and it didn't come. So, I decided to use the wagon, taking Little Bud with me.

We drove the team and wagon out onto the ice, parked the wagon and unhooked the team, and I tied them to one of the wheels and proceeded to cut our load of ice. We pushed and pulled the blocks to the wagon, and then pulled them up on a trough like plank with cleats on both sides. The cleats kept the ice from sliding of the sides. Then, after the wagon was loaded, I untied my team of horses, hooked them up and climbed up into the seat with Buddy alongside me.

I signaled my horses to go and just as we started to move, I could feel the wagon starting to settle. I thought, "Oh, NO! We are going down!" It took only a few seconds and we were at the bottom of the lake, wagon, team and all.

We were very fortunate that we were not farther out onto the ice, as the water was not quite up to the horses' backs. And Buddy, sitting up in the wagon seat, was still clear.

This was the occasion when I found out how cold that water was in the winter time!

To free the horses from the wagon I had to get down into the water, pull the pin out of the doubletrees, and then unhook one horse from his side of the doubletrees. Then I had to go to the front of them, get down and unhook one of the horses from the neck yoke, and do the same thing over again for the other horse. Wet and very cold, I grabbed my ice saw and axe off of the top of the load of ice and started to saw a channel to shore — I had to do my best to save the horses.

I would saw about ten feet and then go back and cut again about three feet from the first cut, just wide enough for the horses to get through one at a time. Then I chopped that long piece of ice up into chunks small enough to pull them out with my ice tongs. And I worked furiously because I knew that I didn't have a lot of time before the horses would get so cold they would start to stiffen up and not be able to get out. But those horses were smart enough that, as I sawed a strip of ice and pulled it out, they followed me, each time getting to a little more shallow water.

When I got enough ice cut so they were finally able to get out, both of them were shivering fiercely. I had been working so hard that I didn't really notice the cold, but we left everything there and headed for home, with Buddy and me walking and leading the horses. After going for about a mile of the three that we had to go, the horses started to limber up, so Buddy got up onto one of them and rode the rest of the way. I knew that, as wet as I was, I had better keep walking even though I was fagged out — and I also knew that we were very lucky that it was sort of a mild day.

The next morning I gathered some chains and a long cable, and fashioned a little pole with a hook on the end so that I could fasten a chain on the tongue of the wagon. That way I would not have to get wet hooking on.

When I started to saw the ice, I discovered that I was stiff from the labor of the previous day, but this time I had to saw the channel wide enough for the wagon to come through. I finally got it pulled out with the long cable, but part of my load of ice had floated out of the wagon, so I had to get it back.

I hooked my team back onto the wagon, but they were reluctant to even get close to that ice again, so I just made a circle close to the edge of the ice with them and then backed my wagon onto the ice and stopped the team of horses when their hind feet got to the edge. Then I went out, about forty or fifty feet to where the ice blocks had floated, and pulled them back one at a time. After I got a trail established, they slid right along. I tried to float some of the blocks along the channel that I had cut for the wagon, but that was too slow as there was a lot of broken ice chunks left in the water.

Then I had to lift them onto the wagon, and head for home — and those horses were stiff for a long time after that.

Incidentally, the last old ice house that I made from logs is still standing today on Buck and Cheryl's place.

Packing and Planting Fish

Shortly after we moved up to the Plant place, I started to take hunters into the Bob Marshall Wilderness and we began to take sightseeing and fishing trips into the Mission Mountains. About this same time I started to plant fish in the Mission Mountain lakes and on one trip Adelle and three of our neighbors, Ernie Landquist, Frank Grant and Swen Wintsel, helped me.

Early in the morning we met the fish hatchery truck at the McDonald trailhead with eight or ten pack animals, most of them mine. We used ten-gallon cream cans wrapped with burlap to keep the water cooler and we dipped the little fish, about an inch or so long, out of the truck tank and put about 5,000 in each can. Then we loaded the cans, one can on each side of the packhorses, working as fast as we could to not waste any time, and took off with them.

About half way, we stopped at the upper cedar grove on McDonald Creek and added more water to each can. While there, one of the horses laid down to try to roll the pack off and spilled some of the fish out. We just picked them up and threw them into the creek, and that made a good fishing spot a little later.

As we came to Moon, Long and Frog Lakes, two cans of fish were put in each lake. Four cans of fish were put in Summit Lake, and, having lost only lost three or four fish by that time, we added water to the remaining cans and started for Elk Lake.

When we were approaching Elk Divide Lake, I noticed that the fish were dying very fast, so instead of following the horse trail to the far end of the lake, in order to save time and because it was too steep for the horses to go down, we each grabbed a can off the horses and went down on foot, putting the fish into the lake as fast as we could. Then we had to carry the empty cans back up that steep mountain to the horses.

After that we went down and made camp at the outlet of the lake and an hour or two after we had dumped the fish, Adelle and I took a walk around that beautiful lake. We sat down on a point of rock at the water's edge and all at once we noticed a whole school of those little fish coming right by us. It was such a good feeling to see them. They had come about a mile and a half from where we had dumped them and were checking the shore line like a bunch of little soldiers.

We also planted Mollman Lakes and Terrace Lakes and a lot of people subsequently reaped a lot of good fishing. It also helped our business.

Hunting With Family And Friends

A few years later, a group of our friends came in on a hunting trip during some slack time that I had during the season. The group included four couples and one single, Grace and Alton Ingraham, Luela and Evan Kimmel, Ana Mae and Floyd Cheff, Herman Byrd, and Adelle and I.

Alton was an expert with a sling-shot, a wooden crotch with a rubber pull. As we were preparing to leave, Herman said to Alton, "Here's a five dollar bill if you can hit that little bird in the very top of that huge high pine tree." It was quite a ways away, but Alton grabbed his sling-shot, picked out a good rock and let fly. That bird came tumbling down; no one thought he could do it, but he did. By the time we got into our camp, which was twenty-eight miles away, he had grouse hanging all over his horse. He is eighty years old now and still uses that sling-shot wherever he goes.

While on this trip, I was using one of my friend Thurman's horses. We often used each other's horses, and this was a good, well-loved horse, but he had been known to take off for home, so this evening we hobbled him when we turned out the horses to graze for the night. In the morning when I went out to wrangle, I couldn't find Thurman's horse. I checked the tracks on the trails leading home, but he hadn't gone out. Then all of us men went to look for him and it was quite a while when Evan finally found him.

This horse was an expert with hobbles on his feet, but he had tried to jump a huge log with several knots and broken limbs sticking out, and, as he jumped, the chain on the hobbles caught onto a six- or eight-inch-long hard limb and flipped him over. And there he hung. The horse had been fighting so hard to try to get loose and free himself, and had beaten his head against some of those sharp knots, that the bones were exposed on his jaw and on his temple. The hide on his hip was rubbed clear through to the bone. What a sad looking horse!

We got him loose and free of the log and then we managed to get him into the camp where we bathed his wounds with warm soapy water, then with clear water. A forest ranger happened to come by our camp that day and told me that he had just gotten in some new horse medicine called Scarlet Oil. He had an extra bottle of it, he said, and I could have it if we'd come down to the ranger station and get it. So, I did and we painted all of that horse's wounds with this reddish-colored oil. Before we used the oil, his head and hips had swollen badly.

The first night I stayed up all night, putting packs on his head to try to get the swelling down so he could get his mouth open to eat. Finally, he was able to open his mouth and we fed him all the rolled oats that he could eat. What a pitiful looking horse! I felt terrible to think of using my friend's horse and to have it get into this sort of condition; everyone in camp was sad about it.

I kept this horse in camp for about thirty days before I brought him out and I think the scarlet oil did a good job helping the wounds to heal. Fortunately, the horse was a tough one with a lot of spunk and he finally healed to where only faint scars showed.

Also while on this trip, I took Adelle and went up Bartlett Mountain to see if we could find us an elk. We only had one gun between us and the plan was that if we saw anything, I would give my gun to Adelle. About mid-day, I spotted a big bull elk get out of his bed and start across the ridge at a fast trot. I quickly handed Adelle my gun and told her to get him.

The elk was about 150 yards away, going through a stand of larger lodgepole pine. It was difficult shooting. Adelle shot two shots. The bull kept going, but seemed to be slowing down. She handed me the gun and said, "Take this gun, I can't hit it!"

By then the bull was gone and out of sight and we started down to where we had last seen him and I could hear him wheezing. When we got to him, he was laying out flat with two bullet holes, about two inches apart, in him. Two perfect shots, just behind the shoulders! I was proud of her shooting. She'd done better than I could have done as it was hard shooting between all of those trees.

I still think that some of our group doubted that she had done the shooting, but she really did, and did a good job. On this trip, we had so much meat that part of the group took turns walking out of the wilderness area so we could use their horses to pack out the meat. And we all had a good memories of this trip.

Getting Cows In and Milking
While we lived on the Plant place I was milking several cows and part of the time I would be working on an outside job. I would have to get up in the mornings at 4 a.m. and would light the old kerosene lantern, but sometimes it would be so dark out the lantern would only shine a few feet away and I was unable to locate the cows.

I had cowbells on several of my cows and sometimes, when they were not far away, and I could hear the bells.

It was a good thing I had old Pat to help me. A half collie and half Australian shepherd, he had been my mother's dog and she had trained him to get her cows before they moved back east. When they left, I took Pat. All I had to do was say, "Get the cows, Pat" and he would take off like a flash. And he would never come back without the cows.

Sometimes they would not be too far away, but on other occasions they would be a mile and a half up on a big ridge and it would take quite a while then. But I would be able to hear the bells as he brought them down the side of that ridge. He never ran them, but always kept them coming at a good, fast clip.

Pat always seemed to know exactly where they were, and he never left one of them behind; he put every one of them in the corral. Without that dog, I would have never been able to take care of those milk cows and still get to my job on time.

He was not a noisy dog; he only yipped once in a while if a cow wasn't doing what she should and he was also a top-notch pheasant dog.

Adelle's New Horse

We were still paying on our new car that we had bought while I worked on Kerr Dam and I was making $44.00 per month, and we had car payments of $39.00 a month, which left us $5.00 to live on — besides the $5.00 worth of cream a week we sold.

We didn't drive our car then unless it was absolutely necessary. We always walked for the mail, and to the neighbors, and one day I traded a load of hay to Perry and Joe McConnell for a new saddlehorse. When I went to get him, I took my saddle so I could ride him home. We caught the horse, and they asked me a couple of times if I wanted to put him in the corral to get on him. I never took the hint, and said, "No, I'll get on him right here. I got on, and rode him home. He never bucked. But those guys watched until I was out of sight; I knew they expected me to get bucked off.

The horse reined well, and was a very good traveler and when I got home I told Adelle I had just the horse for her. I thought this horse looked like a horse that I had seen someplace before.

Well, the next morning I saddled the horse for Adelle to ride. At the time she had a bad cut on her finger, and I had put a splint around it for her — in these days a person had to be dying before going to a doctor — and Adelle got onto the horse while I was holding him. She no more than hit the saddle when the horse took off, jerked away from me, and bucked her off. Thank goodness that even though she was bruised up, she didn't break any bones.

It made me mad that he would buck her off, so I got my spurs and caught him again. When I got on he gave me quite a ride, but I was determined to stay with him. I gave that horse my spurs until he couldn't go anymore.

Adelle named that horse Knot Head. I rode him for two weeks to the highway, which was four miles, where I would tie him to the fence and catch an old school bus that hauled the men to work. I would leave the horse tied there all day. Then, after work, I would untie him to ride home. Every morning and every night he tried to buck me off and this routine went on for about a week, when he finally gave up. After that, I could do anything and he just wouldn't buck with me.

But I finally found out that he was one of Hector McCleod's trained bucking horses. I knew that I had seen him somewhere, and it was in the rodeo. But I got him to where he would not buck with me anymore, but he bucked off everyone else that got on him.

Mrs. Romer

During this period Mrs. Romer, who was a millionaire lady, built a summer home down on the south side of Post Creek. She hired me to come and give her grandchildren and their friends riding lessons. Charlene, one of the granddaughters, just adored Adelle and spent half the time at our place. We packed all of Mrs. Romer's guests into the mountains.

Adelle in Hospital

One year as we were getting ready to come out of the Mission Mountains with the Romers and some of their friends, Adelle got a terrible stomach and side ache. She had a very hard time riding that horse out of there.

When it would hurt too badly, she would stop her horse, and then, when it eased a little, she would come on. I got sort of aggravated at her for the way she was coming with her horse, instead of keeping a steady pace on the trail, but I didn't know how bad she was. She was not one to complain about how it was hurting her.

After we got to the foot of the mountains, in fact right where we are living now, Adelle took a short cut home while I took the people and the packstring to the Romer Ranch and unloaded their gear. Then I took my stock home through the woods and when I got home, Adelle was very sick. She thought she had the flu, but the next morning when she was not any better, we went to the doctor, Dr. Lowe. He had us rush her right to the Mission Hospital, where he operated on her. She had a ruptured appendix, and the poison had spread throughout her, causing a miscarriage. She had to have blood transfusions, with her dad giving the blood.

Our kids, Viola Mae, Buddy, Kenny and I had a little funeral for the little boy baby of three months that Adelle lost. We dug the little grave near the old wild apple tree in the woods north of our house.

We very nearly lost Adelle, too. She spent over a month in the hospital and after that she stayed a week at her mother and dad's place.

I found out quickly that it was quite a job to try to take care of three little ones and still get my work done. We didn't have any insurance; in fact, we hardly even knew what insurance was. When I would go to visit Adelle I always went late in the evening, after the hospital door was closed and locked for the night. But I would rap on the door and Sister Marciana, whom Adelle simply loved, would come and let me in. Several times I brought the kids along to see their mother and Adelle still laughs at the way I had them dressed, and how I had their hair combed.

Mrs. Romer came to see Adelle two different times and both times left a check to help us out a little — we sure did appreciate that. She filled the hospital with flowers and brought ice cream enough for everyone, one of the many things that dear lady did to help pep Adelle up a little.

While Mrs. Romer lived near us, she always invited us to her parties. We were sort of reluctant to go as she always had some wealthy people there, but she always insisted we come. She treated us like we were royalty of some kind.

After Adelle got well, we all realized that it was nice to have her home again.

Adelle And Charlene Baker

About 1942, the millionaire lady, Mrs. Romer, sent her granddaughter, Charlene, from New York City to go on a hunting trip with us. Charlene was only fourteen years old, and she came not to hunt but just to be along in the hunting camp, going with us into the South Fork of the Flathead.

Charlene was riding ahead of me as we were going down the trail to the South Fork River when a huge bull elk came onto the trail. A short ways ahead of us, it threw back its massive horns and let out a squealing bugle, and then some loud grunts. It scared Charlene half to death and she quickly rode back to where Adelle was riding; she thought that big bull was going to charge us. If a person has never heard one close, it is sort of scary and also a big thrill.

A couple of days later as we were riding into one of our camp sites, a big bull elk was bugling quite a distance up on a sidehill. I handed Adelle my old 30-30 Winchester single-shot rifle and my knife, and told her to go up and get that elk. Adelle, with gun in one hand and knife in the other, with Charlene right behind her, started up the mountainside through timber and down logs. The rest of us unpacked and unsaddled the stock.

It was getting late, almost getting dark when "Bang!" went the old gun. A few seconds later, I could hear Adelle calling, "Bud, Bud!" She sounded sort of excited, so I charged up to where they were. Adelle had shot the big bull in a little ravine up the side of a steep mountain. The big bull had come charging and rolling right down

Charlene Baker (left) and Adelle at one of the high country camps in 1942.

at her and Charlene, who was just a ways behind her. This was a big six-point bull, but it only had one horn. The other had been broken off, maybe in a fight some time earlier.

As I dressed out the elk, I realized that it would have been quite a task for those two girls to gut that big bull. And I was proud of them just to get it down.

Buddy Hanging From His Saddle Horn

One time we had some cattle missing. Buddy was then about six years old and he was doing a good job on a saddlehorse, so he and I went north from our place to look for the missing cattle. I sent him through thick timber parallel to the big canal, as far as a big swamp. He was to go about a mile farther, and then go back through the woods toward home. We had just gotten him a good pair of buckskin gauntlets, made by Mary Katherine Mollman.

I went about two miles west of where I sent him, then east in his direction, then toward home.

As I went east some distance I thought I could hear a voice mumbling and saying, "Whoa". My horse also knew there was something up there in the woods, so I rode up that way — and there was Buddy.

He had come to a place where the thorn bushes had grown thick across the old trail, too thick to ride through, so he decided to dismount and lead his horse through the bushes. His saddle had a high and small saddle horn and when he was getting off his new leather glove slipped over the saddlehorn, binding his wrist tightly to the horn. He was unable to get back up on his horse, and when I found him (and it was just by accident that I did), old Shorty, the horse, was walking slowly toward home with Buddy dangling on his side.

When I got him back on his horse he was okay except for a sore arm. Maybe it was a good thing that Buddy didn't holler or scream, as it may have gotten the horse excited. He had traveled for quite a distance hanging there and it goes to show a person how easy it is to get in a predicament that one would never dream about.

Conko's Horse

One year I wintered one of Eneas Conko's prize Thoroughbred stallions since he didn't have a good place to keep him. The horse would get half-way mean during breeding season, so while I had him loose in a small pasture, he was dragging a halter rope. Then, one day, Adelle looked out and Kenny, our second son who was about two years old, was out there leading that stud around. Adelle about had a heart attack, but, fortunately, oftentimes animals don't act up with a child like they will with an adult.

Adelle's younger brothers spent a lot of time up at our place and one time I was breaking a horse for my brother, Floyd, and that horse and a few others were grazing below our house a little ways. All the kids were playing close by the horses when Adelle's brother, Bob, who was about ten years old, ran up behind Joe, the horse that I was breaking to ride. The horse kicked him with both hind feet, right in the belly. It made a loud crack and threw Bob backwards about ten or fifteen feet, flat on his back. We all thought he had been killed, but he was all right after a while.

Fun Times: Adelle and Ugly Pigs

Adelle and I had ridden horses over to the neighbors for something, I don't remember what, who had a lot of ugly pigs running loose in the woods. On our way home, we were in a hurry, and were galloping along at a good clip when, suddenly, one of those little, ugly pigs ran out from behind a bush, right in front of Adelle's horse.

The horse bolted sideways, but Adelle kept on straight ahead and landed seat first on a big, flat rock. Again, since she wasn't dead, she wouldn't go to the doctor, but I think she broke her tailbone. She has been bothered with that ever since that tumble and, once in a while, even yet when it is bothering her, she will say, "That darn scrawny pig!"

Ida Mae in the Pig Pen

One time, Adelle's sister, Ida Mae, who is a few years younger than Adelle, came to stay with us for a while. She was a little, active, ambitious gal, and always looked nice and neat. She always liked to help with the outdoor chores.

Her visit was the spring of the year, and we had just gotten a heavy rain. One corner of my pig pen got very muddy and the pigs had tipped over their feed trough, so Ida Mae was going to tip it back up right. She was short, and as she bent over the top rail on the fence, her feet were off the ground. As she reached for the trough, she lost her balance and flipped over the fence, making a somersault right into that deep mud. As she tried to yell and squirm herself out of that mud, she didn't look near as neat as she usually did — or smell as good either. Too bad we didn't own a camera at that time.

Ruth

Adelle had another sister, Ruth. One time when she was visiting us for a few days, both she and Adelle were pregnant and they were about the same size and both were quite a ways along. I had a habit of snapping Adelle's girdle all the time, and one day Adelle was to my side and a little bit ahead of me, doing something in the kitchen, so I reached down with one hand and gave her girdle a big snap. As Adelle turned around, I very nearly got a big slap on my face! It was Ruth instead of Adelle.

Adelle And I Plan A Swim

One summer night while we were living at the Plant place, Adelle and I went to a dance. It was nice and warm on our way home, about one or two in the morning, and after getting inside our own land we decided to take a swim in the canal before driving up to our house. We drove over along close to the ditch, parked, and got out, stripped off all our clothes, and walked to the edge of the water, ready to jump in. Suddenly we found ourselves spotlighted by two cars parked across the ditch from us.

We both turned and ran for the car with our fannies shining in the car lights. We jumped into the car and took off. At daylight I had to go back there and gather up our clothes, which were all strung along the ditch bank.

We had seen those same cars parked in that spot before, but had forgotten all about it. And we never did find out who they were.

I built an Indian sweathouse on our place and one time I took Adelle with me for her first sweat bath. She went in first, and I got right next to the doorway. When I started to sing an Indian song and sprinkle the water on the hot rocks she said, "Let me out of here." I wouldn't let her by me to get out, so she tore a hole right out through the side of my sweathouse. She gets claustrophobic in tight places, and she sure didn't like the Indian way of taking a bath.

Floyd Scaring Vela, My Brother

One of my younger brothers, Vela, came from Detroit and stayed with us one winter, going to school in Ronan. A married brother, Floyd, and his wife, Anna Mae, came to see us one day and he took a bear hide that I had, and hid behind a big log near an apple tree at the edge of the woods. When Vela came home from school, I gave him a bucket and asked him to run over to the apple tree and get Adelle a few apples.

He gladly went, and as he got there and started to reach for an apple, that old bear growled a little, and raised up from behind the log, about fifteen feet away. Vela dropped his bucket and charged for the house, jumping the yard fence, and running into the house. He hollered, "Bear!" and grabbed my 30-30 rifle, and started back out the door. I said, "Wait, I will go with you." Floyd was out there, sitting on that log and laughing. I told Vela to go ahead and take a shot at him, and he said, "I think I will!" But of course, he didn't.

Our First Trip Out Of State

In the winter of 1941, Floyd, who was just younger than I, and his wife, Anna Mae, and Adelle and I took at trip to Michigan. We had received invitations to our younger brother Louie's wedding. The Depression was far from being over, but we four started to plan a trip to Detroit, which is where most of my family were living then, for the wedding.

None of us had very much money, but Floyd and Anna Mae did have a fairly new Chevrolet sedan, though their license was about to expire. I had just gotten a new license for my car so, in order to save money, we dumb kids put my license on his car. We loaded two big boxes with frozen elk meat from our fall hunt to take out to the family in Detroit and I also took along one of my bottles of gold that I had mined out the winter before, just in case we should run short of money. We loaded what little bit of extra clothes we had and took off. It was the coldest part of the winter.

We were somewhere in North Dakota in a blizzard when we came onto a car full of young people that had run out of gas in the middle of the night. We had a five-gallon can of gas with us, in case we should run out during the night, as we planned to drive straight through, but we stopped to help these people and gave them our can of gas. They poured the gas into their car, and it started right up and, after we were good enough to stop and help them, they speeded off in the opposite direction with our new gas can.

It was early in the morning when we went through Chicago. As we approached PawPaw, Michigan, about eight or nine in the morning, a police car that was teaching a young officer how to stop cars pulled us over. Apparently there had been a big robbery in Chicago during the night.

Floyd was at the wheel when they stopped us and when they asked him his name, he gave them mine since we had used my license on the car. They took us all out and questioned us all separately and I guess we all got excited. Our younger brother, Vela, was also with us. When they questioned Anna Mae they asked her who her husband was, and she said, "Bud."

Then, when they asked Adelle who her husband was, she also said, "Bud." They said, "How come you are both married to Bud?" When they asked Adelle how many years she had been married to me, she said nine years. When they asked me, I said eight years. They asked, "Are you even married?" We did both say we had three children.

The week before we had left home, Anna Mae's sister's car broke down. Her name was Fern Moore, and she had been using Floyd and Anna Mae's car, so had attached her driver's license to the steering post of the car. It was still there — and the officers took it off and found the name Fern Moore.

We were all trying to explain what we had done, but they wouldn't listen — they carted all of us off to jail. They thought we had a stolen car, and that we were not even married. The police locked Floyd, Vela and I together in a cell, and put the girls in the women's quarters. They finally turned us loose the next evening, but would not let us have the car.

One officer told us he was going to Lansing, and three of us could ride with him that far. Floyd, Anna Mae and Vela went with him, and Adelle and I decided to try to hitchhike, as we didn't feel we had enough money for a bus. This was our first experience at hitchhiking. It was very cold, and Adelle would not try to get a ride until she got so cold that she could not stand it much longer. Finally, a Model A Ford sedan with three teenage boys stopped and gave us a ride for about fifty miles.

The road was a solid glare of ice and Adelle and I huddled together in the back seat, hanging on to each other for dear life. The young driver drove most of the way with only one hand on the wheel and we were sliding back and forth across that road. The three young fellows were waving their arms and talking and laughing all the way. We were both wishing we were back out on the road in the cold and what a relief when they finally let us out.

A few minutes after we were out, a police car pulled up near us and wanted to know what we were doing there. He asked me if I knew who he was. I said, "Yes, I saw you back in PawPaw." We thought for a while he was going to take us back there, but I finally convinced him that they had turned us loose and that we had not escaped. Then we caught a ride with a big cattle truck loaded with cattle where they took us to the edge of Detroit. We then caught a bus on in to our destination.

Then we learned that the elk meat in the trunk of our car the cops had impounded had thawed and the blood had dripped out the back of the vehicle. Then they thought we had killed someone but a few days later they got the report on us from Montana, and decided that we were not complete outlaws, and that we owned the car. Someone drove Floyd back to retrieve the car.

While we were in Detroit we did run short on funds, so one day Adelle and I took my bottle of gold to a big jewelry shop and asked if they would buy some raw gold. They did, and I saved one of my larger nuggets that was shaped like a heart; this I gave to my dad.

One of the women that worked in this place poured some gold out of my bottle into her hand and was showing the raw gold to several of their customers. But when she got done showing it, she poured it back into the bottle and some of it stuck to her damp hand. She just slapped her hands together and let the gold fall to the floor. Adelle thought I was going to jump over that counter.

They melted my gold into a little gold bar of several ounces and paid me $32.00 an ounce.

This was our first trip to the big city and although we went back a few more times, we didn't do any hitchhiking and we didn't get put into jail. Adelle didn't want anyone at home to find out that we got put into jail, but when we got home everyone knew about it.

I also learned that my father had the nugget I gave him made into a stickpin, and always wore it on his lapel. But, one evening while in a bar having a few drinks, someone plucked it off of him.

Bannack

In the fall of 1941, after hunting season, we went with my friend, Clifford Artis, to Bannack. He was the fellow who I oiled for at Kerr Dam and he wanted me to oil for him on a big fifteen-yard Monagon drag line and dredge used for mining gold on Grasshopper Creek, which was five miles below Bannack. Ralph E. Davis had a mining camp at Bannack, and this was part of his operation.

We lived in a twelve by fourteen foot tent set over a frame with about three feet of board nailed up on the sides and we burnt mostly sagebrush for fuel as there was no timber close by. The weather got down to forty degrees below zero for a while.

Cliff and I worked the night shift. The machine, or dredge, sat on big pontoons in the water. As we dug in the creek bottom, all of the gravel and dirt were dumped into a big hopper on top of the dredge. Then it went into big screen tubes set on a downward angle with water spraying all over this long tube screen. The bigger rocks went straight on through the first tube after being washed, but the finer stuff went through two more screens that rotated around the outside of the first screen.

All of the fine sand and gravel fell down on some flat shaker screens that shook all the gold down into a sluice box with riffles that held the gold from going out. All the rocks, gravel, sand and dirt went out the back end of the dredge and formed a dam behind us. We worked up the stream, forming a pond for the dredge to float on, going in steps, moving the drag-line from thirty to fifty feet at each move. Then we stopped and pulled the dredge up toward us, the same distance we had moved the drag-line.

One night as we went to work, the crew just ahead of us were finishing cleaning the gold out of the riffles. I don't know how much gold they took out that evening, but we worked until lunch time, four hours. When we stopped for lunch, the riffles were all yellow with gold so we called the camp and told them that we must have hit a good spot. The head guys came right out and we cleaned the riffles again. They estimated we got out about $86,000.00 worth of gold. What a sight, with the price of gold at $32.00 dollars an ounce!

This was about the time that Pearl Harbor was bombed and World War Two broke out, and in a few days the government had us shut down. Our Monagon was torn down and sent to the coast for defense work.

While at Bannock we had a lot of fun with the work. We did a lot of skating on backwaters formed by the creeks where the water backed up.

An old miner hermit who lived a mile or so downstream from us invited us to come work by hand in his mine. So, we would walk down there and dig, following the bedrock. Then we would put our diggings in what was called a rocker, made on the order of a baby cradle and would rock it back and forth by a wooden handle that was fastened to the rocker. At the end of the day we would clean the gold out of the bottom of it.

He told us a story about one time when he and his wife lived in Butte and had a school teacher boarding with them one winter. Like most people they used a chamber pot at night, and Mr. Pentagraff decided to play a joke on the school teacher. He put a handful of carbide in the bottom of her dry pot and in the middle of the night when she used the pot, the carbide started to sizzle and smoke, turning blue. It scared her to death, and she came out screaming for Mrs. Pentagraff. She thought something was wrong with her.

We lived about 200 yards from the office at camp, and this was where we got our mail. One evening Adelle was going down the hill to get the mail. There was a little stream about three or four feet wide that went across the road just a short ways from the office and, as she came to the stream, she decided to jump it, but at the edge of the water both her feet flew out from under her and she lit on her seat in the middle of the creek.

I don't know how many people saw her, but she came back without any mail.

One day Cliff and I went duck hunting down Grasshopper Creek. We were having good luck when we came to a cliff where we were unable to continue on our side of the creek. I only had low boots, but Cliff was wearing hip boots and I told him to go across and I would work back. "No," he said, "Come on. I'll carry you across." I said, "No way, I am too heavy."

In lots of places the stream was not over two feet deep and quite wide, but neither one of us was familiar with this part of the creek. The water was murky and we couldn't see the bottom, but Cliff got into the water and backed up to the bank. "Come on, jump on my back," he said. I didn't want to very much as I was nearly as heavy as he was, but I finally eased onto his back. We had two shotguns, a few ducks and me riding quite high.

Cliff started to stagger across the creek with his big load and we got a little past the center of the stream when he stepped into a deep hole. As we were going down, I tried to climb a little higher onto him.

We climbed out on the same side we went in on and both of us were soaked full length, and so were our shotguns. We headed for home in below freezing weather, about a mile away. (By the way, many years later I was dumb enough to let my grandson, Bill, try to carry me across the ditch on our lower place, and the same thing happened, only it was not quite so cold.)

One Sunday Adelle, our two sons Buddy and Kenny and I went for a walk from our camp to the ghost town of Bannack As we walked, we saw dead jackrabbits laying all over; they apparently had some kind of a plague. Then, the first thing we knew, Buddy had picked up a dying rabbit and was cuddling it. We made him put it down and go wash in the creek, afraid he might contact the plague.

While we were at Bannack, our daughter Viola Mae was staying with Adelle's mother and father in Ronan so she could go to school. At Christmas time she came to visit us, and took the bus to Missoula where she was met by a relative, Lorraine Rogers. Lorraine took her shopping and bought her candy before putting her on the bus to Butte. Then Viola Mae had to change buses again at Butte, for Dillon, where we picked her up. But people fed her candy all the way and when she got to Dillon she was real sick. We didn't know at the time that she was coming down with sugar diabetes.

When Viola Mae was eight, she became very ill and kept vomiting and couldn't get enough water. We took her to a doctor, who said "Sugar Diabetes!" and sent her to the hospital. There she went into a coma; her veins had collapsed and it was some time before they could get an intravenous started.

We knew of no one in our families with sugar diabetes, but when Viola was four years old, she had smallpox and ran a terribly high fever. The doctor thought that must have burnt up the pancreas, which resulted in the diabetes. Now we were told our lovely little daughter, "Ola" had developed it. It was so sad to see her have to do without sweets, and learn to give herself shots of insulin — but she was a brave little gal and in a very short time was giving herself the shots. Adelle would cry each time she had to put the needle in her and I could manage it, but I never liked doing it.

Buddy Falling Under Sled

One time we got a real deep, fluffy snow and went to the neighbors, Allards, for something with the team and sled, and on the way home we stopped to go through a gate at the east end of the big bridge over the canal. My team seemed to love to pull the sled and they were really snappy, always ready to go.

When we left the gate, they took off in high gear, but after we had gone a short ways, Viola Mae started to scream, "Buddy fell under the sleigh!" We had gone on quite a distance before I could get the team stopped and I ran around to the back of the sled to see if I could see him anywhere. I couldn't see him but from the marks in the snow it appeared that I was dragging something. The snow was so deep I couldn't see under the sled, so I lifted up one side of the back runners, and there he was.

We had dragged him with the back roller for quite a distance. He was sort of breathless, so we put him on the sled and went on home. We thought maybe he had some broken bones, but he was not hurt a bit. It was a lucky thing that new snow was so deep and soft.

Going to Grandma's for Thanksgiving

One Thanksgiving morning we got up and found about fourteen inches of snow on the ground. We had been invited to Adelle's parents for dinner, so we decided to hitch up the team to the sled to make the trip.

Adelle started to heat up all her old irons while I loaded hay into the sleigh and then we wrapped the irons in burlap and put them into the sled along with some old blankets. We tucked the kids in the sled with the irons at their feet, got in and away we went to Grandma's house, over the rivers and through the woods. We had a great time singing songs all the way.

We got there in good time, and had a great dinner. But shortly after dinner, a warm breeze started to blow. We didn't get to visit too long when I told Adelle that we had better head for home or we might have to walk. So, we hooked up the team and started for home,but before we got there the poor horses were dragging us across a lot of bare ground.

Our Old Place

About 1942 we heard that the land adjoining the Plant place was for sale for $800.00. It was "Tax Deed" land and we were interested in trying to buy it.

We went to the Ronan State Bank and they let us have the money, so we went to Polson to the courthouse and when we got there the price had been lowered to $400.00. They had another eighty-acre tract just a half mile below this one that laid north and south across the creek. I could have bought that one for $400.00 also, but we were so dumb — we already had the money, but we were so afraid of how we were going to pay all that money back to the bank we only took one piece of land, rushed back to the bank and gave them the other $400.00. Someone else bought it, but then some years later our son, Buddy, bought that same piece of land, but had to give a lot more money for it.

Shortly after we passed up that chance, things started to get a little better. One day Adelle and I walked over to our new land to start to make plans on what we were going to do with the place. Adelle picked up my axe, which I always kept razor sharp, and said, "Our land, our trees!" She started to chop into a log but she missed the log and the axe went right through her shoe and chopped her foot.

She wasn't dying so we didn't bother about going to the doctor. We headed for home and Dr. Cheff bandaged her foot.

Pulling Trees on Our Place

That spring I took my team of horses and started to pull out trees. The place had a lot of trees about twelve feet tall all over the area below the ditch and I pulled them out first. Then I started on the big tall trees that were from ten inches to two feet around.

I had a long ladder that I would lean onto a tree. Then I hooked a long cable as high up on the tree as I could reach. Next I hooked my team onto the end of the cable and pulled the tree over. If the tree didn't come, I would have to try the other direction. Sometimes I would have to pull from three or four directions, but I managed to get almost all of them out and this way I didn't have a lot of stumps to contend with. All of the good, straight trees I saved for house logs.

That winter I went back up to Suzanne Creek, way up on a little bench on the north side of the canyon, and right up close to the very steep part of the mountains to get more logs. I would saw the trees down with my crosscut saw, skid them one at a time to my main trail, and then take three or four at a time the rest of the way down to where we decided to build our cabins on our new land. The worst place to get them through was over the canal bank.

This recent photograph shows Bud and Adelle in front a recently-renovated log cabin they originally built in 1941, just before their son, Bucky, was born.

I then peeled my logs and started to build a two-room cabin.

I finally got this cabin done, and the next thing was to build an outhouse. I built quite a nice one, it was a three-holer. When it came time to cut out the first hole in the seat, I tried to get Adelle to sit down on the bench part so I could draw a pencil mark around her seat; then I would know where and how big to cut the hole. But I just couldn't get her to sit there while I marked around her.

Finally, I decided I would mark around my own seat, so I did. Then I proceeded to cut the hole out to my marking. I thought, "Well, this hole may not fit her seat, but it sure will fit mine." When I got the hole cut out and looked at it, I just couldn't believe that my rear was that big. I could have thrown the dog and a couple of kids through that hole! I couldn't leave it that way or we would have lost our kids one at a time on their first trip out, so I had to build a new top. That time I got measurements from another toilet, and redid it with two holes for grownups and a little, low hole for the kids.

Once fall Adelle decided she was going to milk a cow while I was in the hunting camp. I had a corral above the canal by the fence and we had a nice little Guernsey cow, but I only had a footbridge across the canal made of two logs, one smaller than the other — and Adelle was pregnant and real big with Bucky. That footbridge was quite shaky when a person went across and to keep from falling off the foot bridge, Adelle would crawl on her hands and knees with her belly dragging.

She got tired of that before long, especially when the foot bridge was covered with snow, and it didn't take her too long to dry that cow up.

Bucky was Born

On December 29, 1943, another son, Roger Charles, was born. Adelle was at her parents in Ronan, and Dr. Venaman delivered the baby. Buddy wanted to name him Buck Rogers, the first space man of the comic books, but Adelle said she would name him Roger, after her maiden name, and we would call him Buck.

Built My Cellar

After digging a good, big, deep hole in the ground, my hands and arms were in pretty good shape, so I started to dig a hole for a root cellar.

I dug a good-sized hole for the cellar that was about three feet deep. Then I lined the dirt wall with logs and went another two or three feet above the ground level with the logs. The front and back had logs clear up to the peak. I put a ridge log on top that reached from one end to the other and then put a good post in the center of the cellar to help support the roof.

I made a pitch roof, covered with poles side-by-side. Then I put a little square hole in the center for an air vent and covered the roof poles with black tarpaper, and then a layer of straw. I shoveled all the extra dirt over the top and sides. I had a double door on the entrance to the cellar.

Next I built an ice house, and a horse and cow corral.

We Moved To Our Own Place

In 1943 we moved from the Plant place to our new cabin. We bought a new living room set and a new heater stove. Before we moved, Adelle washed all of our clothes and bedding in boiling hot water to make sure no bed bugs were brought into our new place, and we never had another bed bug, thank goodness!

One time to celebrate our anniversary, we went to Missoula and stayed all night. We got a room at the Missoula Hotel and shortly after we'd gone to bed that night, I told Adelle, "There are bed bugs in this bed. I can tell when a bed bug bites me!" She said, "No, not in this nice room. I got up and turned on the light. Bed bugs were running everywhere!

I got so angry I just smashed them all over on the white walls and the white bedding, and we went home.

Our Home

Our new home wasn't fancy, but Adelle always kept it neat and attractive. Everything in the kitchen I made, and me being a very poor carpenter as I had never done any of that kind of work before! But we managed to get by and it was all our own.

We didn't have any electricity at all. To keep our milk or any other food cool, I had to dig a hole in the ground just outside of the back porch. We had a big, metal box in that hole and we always kept a chunk of ice in it that we would get from the ice house.

I built a set of bunkbeds out of poles for the kids to sleep in, and we put it out on the porch. We had curtains that could slide back and forth on the bunk beds, which kept the snow out during the winter. The three older kids slept out there all winter long and none of them ever had a cold, but if we were to do that today we would be put up for child abuse.

We had no inside plumbing so we had to haul our water from the canal in buckets. The banks were very steep and it got real slick at times and there were lots of buckets of water spilled when someone would fall.

Another Son
Edward Rex was born July 28, 1945, at my sister Bernida's place in Ronan. Dr. Veneman delivered him, too. We have called him Micky ever since he was born because I always liked that name, but Edward Rex was named for Adelle's oldest brother Edward, and my oldest brother, Rex.

Some Gas For The Car
One day Adelle was getting ready to come to Holland Lake with more supplies for hunting camp and our son, Bucky, and Adelle's sister's son, Jimmy, and my nephew, Mark, thought they would help Adelle out, so they were going to fill the car up with gas.

They got some old, dirty buckets and hauled several loads of water from up in the canal, and filled the gas tank to the top. Adelle had to go to the neighbor's for help and Mr. Landquist and his son Clarence came, took the gas tank off, cleaned it and the lines, and put them back.

Helen Got Rooted
I always raised a few pigs and one time we had a little runt, as is common. We raised the runt on a bottle and by fall it was pretty good-sized and had the run of the place, since the garden had all been harvested. One evening Adelle's brother, Ed, his wife Helen, and her sister, Ruth, and her husband, Phil Bratton, came to visit. We didn't have inside plumbing and the outhouse was a ways out.

Adelle, Helen and Ruth headed out there, but didn't go all the way, stopping instead under some big trees. All three squatted down when all at once Helen let out a blood-curdling scream that was heard all over the side of the mountain. The loose pig, without making a sound, came up behind her and rooted her from the bottom, right up and off her perch. She thought for sure a grizzly had her.

Losing Our Fruit
Adelle used to can a lot of fruit and we always bought a lot of staples, extra flour, sugar and such early in the fall of each year. For several years, someone had gotten into our cellar and stolen a lot of the fruit and other foods.

I had a pretty good hunch who was doing it and one fall I met two fellows on the road and stopped to talk to them. We were all horseback. I mentioned to them about losing my fruit and other things and I told them that I kept thinking that someday I would catch them, but I hadn't been able to so far. "But," I said, "this year I will catch them because I am going to poison a lot of it." After that, I never lost any more fruit.

Another time, after we had moved to our new place, I was over at the Plant place, plowing with the horses. At noon I would unhitch my horses and tie them to the fence, letting them feed and rest for an hour while I walked home for lunch. Before I left, I laid my tools, a crescent wrench and a couple other tools on my plow seat. When I got back from lunch, I noticed saddlehorse tracks had come by and my tools were gone.

This made me quite aggravated, so I jerked the harness off one of the horses and jumped on him and took off at a good gallop after the thief. I finally caught up with them a short ways before they got home. My wrenches were sticking out of their saddle bags, but they used the excuse that they were going to use them and then bring them back.

Cutting House Logs

In the summer of 1943 a D-8 caterpillar was coming through the woods heading south to do some work in the area beyond Post Creek and I got the guy that was running it to dig me a hole for a basement. We planned to build ourselves a big log house.

I spent all winter getting a set of house logs. This time I went up Mollman Canyon to cut them and I got them way up where the slide rock starts, working alone as I always did, but sometimes Buddy, my son, would come with me. I would saw the trees down with my crosscut saw, chopping the limbs down with my axe. I shod my team of horses with NeverSlip corked shoes — and some of those same shoes are now welded in a frame used to hold logs in the fireplace up at the Guest Ranch.

There was a lot of snow that winter and my skidding trail got very slick. This was good in one way, as I could drag several logs at a time along the icy trail, and Buddy would have an exciting ride down. But it was hard for the horses. I piled the logs on the upper side of the canal, just below where our son, Bucky, and his wife, Cheryl, now have their house, and peeled the bark off there. Those were real good house logs.

I milked my cows not far from the log pile, at the edge of the meadow. We always gave one of our neighbors milk and I would leave a jar full there on a post each evening, and they could come and get it. Then they had the nerve to ask me if I would bring it over to their place every day, about a half a mile. I told them I couldn't bring it over, as I had too much to do and didn't have the time. They got mad at me and the next day set my pile of house logs on fire.

Luckily, I saw the smoke and managed to put the fire out, but I lost some of them. And I knew who'd set the fire because I could see the tracks; they were the same ones that had come to get the milk.

Part Four

HUNGRY HORSE DAM AND OTHER STORIES

Moving to Martin City

During the summer of 1944 there was quite a bit of talk about the chances of a dam being built on the South Fork of the Flathead River and my sister, Bernida, and her husband, Herman, and family decided to go to that area and start a grocery store. They approached us to come and put in a meat market adjoining their store. We thought about it for a while, and finally decided to try it.

The year before we moved, I had sawed down about 20,000 feet of trees right here on our own land, and hauled them down on Marsh Creek, to the land that Culps now own. There was a little sawmill there, and I had them cut the logs into lumber for me. We had the lumber and our house logs ready to start building a nice big log house, but instead of starting to build we decided to have a sale.

We sold all of our cattle except eight or ten head, but kept a big share of the horses. I did sell quite a few pack saddles and a few riding saddles. Then we started to make preparations to go to Martin City.

This was a town that was built on land that belonged to the Gaspar Martin family and they were related to my family. We moved there during the Christmas vacation of 1946 and we lived in a little cabin that belonged to Bernida and Herman. The snow was about three or four feet deep at the time.

We bought a couple of lots and I hired a bulldozer to plow off a spot big enough to start a house. I hauled all the lumber from Ronan to start our house in Martin City. All of the logs that I had spent the winter getting, I left there. I gave H.O. Bell enough to build a bridge across the canal. I took a load of hay and a milk cow so that we could have milk for the family. We were pretty well moved and settled by New Year's.

By this time other members of our family had moved there and we all decided to go to the dance at the Deer Lick Bar. No one had much money and times were really tough, and after this night at the bar, which was the only place in the town to go, Adelle was ready to move back to Ronan. The people in the bar were a rough looking and acting bunch.

I Build Our House

This was my first time at building a frame house and Herman helped me a couple of days and also gave me some advice as he had just finished his house. The new house was located about a block from where we were living.

One day while I was working on it, I looked through the open door and saw our son, Bucky, who was about three or four years old, coming over, walking on top of the snow. Before he got to where I was, I threw an old tarp over me and crouched down in the corner of the front room. I was peeking out of a little hole in the tarp when he came in and hollered, "Daddy!" I didn't answer, but moved a little bit toward him. He ran over to my hammer and grabbed it up. I moved a little closer to him, and he held up that hammer again.

Each time I moved closer, he would say "No, no, no! I'll pound-pound you." He would not back up or run. I got sort of worried that he might let that hammer fly at me, so I threw off the tarp so he could see it was me.

It didn't take too long to build the house. It was a two-story one, and I made a lot of mistakes on it, but when we got it done, it looked like a house, believe it or not. As soon as we got moved in, I started to build a butcher shop and locker plant all under the same roof. It was tight against the grocery store with a large open door between the two buildings.

Butcher Shop
Finally, we had a fair home built and were living comfortably in it, and now we had the butcher shop and locker plant ready to go. So, we opened up for business (I don't remember the date). I was sort of green at this, as I was not a meat cutter by trade, and most of what I knew I had learned watching others and studying different meat cutting books. Furthermore, I was not cut out to be a businessman.

People came in with hard-luck stories and I fell for all of them, and I trusted everyone as good, honest people. For example, the Sunset Guest Ranch got me for a beef and a half; I never could collect a penny of it. And many people would promise to be in to pay. Some did, but a lot never did pay.

I still had a few head of cattle, so I butchered them and sold the meat in the meat market and we did fair on the locker plant, although several of those people also didn't pay.

After Adelle and I both worked in the shop and couldn't make a decent profit, we decided to rent it out. I had purchased a dump truck shortly after we moved to Martin City, and I used it to work on the state highway off and on. Then I decided to join the Ironworker's Union and go to work on the dam just as they were starting on it.

A Daughter
Our second daughter was born April 23, 1948, in the hallway of the Whitefish Hospital because the labor rooms and the delivery room were full. This was our first child born in a hospital. Viola Mae named her; Adelle had planned to call her Roxanne, but Viola wanted it to be Roxena Adelle. And we were tickled to get another girl.

Hungry Horse Dam
I first worked on putting up big Quonset buildings for the main camp machine shops, warehouses and office building. When we finished this, I went to work at

tying reinforcement steel in the diversion tunnel and when that was finished, I went to work as a rigger. We unloaded railroad cars that brought in material for the dam, and hauled it all up to the dam site. I worked on putting up the four high lines, which were 800 feet above the river bottom, across the river.

One of my first jobs on this part was to take down some very tall trees for a place to put in big anchors to hold the high-line cableways. A caterpillar pushed in some crude, steep roads to take our crane up to that location and we had to take the trees down without hitting the power lines. Fortunately, we had a real good crane operator.

One evening as we were going down off the mountain in pickups with the operator's superintendent driving one of them, our operator, not knowing that his superintendent was deathly afraid of any reptile, put a life-like lizard on the driver's leg. When the driver saw the big lizard wiggling on his leg, he simply let out a big yell and jumped out of the pickup while it was still going. One of the other guys got the pickup stopped and no one got hurt, but our good operator got fired.

The next morning we had a new operator, who was not very good and was very afraid of working on the steep ground. I told the guys that we needed to be very careful because we would be working close to the power-line that day. I had the operator take me on one hook to the top of a tree, where I hooked a cable to its tip and then hooked another short cable into the other hook on the end of the boom. Then I came back down.

The tree then was cut off at the ground. My partner, Vern Drake, was a good rigger and he was down on a skidding road below the crane where he was to unhook the tree as I sent it down to him. I directed the operator to swing the tree, which was hanging straight up and down, to the spot where Vern was to land it. He would just sit the butt of the tree down on the frozen ground and let it slide down the road instead of swinging it around and laying it down. By the time the tree was down, it had pulled the boom cable into the power-line — and neither the operator nor Vern noticed what was happening.

I started to run and screamed at them to try to stop them, but they couldn't hear me. Vern walked toward the hook to unhook it. I screamed and waved my arms for him to stay away from it, but he looked at me, and went right ahead and touched that hook. It knocked him flat.

The operator still didn't know what was the matter and I had to have him boom up to free the cables from the power-line before we could do anything. It was a good thing he didn't try to get off the rig or he would have been dead also. I rolled Vern over and started to work on him. I tried to revive him until the ambulance came, but he had died instantly. Both his shoes had a big holes blown out of the soles. I don't remember how many volts hit him, but it was a lot.

After the trees were all removed, I went to work on a raising gang putting up the towers for the cable-ways. We built six towers that would run up and down on big tracks. Two others were stationary head towers where the big electric motors were located. One of them was over a hundred feet high.

As we were about finished with it, one of our men (we called him Wick and he was a nice young, active man and hard working) was going to move a piece of reinforced plywood sheet called a float around to the opposite side of the column.

He was a cat-quick fellow, but just a little bit reckless. He gave the float a pull but it didn't come, so he gave it a real hard pull and it flipped around the column faster and harder than he expected. It hit him on the temple and knocked him off the iron. I was on the ground watching him, ready to send more iron up to him. As he fell, his body hit one cross beam and flipped off it, and then another and another before he hit the ground. His body was badly beaten up.

About two weeks later, a crew of drillers and laborers were working a short distance from our crew of riggers. A whistle blew a signal for a blasting shot and everybody ran for cover. I got behind an eight-yard concrete bucket, watching the drilling crew hide behind some big boulders. One young fellow apparently felt he was not safe where he was with two or three other guys, so he got up and started to run for another boulder just when the charge went off. A big chunk of rock hit him on the side of the head and killed him instantly. This was his first day at work.

It was heartbreaking to see some of these healthy young men lose their lives.

Cable Way

After we got all the towers put up, we started to string cable across the river. First we threw a long chalk line with a weight on the end across the river and then several guys tried to throw it to the other side, but no one was able to. A big tall fellow from Arkansas said he would like to try it, as he had hunted squirrels a lot in his home state with a sling shot. Well, he picked up that string, gave it a couple of whirls and threw it across easily. Then we tied the string to the end of a rope, tying the rope to a cable one-quarter inch by 2,400 feet.

The cable was pulled up the mountain by hand to the head tower where the electric motors were and the end was fastened to a big drum, and then all the larger cable were pulled. An endless cable was finally put up.

This cable was over 4,800 feet long and was strung from a drum on the head tower, and then put over a big pulley on top of the tail tower 2,400 feet away, across the river. The end was pulled back across the river to the head tower where that end was fastened to an identical drum that was just above the first drum.

We fastened one end to one drum, the other end to the other drum. When the power was turned on one drum turned one direction, the other drum turned the other direction. When one cable went out of one drum the other drum would be taking in the slack so there was the same amount of power either direction. Next, with this endless cable, we pulled up what we called the gut cables, which were from three and one-fourths to four inches in diameter and 2,400 feet long. These were very heavy cables to string up and they were strung tight across the river, 800 feet above the river bottom, from one tower to the other on the opposite side of the river. We had what we called a skip that was big enough for four or five men to get into, along with all the tools that we needed, and this skip was hooked to the endless cable so that we could go back and forth across the canyon.

After we got all four of the cable-ways finished and working, my good friend of a life-time, Alton Ingraham, was put into the maintenance gang of about six or eight men. They worked days but could be called out anytime during the night if anything went wrong with the cableways; they had to be men of experience.

Twelve men were needed for the hook tending jobs and there were only two that had any experience at this work, Stub Russell and a fellow we called Whiskers.

The superintendent asked me one morning if I would like to try out to be a hook tender. I told him that I would, so I was given a paddle that was colored bright yellow, made of thin plywood, and round, about fourteen inches in diameter. It had a short handle with a ring in the end to snap onto my rigger belt. The operators were each in a cab, with their rig sitting on a wooden tower just above the dam. About half or more of the time the operators could not see us, so there was a signal man on the ground or where he could see us when the operator could not.

Each hook tender had a signalman, who we called a bellboy. They held a hand signal in their hand with a button to punch and when we were in sight of our operator, we gave the signals directly to him. When he could not see us, we gave our signals to our bellboy — and we did this with the yellow paddle that we always held in one hand as we were out over the canyon.

When we wanted to signal to go up, we held our yellow paddle up overhead. That meant the operator was to start hoisting up. As soon as we were clear of the ground or anything we might run into, we would give our paddle a wiggle that meant for a highball, or going fast. The signal to come down was to swing our paddle in a downward motion, and to go toward the head tower, the paddle was swung back and forth over our head. To go toward the tail tower, we swung the paddle behind us. And sticking the paddle straight out always meant slow down.

One end of the cable was on a big track so we could move our loads up or downstream. To go downstream we stuck our paddle out three times and if we wanted to go upstream we stuck it out four times in the upstream direction.

When we were working in the blind from the operator, the bellboys would relay our signals to the operators. Each time they pushed the button, a red light and also a beep would flash in front of the operator and one always meant stop.

High Lines

When I first started I was sent with Stub Russell, an experienced hook tender, and we hooked onto a large sand hopper that sat up on legs. We picked it up off of a large truck and took it down to the keyway for the dam. Stub was a man of few words, but he did tell me to watch him closely, which I tried to do. Then we went up and hooked onto a much smaller hopper, which had a rubber tube or spout on the bottom, filled with sand. We took this load of blasting sand down and he put the tube on the bottom of the hopper that we were riding on into a two foot by two foot hole in the top of the big one we took down first. I climbed down on a little ladder on the side of the hopper and opened the trap door, dumping the sand. We made about three or four loads.

On the last load I thought he was going to miss the big hopper which he did, but on purpose. We landed down on the ground and he got off. He said, "Okay, it's all yours. Take this hopper up and put that spout in the two by two-foot hole and dump the sand." And he went over to a big rock and sat down. Well, he hadn't explained anything to me. I knew the signals, but I didn't know or realized that there was a lot of swing in the lines when they hung down below the carriage, 500 to 700 feet below.

I had my signal paddle in one hand, and I was standing on the corner of the hopper holding onto one of the four cables on each corner of the hopper. I gave the signal to get up. I stopped the hoisting when the hopper was high enough to clear the big sand hopper, and then I gave the signal to travel downriver. When I got in line with the hopper, I gave a stop signal, but I kept on going! I was thinking that the operator was not taking my signals, but he was doing exactly what I had asked for — what I hadn't realized was that when the tower started to move, I was hanging so far down on the lines that the tower had already gone quite a distance before I started to move.

When I gave the stop signal as I got to my target, the traveling tower was already way past my target. And when I gave the stop signal, I swung on for another 100 feet. I should have run the tower back when I was about at the end of my swing. Then I could have stopped my swing by stopping the carriage directly over myself or load.

Then I tried to get my hopper in line with the big hopper, as I was about fifty feet off. Again, I gave a signal to move toward the head tower, and when I got in line with the hopper I signalled to stop the carriage. Well, again I swung way too far out past it.

So now I did have a mess, caused by moving the carriage while my load was still swinging back and forth. This caused my load to go into a big circle, so I was going around and around. Finally, I got nerve enough to look down where Stub was, and he had his hat off, laughing his head off. Stub's brother, Russell, the operator, later said he got so tickled his belly was hurting. I sure am glad that there was no one there with me to get a picture of the confused expression on my face.

Finally, I snapped my paddle signal onto my rigger belt and gave up. Then Stub took his signal paddle off his belt and got the load stopped and it took him only a few moves to get it under control, and the spout down into the hole in the big hopper. I sure found out fast that there was a lot more to it than there appeared to be. But after you know how to do it, you can stop that 200 or so feet of swing by moving the carriage one time. There was a lot to learn on this job, but after a few weeks everything seemed to come together naturally.

In order to get the rock out of the keyway, where it not possible to use cats and trucks, we used skips. They were huge truck beds with a big cable fastened to each corner, which in turn went into a big ring that was hooked to the cableway hook, which lifted them out. These skips were placed all along the keyway and the muckers, who were men that shoveled the skips full of rock, would fill them. As soon as they were filled, we would haul them out and dump them, and then return them to the keyway.

All of the material that went into that dam we put in with those four high-lines. We hauled pumps, pipes, welders, sand blasters, forms, both steel and wood.

For the first few months, after unhooking from a load I would simply step into our cable slings with one foot, hold onto the cable with one hand, signal paddle in the other hand, and go for the next load. We always worked just as fast as we could, but the bosses finally stopped us from riding in our slings, so we had to ride our spreader bar. This was about six feet long and six inches square with our hook on the bottom of it. A cable went up on each end of this bar to another one that had the cable drum, or shivs. We would ride on them and it was a lot more comfortable than standing in a cable, one foot on the flat iron and one wrapped around the cable.

I Take A Northwest Shovel Across The Canyon

One day the bosses wanted a Northwest shovel taken across the canyon and they sent Johnny Ingraham to help me. We hooked onto the shovel, with both of us on top of it, and I gave the signal to start lifting. I could hear the shivs turning for a long time before we started to come off the ground.

I gave the signal to start across the canyon slowly and we were sort of going up and down. As we went, I could tell that all of the cables were stretched to their limits. We were both hanging onto a cable on opposite corners and I looked at Johnny; he was real pale. I said to him that I knew a place that I would rather be. He said so would he! I was almost afraid to move for fear something was going to break, and this is one time I wish we hadn't ridden the load, and had walked down to unhook it.

The mud or concrete for the dam was all poured in a series of many blocks, each five feet thick. The pours were made with eight-yard buckets.

All the materials had to be constantly moved from one block to another and a big tool repair shed built on log skids needed to be moved every three or four days. One time when I needed to move it, I just flew over it and came down on its roof as I always did, and hooked on to it. Each time it was moved, the men working inside would come out and walk to its new location, but this time, as I started up with it because I thought everyone was out, a man appeared in the doorway.

I hollered at him to just stay in there as I had already given the signal for a high-ball move, but the fellow jumped out anyway. We were already up about thirty feet when he jumped, but he landed in the wet, soft concrete so he didn't get hurt too bad.

Once in a while a crew of men would need to be moved to the opposite side of the canyon and if I should happen to have an empty skip, I could bring them across on the high-line. And once in a while, someone would ride with me, but most of them would not get in with me. They would rather walk or have to be taken around by truck, about twelve miles. Most of the time, those who did go with me would take one look down and across that canyon as we started out, and either sit or lie down in the bottom of the skip so that they couldn't see out. Once in a while someone would have the nerve to look over the edge.

We hook tenders always stood up on the edge of the box or skip, and hung onto one of the four cables on each corner of the skip, so that the operator or bellboy could see our signals. My brother, Chris, was also a hook tender on one of the other rigs.

Our superintendent was a man by the name of Jack Johnson. He had spent all his adult life as an ironworker, or rigger, and he knew his business. He was a man for safety, and fair with all his men, and he didn't want any man around the cable ways that were smart-alecs or show-offs, as this was no job for anyone to be playing around on.

One time I very nearly got thrown off my hook. The company was breaking in a new operator, and my operator needed a toilet break so he left the new man at the controls while he went As I was coming across the canyon on my hook quite fast, upon nearing the spot to where I wanted to go down, I stuck my paddle out to signal slow down. The new operator pushed the wrong lever and stopped the carriage still, which caused me to swing very fast out past the carriage. He realized that he had done the wrong thing, and got excited, and put the carriage on power again, which then caused a double whip in my lines, or cables. I was riding on just the four-inch-square spreader bar and it started to flip one way and then the other. I had to drop my paddle in order to hang on; I was hanging on for dear life, with my legs wrapped around the cable and every time the cables snapped, they would nearly snap me loose. I had to keep re-grabbing for new holds. Fortunately, the old operator heard the cables popping and saw the commotion and he ran back into the control room, grabbed the levers and finally got things straightened out. I came so close to falling several times as I was flopping back and forth.

I had another close call once when I picked up a big square platform about twenty-four by twenty-four feet with a cable on each corner to pick it up with. These pads were used to haul a lot of the tools, such as vibrators, to the men. I picked up the pad and started for the other end of the dam, where it was supposed to go. I had to take it up high to get to where I was going with it and the thing kept turning around and around with me.

I couldn't see my operator, so I had to give my signal to the bellboy. But as the pad turned with me, I was going out of sight of my bellboy, and he couldn't see my signals. I glanced at the cable on the corner straight out to my left, thinking I would have to walk over to the other cable so I could see my man. Well, I started to walk over there, forgetting that this thing was turning with me, and that cable was not to my left anymore but was already behind me — and I was stepping off into mid air! I just barely caught that cable with the ends of my fingers, and managed to pull myself back on. It scared me so bad that I had to hold onto my stomach for a little while before I could give another signal.

Nearly Froze on Cable Way

One evening as I was going off shift, I gave my relief man my hook and got on with Warren Aycock, the hook tender on the high-line next to me, to ride across the canyon to where our cars were parked. He was hooked onto a very large skip heaped up with rock, a load that was really too big.

The weather had been real nice so we were not dressed too warmly and when we were about half way across the canyon with that big load it blew an overload on the motor, stalling us in the middle of the canyon. The sky got dark, and a very hard blizzard came on us suddenly, and we had absolutely nothing for a wind break.

When the motor was finally fixed, no one could see us up there in the air, it was snowing so hard. A signalman was put along at different places to watch as they brought us in, just creeping along so that we would not run into anything, since no one could see more than a short distance. When we finally got in, we were so cold we could hardly get off. But oh, what a good feeling to be back on the ground. And I told Warren that I would never catch a ride with him again.

One night as I was working night shift, I rode a concrete bucket loaded with eight yards of mud down into the canyon. We stood on a little ladder on the side of the bucket and hung on; and I did what I had to do, and then sent the bucket for another load of mud.

When the bucket came out from the mixer and started across the canyon, the endless cable, which was used to pull loads back and forth across the canyon, broke. When it snapped, the loaded bucket went flying across and downward into the side of the rocks with the tail of the cable whipping back and forth as it came down, all the way across the dam. Only one man got hit by the cable and it cut his arm right off at the shoulder; I was lucky to have been on the bucket just before this one or I probably would have been killed.

One day I brought my hook into where we picked up a lot of the material to go down onto the dam. I had just stepped off my hook when Elmer Ingraham was coming in on his hook and I thought he was coming in a little lower than he should be to be safe. I was standing there watching when his carriage stopped and he swung in and out, just barely touching the cliff on the side of the mountain. As he swung back out, the carriage went the wrong way and slammed him hard into the rocks, and them slammed him into the rocks a second time, cutting one of his legs off. Either the signalman or the operator made a mistake — when he swung out, the carriage should have moved out to stop him, but it went in instead. (Neither man would subsequently admit responsibility for the wrong move.)

I was the first man to get to Elmer to help him take off his hook and try to keep him from bleeding to death until the ambulance could get there. He was a strong man to have been able to hang onto that cable and not get thrown off when he hit the rocks.

High Lines

While I worked on these cableways, I got more overtime than I really wanted but all overtime was double pay. When we were working with the high-lines, we were expected to work and move the material as fast as we possibly could, although when our rigs were pouring concrete we sometimes would not make a move for several hours.

We had a shack we could sit in, but had to be alert at all times. When the pours for a block of concrete were finished, the bucket would be sent up to our landing and we would go on the run, unhook the concrete bucket, and jump onto our hook.

For the rest of the shift we would be moving materials, as fast as we could go. We had a few men that were bad drinkers, especially on payday, and nearly every payday I would have to work a double shift. Many times I would just get home from work and our superintendent would call me to see if I would come back to work another shift since someone did not show up. Many times I didn't feel like going back, but I never refused to go. I knew, and everyone else, knew that this was a job that not just anyone could do — it took an experienced man.

In all of my life, I can remember missing only one day's work. This happened once when I jumped off a crane onto a skip and kinked my back. On any job that I have ever had, I always did or tried to do whatever I was asked to do, and tried to do it well. This sure did pay off for me on Hungry Hose Dam, as I was the last rigger working on this project. I worked all by myself with the crane operator for a year after everyone else was gone, loading and shipping out everything left on the site.

After I finished on the dam, I bought one of their old D-8 caterpillars and had it moved down to where the ranch is today. I then went from the dam to the aluminum plant at Columbia Falls as an ironworker and on that job, I was on a crane most of the time.

We spent about ten years at Martin City and while we were there I spent a lot of enjoyable days with my older boys. We did a lot of fishing and hunting for ourselves, and I packed out a lot of game for other hunters. We had a bunch of lion hounds, and hunted lion and bobcat and I still took hunters into the Bob Marshall Wilderness each fall, returning to my work on the dam when hunting season was over.

Hunting Mountain Lions

A mountain lion is an animal that people seldom see in the wild and bobcats and lynx are also seldom seen, even though these animals may be close by. When Buddy was in high school, he sent a mail order to Indiana to Maple Hills Farms and bought himself a black and tan female hound. He then had this hound bred to a blue tick hound that was a good lion dog, and she had thirteen pups.

These young dogs turned out to be some of the best of their kind after they gained experience catching a few cats.

There was an old female mountain lion, called the "Desert Lioness," that ranged in a six-mile radius on Desert Mountain. She had been chased several times by a good old lion hunter by the name of Ed Waldon, who we often hunted with, but he'd never caught up with her. One cold winter morning, my son, Buddy and I made ourselves each a lunch, took food for our dogs, and set out to catch the Desert Lioness.

We put the food and our .22 pistols in our backpacks and strapped our snowshoes on the packs. At that time we were living in Martin City, a little settlement named after an uncle of mine. It was about 4:30 in the morning when Buddy and I each took two hound dogs on leashes, letting old King go along loose, and headed for Desert Mountain on foot. The road was plowed clear of snow through the main street of Martin City, and on past it about two miles, so we walked up this street to get out of town. As we went, however, it seemed like every dog in town came out to challenge ours. A big share of the dogs knew King, and would retreat when they saw him, but finally three big ones ganged up to challenge him, and King threw those three dogs every direction. He was a dog that never looked for trouble, but if anything came his way he was ready and could easily defend himself.

When we got to the end of the plowed road, we strapped on our snowshoes and headed up Desert Mountain to see if we could find the big, mean feline known as the Desert Lioness. She had whipped up on a lot of other people's hounds and had quite a reputation.

We climbed nearly to the top of the mountain, but found no tracks in the snow except an old set that was going in a northerly direction. Later in the afternoon, we decided to split up and each of us took two dogs and traveled along a pair of ridges that ran parallel to each other.

As I came down off the mountain I saw quite a few elk, deer, and coyote tracks, and on the way up, we had seen a large wolf track. I got back without seeing a lion track and when I got home at dark, Buddy wasn't in yet. However, he came in not too long after I did and he told how he found the old lioness's tracks, and followed them to where she had just finished killing a large cow elk. It was already dark, so he had left her trail and come on home.

The next morning was a Monday and I had to be on my job at Hungry Horse Dam by 8:00 in the morning and Buddy was supposed to be in school at 9:00, but he decided not to go and instead took two of his hounds and went back up Desert Mountain by himself. When he got back to the elk kill, the old lioness heard him coming and took off.

She did the same thing she had done on previous chases, making a big circle and coming back to hide near her own tracks. Then, as the dogs came by, she would jump on them. Buddy hadn't turned his hounds loose yet, as we like to wait until the cat starts to run, because this usually enables the dogs to overtake the cat quickly. But this old feline was different than most cats; she would rather fight. As Buddy followed her tracks, he very nearly went past her without seeing her. She had made her circle and was hiding under a tree that had blown over but was held up off the ground a little way by the roots. The snow was three or four feet deep, and had drifted up near the log, making a perfect hiding place.

Just by luck, Buddy saw the very end of her tail moving back and forth on the far side of the log as she got ready to spring, but while the dogs could smell the cat, they couldn't see her because of the drifted snow. Then Buddy made out her face under the log.

He got his .22 pistol out of his holster, but because he was training the young dogs he didn't shoot her. She was about five or six feet away, so he kicked snow in her face, but she didn't move. He reached for a root of the tree, grabbed a chunk of hard snow and threw it in her face, giving a yell at the same time. She took off,

Buddy Cheff and a mountain lion.

and he quickly turned his dogs loose after her. That old girl was so full of elk meat that she couldn't run very fast or far, so the hounds treed her before long. Then Buddy shot and killed her.

I went back with Buddy and got to see what happened by the tracks in the snow. The cat had crouched in a game trail, and a big cow elk had come that way. The elk's tracks skidded to a stop about twenty feet from the cat and the cat had then sprung up the grade right onto the cow's face. The elk had made one jump off to the side of the trail and then the cat broke her neck, and her lower jaw, which was pulled out at a forty-five degree angle, also broken. When Buddy had come along with his dogs, the lioness was probably hesitant of tackling a man and two dogs, which was lucky for Buddy.

My sons and I have had a lot of hard work and fun chasing all kinds of cats. Some people say that a lion will only kill young or weak animals, but these people haven't been around lions very much. A cat is not a bit choosey and we have found that they will kill the first thing they come to.

The East Shore Lions

One winter evening as Adelle and I were driving along the East Shore of Flathead Lake, I saw what I was sure was a lion track crossing the road — something I'm always looking for as I drive along.

I didn't stop to make sure it was a lion track, but lion tracks are easy to identify once a person is used to seeing them, so when I got home, I told Buddy that I had seen a lion track cross the highway, and the next morning he went to check it out. He found the track and followed it to where the lion had killed a big mule deer. The next morning, we went to see if we could get it. At that time there was a $50.00 bounty on cougar, but we were thinking of taking it alive, which we have had a lot of fun doing.

When we got to the deer kill, we found that the mule deer had been eaten up, and the bones were left in a single pile. As we scrutinized the tracks around the kill, it looked as though there was more than one size of prints and we surmised that there were several cats in the vicinity. We made a circle of the area, but only found one set of cat tracks leading away from the kill. We followed this set of tracks for quite a distance when, all of a sudden, another set of tracks stepped out of the first ones. Then there was another, and another, and another, until we could tell that five different lions had been stepping so perfectly in each other's tracks that in the deep snow it looked as if there was only one cougar for the distance of a mile or two, where they must have decided to start hunting.

All the lions were going in the same direction, but had spaced themselves about a hundred yards apart.

We followed the inside tracks as they made a big circle, and came back to the same tracks where we had already been. Now the lion tracks were following our tracks, so we knew they were quite close, and the dogs began to act excited and smell the air for the cats' scent. The lions had already followed our tracks about a quarter of a mile when we caught up with them.

We turned the dogs loose and in a few short minutes they had all five of those cats in different trees. We concentrated on only one lion, which we wanted to take alive and let the rest go free. Later, however, another hunter followed our tracks into the area and took the other lions.

The cat that we wanted that day had gone up a tall larch tree. There was an identical tree about eight or ten feet away from the one the lion was in, so I put on pole climbers, took the snare and started up the other tree, thinking it was a good place to get the snare on the cat.

The cat went up to the very top of the tree as I climbed closer to it, so I kept on going too. When I was about eight feet below the cat, I took out my snare, which was on the end of a slender, soft little pole, to slip it over the lion's neck, and maybe one leg also. The cat kept snarling and acting like it wanted to jump at me, but I didn't think that it would do it. I took my hatchet from my belt and hung it from a little limb just in front of me in case I needed it.

I had the snare almost on the cat when, like lightning, it jumped right for my head. Luckily, the top of the tree was so small that it sprang back with the lion's weight, and so the cat didn't make it to my head. But it caught me on my pant leg, and I kicked it in the face with my other foot. It fell down, catching itself on a few branches on the way to the ground. The snow was deep, and when it landed it didn't seem to be hurt because it jumped right up, and then took off running. Buddy turned the hounds loose and they treed it again within a hundred yards of the first tree.

This time the lion went up a big fir tree that had enough limbs to climb without the pole climbers and since we always took turns in the climbing because it can be such hard work, Buddy went up the tree to try to snare the lion.

He got about halfway up the tree when the lion started coming to him. I did some fast grabbing for my .22 pistol so I could shoot the cat if it was necessary. When the lion got to where Buddy was, Buddy leaned out away from the tree on the opposite side of the trunk from the lion and the lion stopped on the other side of the tree. For several moments while they were even with each other, and they simply stared at each other at close-range with only a tree-trunk separating them. I was ready to shoot when the lion came on down the tree and jumped the last ten feet to the ground.

I turned the dogs loose again, and again they treed the lion, this time in a huge larch with no limbs for the first forty feet. It was a dangerous tree to climb, and because it was getting late in the evening and soon would be dark, I told Buddy to shoot this one; we would catch another lion later, which we did.

To catch the lion alive, we would fasten the open snare on the end of a light ten-foot pole with a slim copper wire. After the snare was over the cat, we would pull the pole free from the snare and then pull the cat to the ground. Then we would get a dally around a tree.

The snare had to be of light steel cable, about ten feet long, so that the cat couldn't bite it in two. A long rope was fastened to the snare and after we had the cat dallied to a tree, one of us would grab its hind feet and tie them together, as the hind feet are as dangerous as the front. Once the hind feet were secure, we would work on the front feet. We then cut a good hard stick two or three inches in diameter, and about ten to twelve inches long, with a couple of strands of tie wire fastened to one end. We would get the cat to bite it, and then take the wire up over the back of the cat's head and tie the wire to the other end of the stick, so he

Mick Cheff and a mountain lion.

couldn't spit it out. This prevented the lion from biting.

The cat was then either tied to a pole to be carried out, or laid on top of two little bushy trees that had been cut, and then tied onto it. This way we could drag the cat on top of the snow without injuring it.

At our ranch, we constructed a large cage with a partition so we could keep two lions at one time, and we also had smaller pens for bobcats. My boys brought in several cats when I was not with them and they had a lot of fun.

Fish Creek Lion

One year my boys were working iron in Missoula and hunting in the Fish creek area where a big mountain lion tom was killing elk out of a herd of about 16 or 18 elk located in the canyon. One by one the cat had killed them, ripping them open and lapping up the blood, but not eating the meat except for small parts of the liver.

The boys were determined to catch this tom, but for several weekends it stormed badly and by the time they were able to go after him, the tom had cleaned out the herd. Then he moved over a big ridge into the next canyon, where he started on another herd of elk.

Buddy, and another guy who also had been wanting to get this tom, trailed the lion into the next canyon. The other fellow was not as experienced as Buddy at using snowshoes, and was not able to keep up and Bud was so determined to get the lion that he went on ahead with his hounds. Finally, he caught up to the lion at another kill, and with the help of his hounds got the big tom treed.

He knew the friend wanted to take the lion, so he waited for the man to catch up. After about five hours, however, Bud was unable to keep the cat up the tree any longer and it became aggressive, and started down the tree, climbing out on a big limb right over Bud's head. The tom was staring right at him, and Bud could tell it was going to jump, but the snow was so deep that Bud couldn't move out of the way. Then the lion paused for a minute, glowered at Bud, and then jumped for him just as Bud shot.

At the same instant, one of the dogs broke his rope and met the lion in mid-air. The dog and the lion tumbled down the hill and when Bud got down to them, the hound, Hap, was on top of the lion, thinking he'd killed it all by himself.

If this cat had not been destroyed, it is hard to tell how much game it would have killed.

Martin City

While we lived at Martin City, we enjoyed all of our life up there. At first Adelle didn't make many friends, but when she was pregnant with our daughter, Roxy, a gal named Bertha Dever came into the butcher shop where Adelle was working and remarked, "It looks like we have both been eating more meat than we need!" She was pregnant also. They instantly became good friends.

We lived in what was to be called the Byrd-Cheff Addition and so did my sister, Bernida, and her husband, Herman Byrd; my brother, Rex Cheff, and his wife, Mae; my sister, Grace, and her husband, Bill Pumala; my brother, Chris, and his wife Ida Mae (who is Adelle's sister); my sister, Josephine, and her husband, Clyde Schwach; our nephew, Duane Byrd, and his wife, Jody; and our daughter, Viola, when she married Don Lietz.

Also living there at the time were some good friends, Bertha and George Dever, Olaf and Helen Barbo, and Grace and Alton Ingraham.

Martin City was a typical, fast-growing construction boom town, made up of mostly bars. One of these bars was called the Hungry Horse Bar, and had horse shoe tracks on the walk leading into the bar. One day our sons, Micky and Bucky, aged seven and eight respectively, were riding on their horses down Main Street when they decided to follow the tracks right into the bar, and the patrons wildly urged them on.

We had many happy times together, holding square dances, parties, picnics and so forth. Our house was built on the edge of town, and we had a corral behind the house. We also rented a pasture about one and a half miles from town where we could keep some of our horses.

The pasture was along the river, and was a very scenic spot. We had many picnics there, both for the family and school. It was in this pasture that three of our best horses were shot and killed. We never found out who killed our horses or why they'd done it — somebody apparently had a grudge, or maybe they were just spotlighting.

Raising five sons and two daughters in a small construction town was never dull and our kids and their cousins and close friends found all sorts of things to do, some of which we didn't approve.

Dan Donald

On March 5th, 1951, we had a real bad storm and Adelle went into labor and the

Bud and daughter Viola Mae put on a theater program in Martin City for the local Parent-Teachers Association.

snowplow plowed the road all the way from Martin City to the Whitefish hospital so we could get her there. Our baby was born shortly after we got there and we named him Dan Donald. Donald was the name of our daughter Viola's husband to be.

Our new son was the first of our babies to be born in a delivery room, and we have always called him Happy - and he was to be our last baby.

We were proud of each of our children when they were born, and we are still very proud of each of them as none of them are in jail. They all have nice families and are all making decent livings for their families.

Viola Mae Gets Married
Viola Mae graduated from high school in May, 1951, and was married on June eighth of that year. She married a fine young man by the name of Don Lietz. He was a logger and fit right in with the rest of the boys.

Viola and Don lived in a trailer in the North Fork of the Flathead, where he was working, and about a year later I got him a job as an ironworker on the dam.

Dumping the Kids
Sometimes I would unintentionally give the kids a little excitement, like the time I was taking the dump truck to the pasture with our boys and the neighborhood boys piled in the back. I forgot about making sure the hoist was turned off, and as I drove down the road I had kids screaming and hanging on for dear life.

Another time I had traveled quite a distance when a car passed me and the people in it pointed to the back of my truck; I hadn't noticed the bed was up and the kids were hanging all over like grapes. I believe the Lord watched over those kids as never did one of them fall or get hurt.

The Years At Martin City

Those ten years at Martin City filled us with many memories. We had all the kids at home, and each one filled a very special spot.

Kenny was paper boy for a few years, and whenever he collected his money from his customers he had a following of kids. He seldom got home with all the money and it was fortunate that he got a lot of tips, especially from the "Fancy House" on the hill, or we would have been broke paying his paper bill.

He was a kid that was always into mischief, always trying something foolish or daring, such as the time he rode his horse across the river.

He and a friend had gone around the Flathead River on the railroad track bridge. The water was real high in the river and on their way home those two little kids decided to swim the river with their horses. Kenny's friend said his horse couldn't swim, but Kenny said, "All horses can swim, so let me ride your horse." They started across the river and that horse did go under, and just by luck Kenny caught ahold of Snort, our horse, and Snort took both of those kids across the river. That other kid's horse finally got out about one mile downstream and in that cold, swift water they were lucky they didn't all drown.

Another time Buddy and I had taken our saddlehorses across the foot bridge built on the side of a high railroad bridge near Coram and rode somewhere on the back side of Teakettle Mountain. When we came back that evening, we waited for the evening train to cross the bridge so we would be sure that we wouldn't get caught with our horses on that narrow foot bridge. After the train had gone by, we started across, leading our horses. We were right in the middle of the bridge when we heard a whistle blow — a train was leaving Coram and never before had we seen two trains travel those tracks, one behind the other, on the same evening.

We were afraid that the horses would stampede or jump over the edge, or onto the tracks, or even over us, as we tried to get off the bridge, but fortunately the engineer saw us and was able to stop his train, thank goodness, allowing us to go on across.

Micky and Bucky were close in age so they were always together. Micky had a slight lisp, so Bucky would explain what he was saying. One day at school Buck had the misfortune to get caught in his zipper when he'd gone to the bathroom, so Micky went for the teacher. The teacher didn't have any little boys of her own, so she called in another teacher, who brought a big knife with her to cut the pant fabric. One of Bucky's cousins, Jimmy Byrd saw the teacher go into the bathroom with the knife became quite excited, and told Micky that they were going to cut it off!

All the boys were relieved to find out that she used the knife to spring the zipper, but Bucky was so embarrassed over the whole incident that he refused to talk to anyone about it, and was mad if we mentioned it.

I built a little red cutter and hitched our saddle horse to it so we could take the kids for sleigh rides during the winter. When Roxy was about three years old, Santa arrived and was going on up to some friends place. He invited Roxy and Adelle to ride with him. On the way, Santa leaned over and kissed Adelle. Roxy, looking very disapproving, said, "Santa! My daddy won't like that!"

Just across the road in the woods lived an old man named Bob Bales, whom we all called "Old Bob." The winters at Martin City were pretty severe, and all he had for a shelter was a lean-to and he had what appeared to be a long, narrow table on which he slept. There was a cook stove right in front of the table and that was all the heat he had. He would cook a big kettle of oatmeal, and eat that for several days. Adelle often fixed meals and sent them over to him, and being able to see firsthand how hard the living conditions were for those less fortunate than others was a lesson for our family.

These were years that taught us all a lot about life, especially the kids, and it gave them a taste of town life, but we were all anxious to move back to the country. Even Roxy and Happy, who had never lived in the country, were excited about talk of moving back. We would find life much different, with more work, we would miss our friends and all the good times, but still we were all ready to make the move back to the country.

My Cache

Whenever Adelle and I went somewhere, or when we were returning home, I always put what money I had left into a can and then into a big jar I kept buried. When I got the chance to buy the land where the ranch now sits, I dug out my money cache, and got out the jug that I had buried. I poured it all out on a tarp and counted it; I had just enough money to pay cash for that piece of land, 160 acres. There were pennies, nickels, dimes, quarters, half dollars, silver dollars, dollar bills, five, ten and twenty dollar bills.

I went into the house and had Adelle and all the kids come out to my shed to see what I had on my tarp, and they all just stared at it. Adelle knew I'd been saving money, but had no idea it amounted to that much and the kids were so excited because they had never seen that much money at one time. I let them each take a handful of small change and then I gathered it up, went to the courthouse in Polson, and paid for my land.

Going Back Home

Moving back to the country took a lot of preparation as we had accumulated a lot of things in the years at Martin City. We sold our house, our meat market and locker plant and our friends and relatives there gave us a nice farewell party, and presented us with a large painting of Lake McDonald. We were ready to move to the land I had purchased with the money on the tarp.

On the weekends or anytime we had a chance, we had been going to our new place and I had started to doze and level a place with my old cat for a building site. After I got the ground leveled off, I began to build a house.

We had a lot of things already moved down, and we planned to move the rest as soon as I finished working on construction at the aluminum plant in Columbia Falls. We moved to our place near Ronan in 1955 when I had only the shell of the house up, and didn't even have the doors or windows on yet. There was a big pile of boards in the middle of the living room and, in fact, we used that lumber pile as a table for a large family dinner on Thanksgiving Day that year. I managed to finish the building, and then started to build a shop and a storage shed.

When I first began to level and landscape this place, the brush was so thick and bent over that it was impossible to walk through it; we literally had to crawl on our hands and knees. I moved many tons of dirt to get the ground landscaped for the two buildings and for the barn and corrals, and then for the Lodge we built.

One spring morning I took my D-8 cat up above our house to work on the steep sidehill where the ground was covered with needles and leaves from the trees. I had one of the kids with me in the cat, and Adelle and the others were in the house when, all of a sudden, the cat started to slide sideways down the hill, right toward the house, gaining speed. I had not realized that, in the shade of all the trees and under the needles and leaves, the ground still frozen very hard and was as slick as ice.

At the edge of the house there was a straight offbank six or seven feet high, and I knew that if I went over it sideways the cat would tip over. Frantically, I tried to get one of the tracks to take ahold so I could at least get the cat turned enough to go over that bank straight, either frontwards or backwards. Finally, one track took hold in the dirt, and I got the big machine swung around head first, just before we went over the bank.

About six inches of the end of the dozer blade caught the corner of our house as we came flying down over that bank and it moved our house over about eight inches. The family came flying out of the house to see what in the world was happening.

Thank goodness I managed to get it turned or we would have rolled right into the house with 28 tons of moving iron. And we were very lucky no one was hurt.

With my poor D-8 standing on end over the bank, its blade stuck down into the dirt, I had to reeve up several parts of cable from my winch and fasten or anchor them to three or four big stumps and onto my winch line. It took me all day to get enough rigging set up to be able to pull the cat back up over the bank.

After I got the D-8 out of there, I had to bring it down and push our house back into place.

The next project was to get our land cleared of timber. I pushed all the trees down, going one direction from our fence-line to the creek about one-quarter of a mile, and then turned around and went back, pushing the trees down the other direction. I kept going back and forth until I got quite a strip down.

Then I got on the uphill side and pushed and rolled all of the trees and timber into long windrows the length of the field. I let the pile of stuff dry for some time, and later burned it. The whole family got in on the burning as there was a lot of sticks and brush that had to be picked by hand because it was impossible to get them all with the cat. There also were many tons of rock that had to be picked by hand!

It took about three years to get the land cleared off because I wasn't able to keep at it steady with a lot of other things to do. The older boys helped me to fence the land, using posts I had cut at Hungry Horse while we were there working on the dam. The posts, incidentally, were cut from big cedar logs that the people building the dam had given to me.

We dug all the fence posts by hand, and in that rocky ground it was quite a job.

We also had to build our barn and corrals. While we were clearing the land I saved quite a few of the best trees and had a portable saw mill come in to saw them into lumber.

My kids had to learn to work, as there was always lots to be done. When they got home from school I would say, "Hurry up and get your clothes changed, and come and help me." Work hours started at daylight and ended at dark in the evening.

A Lover Of Horses And Cattle

When I was a small boy, animals always seemed to be my highest priority. I loved to ride the work horses while they were being driven by my dad, or by other men in the fields. My sisters and brothers and I all learned to ride at a young age, as it was our main way of travel. We older kids learned how to drive teams of horses, on wagons, and in the fields on different machinery, and we learned how to skid logs in the woods.

When Adelle and I started a family of our own, we always had a milk cow and cattle, and some horses. I started to break my own horses when I was still very young, and I have broken and trained horses for a lot of people during my life.

After we started outfitting, I can only remember buying four horses during the fifty-some years in our business. The first horse that I bought was an American Saddler stallion, whom we called Valentine. He got that name because I had used all our money to buy him, and didn't have any money left to buy Adelle a Valentine's Day present.

So I called her out and told her, "Here's your valentine!" And after that, she always claimed that horse. He was a sorrel with a black spot on his rump, which was shaped like a valentine.

My second horse was a three-year-old, half-broke, baldfaced, stocking-legged mare we called Dolly. She wasn't too pretty, but I think she was a descendent of some of the old Indian horses, and she was a tough, easy riding, outstanding mountain horse. Each year we brought our horses home after hunting season by going from Holland Lake by way of the Jocko, which made a seventy-five or eighty mile trip. Even at a very old age, Dolly was always way ahead of the other forty or fifty horses on the way home. She was a good, faithful mare.

My next horse to buy was a Thoroughbred stallion we called Little Chief. He was also a good horse, and anywhere you pointed him, he would go, through mud, water, brush, over rocks and logs. Nothing would stop him. We got a lot of good colts from Little Chief, who was a grandson of the famous race horse, "Man Of War." There were only a couple of jockeys who could ride Man of War, and Little Chief must have taken after his grandfather, because only a really good rider could handle him.

The last horse I bought was a mare we called Diamond. I worked in Missoula for six months, and each day as I went to work, I would see this mare, all alone, going around her twenty-acre pasture. I felt sorry for her, going around that fence by herself, so one evening on my way home, I stopped and bought her. She was gentle, faithful and tough, but there wasn't a gate or any kind of door that she couldn't open, unless it was tied or nailed shut. She was very hard riding, so we packed her a lot, and we didn't keep her too many years.

In all my years in the business, I bred and raised all of our own horses, and we had a lot of real good ones. We raised hundreds of them, and if there was any that didn't qualify, we got rid of them. There were only a few that didn't turn out, because I only bred our best mares.

I broke and trained and shoed every one of my own horses, and every one that we raised got broke to ride. My boys and I have never seen a horse that couldn't be broke to ride; we have had a few that were rougher than others, but we managed to break them all. We have been very fortunate that none of us have ever been hurt bad.

One time, a few days before I left to go on my hunting trip in the early Forties, a friend of ours named Dude Heath brought me a truck-load of nine mules to break to pack and use. One of them was three years old and the rest were up to six years of age; none had ever had a halter on them, and this was my first experience breaking mules to pack. I managed to get a halter on all of them, and then I tied them all up for the night, letting them fight the halter all night.

The next day I asked a couple of neighbors, Ed Sias and Leo David, to help me lead them to water. We fitted each mule with a pack saddle, and gave each one a name, which we marked on the saddle. We then put a pack on, one at a time, and led each mule around with what we call a "Running W" on their feet as a trip rope. As each mule started to buck, he would be tripped, and after two or three times they would quit bucking. We led each mule from the corral through the woods to get them used to the pack. Then I took each mule, one at a time, and started to shoe it, while Ed and Leo led another pair. I think I was kicked more times while shoeing those wild mules than I have been in the rest of my life.

I spent three days with these mules before I left to go into the mountains with them. We took them over the Mission Mountains to Holland Lake, a distance of thirty-five miles, and it was a real good workout for the mules, and for the rest of the horses, too. And by the end of the season, they were all pretty good mules.

Places I Worked

During the years I often had to go to work away from home, but I didn't like having to be away from my family at all. I am sure they had to sacrifice a lot with my being gone all the time, only getting home on weekends, and sometimes not even then, and when I finished working on Noxon Dam I was done going away from home to work!

I did continue to work out but only after the hunting season each year. I worked on the Higgins Avenue Bridge in Missoula the last time it was re-built and I also worked at the pulp mill there several different times. I worked on the Bonner mill, and a few buildings around Missoula and I also worked on the St. Regis cut-off bridge, and also on a bridge near Superior.

Before we moved from Martin City, I was sent by the union down to Missoula to help unload and set the trusses for the fieldhouse at the university; the crew before us had tipped one of them over.

The boys and I drove back and forth to Columbia Falls to help build an addition on the aluminum plant most of one winter. The roads were very bad that winter and when it was my turn to drive back and forth on the icy road, and after working long days, I would be fagged out. I sure didn't want to have a wreck with others riding with me.

Now, since I am retired I can worry about others — and we worry about our kids who drive to Missoula every day.

We First Took Guests at the Ranch

It was 1958 when we first took guests to stay at the ranch. We housed them in tent houses, new white tents over wooden frames built on concrete slabs, with a clear stream of water nearby.

Adelle had those tents fixed up real attractive and meals were right along with the family. And, since Adelle always was a good cook and the guests were well fed, they loved the arrangements.

We Lose Viola Mae

Viola was twenty-five when her eyesight and kidneys failed her, due to her diabetes, and her weakened condition caused her to die, of pneumonia. She died in her husband's arms.

Viola Mae.

We had feared this day since the time I came home from work one evening and my wife Adelle met me at the door and said, "Viola Mae is very sick." Viola Mae's little face was all sunken in and when I picked her little seven-year-old body up, it felt as limber as a rag. We rushed to the car with her and took her to the doctor's office in town. The doctor was not there but his wife was a nurse and she looked at Viola and said, "I am sure this girl has diabetes. Take her to the hospital. The doctor will be there in a few minutes." Subsequently, the doctor and nurses brought her out of her diabetic coma.

Viola Mae had many, many friends and everybody loved her. She grew up to be a very sweet and lovable girl and it was a sad day for everyone that knew her when she died.

Part Five

GRIZZLY TALES AND HUNTING CAMPS

Ranch Bears

In 1955, we started clearing the heavy timber to make a big meadow and leveling the land for our building site. After we got it all into nice green pasture land, we started to have a lot of bear come around, both blacks and grizzly. We often had seven or eight at a time feeding on clover bloom and dandelion blossoms. In fact, we had so many bear that we had a lot of them named.

One morning, I had my big D-8 caterpillar sitting behind the barn in the horse corral and, when I walked out there, a brown bear was sitting up in the drivers seat of my Cat — just as if he was going to take off with it. Many times our milk cows and some of our mules would take after a bear and run it out of our corrals and meadows, and back up into the woods.

One day one of our mules, Bunny, took after a real big grizzly and ran it out of the meadow, into the woods and up an old skidding trail and stayed after it out in the woods for sometime. All of a sudden, here came that mule just a-flying with her head going from side to side and looking back. The bear apparently decided he'd been chased far enough, and must have turned onto the mule as she was sure moving when she came back.

Another day, I thought, "I will take some pictures of this grizzly." It was usually quite hard to get good pictures of bears, as they seem to always know when someone is close by. But this day I thought I was doing quite well; I had my 16mm movie camera, and was hid behind some bushes and a big grizzly was feeding on dandelion blossoms right past me. Three of our little calves were laying by a brush pile, and this old bear fed to within a few yards of the calves.

One of the calves stood up, looked at the big bear, and then stretched and laid back down. The old bear fed on, right past the calves, grazing like a cow would and when he got his fill, he came back, went right in front of the calves, paying no attention to them, and went back into the woods. I took a full roll of film of him.

After he left, I started back to the house, still trembling with excitement. On the way, I looked down at my camera and realized that I had left the cap over my lens, so I wasted all of that roll of film and the chance to get really good pictures.

Another time, Mick and maybe some of the other boys were up on a roof shingling one of our new buildings when we noticed a large grizzly walking slowly in our meadow. All of sudden the bear started to run to the woods to where a storm had blown and broke off a spruce tree and left a high stump. When he came to this stump, the grizzly battled it a few times with his paw and then stood up on his hind feet and bit a chunk out of the tip of the stump.

I asked the boys, "How high is that stump?" That afternoon, we walked down there to see what he had done and that grizzly had bitten a big chunk out of the top of that stump, just as high as I could reach.

The First Bear That I Caught By The Back Foot

When we were on the ranch, I kept my milk cows in a small pasture behind the barn. One year I had a couple whitefaced cows that were late to calve, so I put them with my milk cows so I could watch them closer, and one of them calved the next morning. When I got up to do my chores, this whitefaced cow was going along the fence bawling. I thought right away that something was wrong. I went to check and sure enough, something was wrong.

I found blood on the grass and a bear had taken the calf into the timber. When I got there, the bear was gone.

Now, when a bear starts to killing calves, a person may as well get rid of it because it will continually kill. I built a pen for the trap and set it.

The next morning as I started out to do my chores, just as it was starting to break day that bear started to beller. I went back in the house and I told Adelle, my wife, to come outside if she wanted to hear a bear beller. She came out, but the bear had stopped.

I stepped back into the house to get my gun, when all at once I thought Adelle was going to tear the door off as she charged into the house. She said, "Hurry up, he is right here in the yard." But he was still some 150 yards behind the barn; that bear had bellowed so loud that Adelle thought he was right close. When these bears bellow, it will make most peoples' hair raise.

By the time I got down there with my gun, the bear must have known that I was coming because I heard him run with that trap and toggle. I heard the toggle hit into a tree and that bear got out of the trap because he had gotten caught by a hind foot. Incidentally, this was the first bear I ever saw caught by a hind foot — and he was caught quite high on the hind leg above the foot. When he pulled out of the trap, all the skin was torn off of his leg down to the foot and it also broke his leg. I felt bad for him to get in that condition.

I saw that bear several times after that, but never had a gun to shoot him. He was easy to identify, as that back leg was real crooked and that foot had shrivelled up to almost nothing. He was a real big bear, but the first year after he got caught in the trap he got very thin and moved down to our son Buddy's place and started killing there. Buddy took the trap down there to trap him, but the old bear was to wise after being caught once.

One Sunday morning, while Adelle and I were attending church and two or three of my other sons and families were in church, the phone rang. It was my son Buddy. He said, "Dad, I have a young grizzly in the trap. Can you come and help me to turn him loose?" I told the rest of my boys about the situation and we left the church to go help Buddy.

*A bear
at the Cheff ranch.*

I went by the veterinarian's and asked him if he could give me something to put the bear to sleep long enough to get the trap off. He gave me a syringe with a shot of tranquilizer in it, and we rushed out to Buddy's place.

There we cut a pole and the boys put the pole over the bear and held him down long enough so I could go up behind him and give him the shot. We waited for quite a while, but he didn't go to sleep so we thought the shot was not strong enough. The boys held him down again, and I put the clamps on the springs of the trap and released the foot from the trap.

Once loose, he got up and took two or three steps and fell over and went to sleep. By then, several of the grandchildren and their mothers and Adelle had come to see what was going on and we were all standing around the bear for a few minutes, feeling sorry for him. We had doctored his foot, which didn't seem to be hurt much, and he finally opened one eye, jumped up, and away he went. We then pulled the trap, because we didn't want to catch any more bear — except the big black bear.

This big black bear killed every one of Buddy's little band of sheep and many of his calves, so we decided to shoot him instead of trying to trap him. We neglected to (or didn't want to) report this bear as on three different times when bear were reported killing livestock that had not been the case.

One time a man reported that a bear had killed one of his horses. It so happened that the horse involved was one of ours, instead of his, and it was real old — it had just laid down and died. But the authorities didn't check with anybody else and set their trap there and destroyed several nice innocent bears for no reason, and we didn't want that to happen again.

Buddy and I saw this big black bear several times, but just didn't get a good shot at him. The bear had all healed up and was fat again, and we were all glad when someone reported that a big crippled black bear was killed at the Job Corps dump; we were sure it was the same one that had bothered us.

We have tried to protect as many of the bears as we could for many years. We always felt that only a very few bear get started killing, but if they do they will not stop and they might just as well be put away. Most people think that a bear is a killer of all things; it is our conviction that most bears will live a lifetime without doing any killing.

Boys and Bear

Happy, our youngest son, was taking some trash to the trash barrel when he noticed that same big black bear at my D-8 Caterpillar. He and his brothers, Mick and Buck, decided to have some fun with the bear and off they went as we watched from the yard.

When they got near, they crouched down on their hand and knees and crawled around toward the front of the blade. Unknown to them, the bear had gotten down on the far side, and was coming around to the front also — and there they met, very nearly bumping noses! The bear whoofed in surprise, blowing slobbers on the boys, and bear and boys each backed off and left the spot in a hurry.

Cheff Guest Ranch

About this time we started to build our lodge. In 1960, I hired Art Powell and his carpenter, Helmar Swenson, to help me frame our new lodge, and to help put in the kitchen cabinets. Another fellow, Jim Trainer, came up and spent about two hours showing me how to mix the mud and how to lay the blocks for my basement.

In February, 1961, our shop burned down. Buck and Cheryl were living in the back half of it and we think the fire started from a leak in the propane stove, or line. We lost everything in the shop, including my packing equipment, all of my tools, my tents, and all of the kid's belongings, too.

By fall we had the lodge far enough along that we decided to start moving into it. Most everything had been moved except for our deep freezer, which was full of meat (we had just finished butchering our pigs and beef for the winter supply), our diaries, several hundred dollars worth of books, and the furniture, when it caught fire too. We had planned to use that house for a guest house, and the furniture was nearly new. Buck and Cheryl moved in for the winter, and were living in it when the fire took place — and once again they lost everything they had, and we lost all we had in there.

We thought this fire was caused by a faulty electrical fixture in the bathroom.

After cleaning up all the mess from both fires, we poured new slabs of concrete over the old slabs and put up two new log buildings, one for a guest house with seven rooms and two baths and the other for a bunkhouse.

The fires were very big losses for us as we had no insurance, so we didn't get everything completed until 1964.

Sent Boys to Chase Bear Away From Our House

One spring morning when I got up, we had about six inches of new snow and when I went outside to do my chores, there were big bear, medium bear and little bear tracks all around our house. I went down to the barn and in my corrals there were more bear tracks there than there were tracks of my animals.

I went back to the house and got all of my teenage sons and one of their friends, Nels Jensen. I told them all that their first job this morning was to take our two lion dogs, and for them to get out there and scatter some bear because there was just to darn many around here.

So, two of the boys went into the woods along our little irrigation ditch, and the other two went down through our meadow with the hounds. When they got quite close to the woods, Nels said, "There is one laying down under the big tree." My son said, "No, that is one of our big black cows." But about that time, a big black-looking grizzly got up out of his bed under the tree and the boys turned the hounds loose after him.

The big bear ran for a short distance, and then slowed down to a brisk walk as it headed towards the mountain on an old log skidding trail. The other two boys were on the edge of the mountain but on the same trail that grizzly was on and they could hear the hounds coming, so they stepped back off of the trail just one step behind some bushes. The grizzly came so close to them that they both said they could have reached out and touched him, but it was so busy watching the dogs that it didn't even notice the boys.

Big Diamond

Dr. Maurice Hornocker, who made a big study of mountain lions, came to us when he started with his study, and had my son Buddy and me catch lions for him. One day we caught five for him and he very much liked the way our hounds worked and on an occasion while I was away, he came to try to buy one of the hounds. He offered my wife, Adelle, a good sum of money for the dog and she said later she wished she would've sold him.

A night or two after that, our last guest had left and there was no one there but Adelle and I and our daughter Roxy. We were getting into bed for the night but our two good hounds were making a real bad fuss, so I put my shirt back on and took a flashlight and went out to see what was the matter.

The dogs were each chained to their separate dog houses, just outside of our yard. When I shined my big flashlight out there, this big beautiful brown bear that we called Big Diamond was about thirty or so feet from me, laying on his stomach, right between the two hounds. He was chewing on one of their bones, totally ignoring the barking dogs. When I turned my light in his face, the bear got up and charged me. It startled me! I jerked my shirt off and gave a yell and whipped him in the face with my shirt, which left me bare naked. Ha, ha, this must have been what scared him — because he turned and left.

But I was the scared one! I started back to the house and realized I better put my shirt back on, as I was going for my shotgun. I slipped my pants on and got my shotgun.

All of this commotion had awakened our daughter, Roxy, so she and Adelle both went back out with me to see what I was going to do. I planned to let the bear get some distance away, and then pepper his butt with buckshot. When we got back out there, he was sitting on a little bank above the hounds and I yelled at him a couple of times. He got up and slowly walked away.

By now I was calmed down and I just couldn't pepper that bear. I think that he was not really after me, but when I put the light in his eyes I had blinded him. But, the very next night he came back and killed our best hound.

There was another smaller bear that looked very much like Big Diamond, that we called Little Diamond — the one that was sitting on the seat, trying to drive my big D-8 caterpillar. Both those bear stayed around here for four or five years and never bothered anything except the dog.

I think they both fell victims at the Job Corps dump, where someone shot them.

The Bear Going Through The Fence

Adelle, some friends and guests, were standing near the barn watching a bear in our meadow a short distance away when one lady said, "Did you see what I saw?"

And yes, they had. All of them had witnessed that bear come to the wire fence, put his paw in the middle wire, push it down, and then step through the fence just like a man would do.

Repairing Fences And Grizzly

One fall some people were cutting Christmas trees for market near our place and they used wire cutters and cut the wires on my brand-new fence in several places because they wanted to drag their trees over part of our land. The following spring I went down to repair my fence about three-fourths of a mile from our ranch house.

We had an old horse that had died on the place also and on this particular day I had taken a young female hound with me. As I was going along the fence on this heavily timbered 160 acre piece of land repairing the fence, my young hound had wandered up toward where the dead horse was and started to bark or bay. I was near the northwest corner of my fence when I heard something hit the wires in the fence that went to the east.

I thought it was probably a bear, but I see bear nearly every day so I didn't pay any attention to it. My dog had come back to me and I followed my fence around the corner and was about halfway along the east fence when I came to where I had heard the fence squeak - and here, indeed, was quite a lot of grizzly hair hanging on some barbs on the wire. This was a common thing in this area.

I continued along my fence until I was done with all of the repair work and was within thirty yards of the big feeder canal that came through the place with a road on top of the bank when my dog wandered out into the woods again. I was wearing a heavy wool shirt that was not tucked in, just hanging loose, and I was carrying a small bucket containing staples, nails, wire cutters and a hammer in one hand and a good sharp ax in the other hand — and I had a good-sized, loose roll of barbed wire on my shoulder.

The dog started to bay again, and then the baying turned into yelps and here she came for me — with a huge mama grizzly right behind her. When I saw them coming, I dropped my bucket and tried to get rid of the roll of wire from my shoulder, but the barbs kept hanging up on my shirt. I finally got loose from the wire or the wire loose from my shirt and was going to try to fight the bear with my axe, but this darned dog ran right between my legs and around them and almost knocked me down.

Everything was happening so fast I let out a bellow, or maybe a scream, I'm not sure, but the grizzly was within two or three steps from me. I was ready to try to hit her with my ax when she stopped and slunk back, turned and went away. I quickly picked up my tools and ran up onto the canal bank. I was still shaking I know, but I had to stop and laugh at myself.

I then started for home on the canal bank and as I was nearing a foot bridge that went across over the water, once again my darned dog went to fooling around in the thick woods below the canal. And, once again, she started to baying and yelped a couple times - and, once again, here she came. I thought, oh no, it is going to happen again but, to my relief, nothing showed up.

But I noticed that the bears had beaten down a trail where they had been crossing this foot bridge to feed on that dead horse. When I got home, I told Adelle about what had happened and subsequently, kiddingly, she would tell everyone that she could hear me screaming all the way up to the ranch — and I'm not sure that if she had been outside that she might not have been able to hear me.

Dad and Mick In A Fight

We finished clearing the big meadow just below our house, burned all the stumps and trees, plowed the land and seeded it to grass. Next, I needed to irrigate it so that it would grow good and fast.

I surveyed my ditches to be sure that we could flood irrigate and got Mick to help me dig the ditches. We took the Ford tractor and hooked up my old walking plow that was made to be pulled with a team of horses and went into the field, with Mick driving the tractor and me walking behind, handling the walking plow.

As we went along, Mick was not driving the tractor quite like I wanted him to drive it so I stopped him just as we got directly below our house, in front of the big picture windows. I told him how I wanted him to drive that tractor. He asked me if I wanted to fight him, and I said yes. Mick jumped off the tractor and made a run at me. We knocked each other down; first I would be down, and then I would get back on my feet and knock him down. All of the time we were fighting, we knew the rest of the family was in the house and we were hoping someone would see us.

Finally, Mick got back on the tractor and we plowed a little ways, but he stopped the tractor, jumped off and ran at me again. We had another fight; no one saw us. We went another little ways and Mick jumped off the tractor for the third time, and we started to fight again. This time Adelle was looking out of the window and she hollered at Buck that Mick and I were fighting down in the field.

She came running out, screaming at us to stop, followed by Buck, his wife Cheryl, Roxy, and Happy. Buck ran past her to try to stop us. But it was all a play fight — we never did hit each other, but they sure thought it was real. Each time we pounded each other, we were missing and faking the falls, and when Adelle and Buck found us out, they were so mad they very nearly beat us up for real!

The Grizzly Carrying A Horse Away

Some friends of ours had a small saddlehorse that got into their rabbit pellets, ate too many, and died from it. This family didn't know what to do with the dead horse, so I told them if they wanted they could haul that horse up here to our place and the bear would take care of it very quick.

So, they got the horse loaded onto a truck and brought it up and we unloaded it near a brush pile a ways from the edge, but still well inside our meadow. The next morning or so, I was setting down in the barn milking one of my milk cows with the barn door open where I was able to see down across our meadow, and I noticed a big old grizzly bear coming out of the woods and going right to that dead horse.

He got to the horse just as I finished milking my cow. Suddenly, that old bear let a very loud bellow out of him that caused all of our animals on the place to come to life. Then he walked all the way around the dead horse, and started back to the woods. I took my milk to the house, and I told Adelle about this big bear, so we walked out into the yard just as this big fellow was coming back. He had gone to the woods to find a good place to put this horse. When he got back to the horse he walked around him again, stopping on the far side; then, he took a big bite into the horse and picked it up in his mouth.

Holding his head up high, the grizzly started for the woods with that horse up off of the ground, its legs dragging along on both sides of the bear. He carried that horse about fifty yards to the fence near the edge of the woods without stopping, laid the horse down next to the fence, and then crawled through it.

He was smart enough to reach under the bottom wire with one paw and pull the horse through the fence. Then he then picked the horse up again in his mouth and took it into the woods. What power these animals have got! This was not a huge horse, but must have weighed 800 to 1,000 pounds, and even so, it didn't last long as food for the grizzly.

Grizzly Chases Doug Up A Tree

We had a young man by the name of Doug McCallister working for us and late one afternoon, Adelle and I had to go to town for more supplies. As we got home we could hear some hollering down toward the creek and toward the lower part of our meadow, but thought it was some of the grandkids playing along the creek, as they did often.

Now Doug liked to go jogging in the evening and he had gone down to jog on this old road and, as he started up it, he saw a bear pulling some bushes down to get at the berries. By this time, Doug had been with us long enough that he was getting used to having bear close by, so he went on jogging up the road. Finally, he turned back and as he was almost back to our meadow and near where the berry bushes were being pulled down, here was old Becky, a grizzly sow and her two cubs.

This time Doug surprised Becky, and she took after him. He was very lucky as there was a nice big tree with a lot of limbs very close by, and he managed to get up and out of reach of the mama bear before she got a hold of him. But old Becky kept him up the tree for quite a while. When we came home from town and heard the hollering, we didn't realize that Becky had Doug up in a tree and we didn't go to rescue him.

Becky finally took her two cubs and walked away and, after she had been gone for some time, Doug got nerve enough to come down out of that tree. Then he

Bud with a packstring in the Missions.

jogged the rest of the way to our house. He came in wringing wet with sweat and affirmed that his jogging in that direction was ended.

Becky is an old sow bear that we named and she has been around here for at least twelve or fourteen years. She spends most of her summers between our house and Buddy's place and I believe she may still be around. She is a good mama, but is protective of her babies as she should be. She has been real productive, raising several crops of young ones, and our son, Buddy, can tell several stories about Becky.

Wilderness Trips

This was about the time that the Wilderness Act was passed and in August that year the National Wilderness Society had their annual meeting here at our ranch. We had everything completely full, and a lot of people stayed at Allentown, a motel about four miles from us. There were people here from everywhere and some stayed for several days.

Adelle's sister, Ruth, her daughter, Cindy, and our daughter-in-laws helped her. We took a big share of the Wilderness Society people on a three day pack trip and our daughter, Roxy, and Cheryl, our daughter-in-law, did the cooking on this trip, and our boys helped with the packing. We used better than fifty head of horses and mules going through Mollman Pass.

At this time we started taking people on walking trips for the Wilderness Society. The guests walked, with our grandkids as guides, some in the lead and some in the back. We packed all the gear on the mules, and set up the camps. Each trip lasted eight days, starting from the Ranch, and we made a big circle into the mountains and ended up back at the Ranch.

We would travel by eleven different lakes, many spectacular waterfalls, and we would see meadows and sidehills covered with all colors of beautiful wild flowers of many varieties, and we passed right by many glaciers and high mountain peaks.

For sleeping, tepee tents were set up with two people per tent. We also set up a cook tent and a large tepee, Indian style, with a fire in the middle. This tepee was big enough for the whole group and each night everyone would gather to tell stories and to sing.

We returned to a big dinner, prepared by Adelle with the help of the other daughters-in-law, and this dinner was followed by Indian dancing, drumming and singing, done by some of our neighbor Indians, complete in their native costumes. This was a great time for a lot of people, and made a lot of good memories. They were fun trips with people from all walks of life and we have a lot of wonderful memories and made a lot of good friends.

On one of these trips, the guests included a man, his wife and two teenage daughters. The man was sort of odd, and quiet, and he was afraid of height and afraid of bears, and all other animals that might be in the mountains. I would guess his age at maybe fifty years, and was surprised that his wife and daughters babied him, and waited on him hand and foot. To get him up the steeper parts of the trails, one girl would pull on him while the other would be pushing on him from behind.

Our youngest son, Happy, and Dan Tuxbury, a friend of his, were doing the guiding for us.

The camp toilet had a pole frame around the stools with a long, green canvas stretched around the frames and one day while we were camped at Mollman Lakes,

Adelle in her cook tent at the Cheff's summer camp in the Mission Mountains.

Happy had the urge to go to the toilet, and when he got there, he discovered that the odd-acting fellow was sitting on the stool. So, Happy went on by the toilet a ways and was standing behind some trees, waiting for his turn. Now Dan, fixing to pull a prank, had not seen Happy go on past the toilet, and thought that he was inside. Dan sneaked up quietly, and then quickly jerked the flap to the toilet open and grabbed the man by the neck, at the same time hollering, "I got you," all the time thinking he had ahold of Happy.

This scared the man half to death, as he was nervous anyway. The man's two daughters thought this was the funniest thing that had ever happened to their dad.

Poor Dan, who was a bashful young fellow, got teased mercilessly for scaring the man off his perch in the toilet and Dan's intended victim, Happy, just stood behind the trees and laughed his fool head off.

Mickey, Mark and Mice

One day at the ranch, I decided to clean out my grain bin down at the barn as I was getting ready to put in a new supply of feed. I started to pick up an old burlap bag and immediately realized there were a lot of mice hiding under it.

I thought, "I will go to the house and get the boys (two of my grandsons) to come down and help me catch and kill that bunch of mice. This should be sort of fun for two young boys."

I did not tell them what we were going to do, but since I had leather gloves on, I told the boys to also put on leather gloves.

The grain bin was about eight feet by eight feet, with the door a little less than standard width. I got the boys inside the grain bin with me and said, "Micky, you stand right here and Mark, you stand right here."

Now I want you all to know that these two grandsons of mine were two husky national champion wrestlers. I said to them, "Be ready, now, and don't let a one of these get away. Catch every one of them." I did notice that they were getting sort of wild-eyed by this time, but I just thought they were anxious to get after them, though I realized I still had not told them what we were after — though I think they were both starting to realize what I wanted them to do.

I hollered, "Get them!" and I pulled up that sack. Mice ran every direction. And both of those big boys hit that door at the same time, and both got wedged in the doorway. They were hollering and kicking and both trying to get out at the same time and the mice were also trying to get out through the same doorway. At that time I did not know that they were afraid of mice and rats.

One fall while Mick was with me in the hunting camp, Karen and the two boys, who were quite little, had a mountain rat get into their house, and it scared them all half to death. These boys are not afraid of the devil, but don't let mice or rats come around! I think this was holdover from when they were small — and I know that if there had been a bunch of little snakes under that sack, I would have been wedged in that doorway with the two little boys.

Mark And Grizzlies

Mick and Karen, one of our sons and his wife, now run the ranch and we live about a half a mile from them. Their two oldest sons, Mick and Mark, played sports after school when they were in middle school — and the only way they were able to do this and be able to get home in the evening was to ride their bikes down the road on the canal bank for three miles to the next county road, and then catch the school bus there for the last seven miles into school, leaving their bikes there until evening.

They then would catch a ride with their aunt Cheryl, another of our daughters-in-laws, each evening to their bikes, and then would pedal back home.

On this evening, Micky, the older boy, had come home some other way and had left his bike there for the night. So, Mark came home alone. The next morning Micky rode the school bus and Mark took off on his bike alone. He was about ten or eleven years old at the time and he was pedaling down the canal as fast as he could and got a little ways past the spot my dog and I had the scare sometime before. Mark came around a sharp bend in the road and canal and right in front of him, right in the middle of the road, were four big grizzly bears.

He managed to get stopped before he ran into them and got his bike turned around while all four grizzlies stood up on their hind feet and started to bellow at him. As he got to going on his bike toward home, he looked back to see them loping after him. Then one of the big grizzlies ran off of the bank, so poor Mark thought the bear was going to head him off on the next bend, as the canal bank was crooked and he was on an S-shaped curve.

So, he really put the pressure on the pedals of that bike and he zoomed down the road. Our place was the nearest house, about a mile and a half distant, and he got to our place puffing and wringing wet with sweat. He wanted to phone his folks as he told us what had happened. Adelie asked him if those bear had bellowed at him,

A government official and Bud putting a radio collar on a grizzly.

and he said yes that is what really scared him. And he was still so nervous and so relieved that he started to cry.

We all realized that it was fortunate that he was able to get his bike stopped before he ran into them, or the incident might have been much more serious.

Helping Radio Collar Bear

A few years back, a bear research team came here to radio collar some of the bear. We caught several of them at Buddy's place and several right here behind my barn and, among others, collared Becky and her offspring.

Early one morning, I saw we had a big grizzly in the snare. I quickly called the research team and they came right out and we went down to collar the big male. When we got close to him, I noticed that we only had him by three toes and he made a lunge for me. When he did, the snare slipped down to where we only had him by one toe. I told the fellow with the dart gun to hurry, which he did. He managed to shoot the bear with the dart before he could lunge again and he soon laid over.

We collared him and took blood samples and they named this particular bear "Old Bud." Two days later, we caught another one that looked like a twin brother and they named him "Oscar." I used to think that all of these bear stayed in this area, but we found out that one day one of these males left the area, crossing over the three ranges of mountains to the east side of the Rockies near Augusta, Montana, where they tracked him by his radio collar.

It seems as the females do not travel like those old males. Old Becky has been close by for all of these years and has never gotten into anything bad except when protecting her cubs.

1932 — My First Hunters

In the year of 1932 a neighbor who had come here from the North Dakota border, Hugh Shepherd, asked me if I would be interested in packing him and three friends into the Bob Marshall for an elk hunt. I was to furnish all the horses and camp gear, and they would bring all of the food, an arrangement would not cost me any money, which I didn't have anyway.

They paid me some money — it could not have been over ten dollars each — and I took them into the Little Salmon area. In those days this area had a lot of game of all kinds but there was one disadvantage with it; the snow in late season could make it impassable. In one area the snow would slide and pile up across the trail so that it was impossible to get through it.

Packing Full Time

In 1937 we were living on the Plant place, as we called it, which was located just above the feeder canal when Adelle and I decided to try to do some packing and guiding. At that time no one had heard of or used the term "outfitting" for the business.

I believe that I probably knew all of these mountains as well or better than most men, as I had traveled with the full blood Indians all through the Mission Range, and had been through a good share of the South Fork of what is now the Bob Marshall Wilderness. I've been on so many trips with the Indians that it would be hard to

*Bud and Adelle
at Summit Lake
in the Mission Mountains.
Circa 1936.*

describe, and would make a very fat book! I have to thank my Indian friend, Bill Conko, and his father and mother, Eneas and Sofia, who treated me as though I was one of their own. They are all gone now, and I sometimes wish they were still here, so I could thank them again for all the experiences they left me.

The Mission Range from the valley floor is as beautiful as I have seen anywhere. And after being able to go into these mountains and really see them from within, I have enjoyed them so much more. I always thought it was a shame that so few people really got to see them: the beautiful lakes, cliffs, flowered terraces, all sorts of glaciers and waterfalls, and wild animals. We felt it was not more than fair to take people who wanted to see the Missions into these areas.

We already had quite a few horses, but we started to raise more. During my life I have bred and raised hundreds of horses, and I can only remember buying two mares since I started packing. My first horses were descendants of Eneas Conko's horses. Some of his stallions came from a ranch owned by the mining magnate Marcus Daly in Hamilton, Montana, which had some of the best horses in the world.

In my young life I broke a lot of Conko's horses and many horses for other people, and during our operation I broke every one of our horses to ride until my boys got old enough to start helping. I also did my own shoeing and leather repairing, which got to be quite a job as we acquired more saddles, pack saddles, and camp equipment.

On one of our early sight-seeing trips to Mollman Lakes, I talked Adelle's dad,

Jess, into coming along. He was leery of horses, but he did very well. I had a group of businessmen from Ronan, but I don't remember who they all were except for Harold Olsson and his son, Don. When we got just above Little Mollman Lake, about two-thirds of the way up the mountain, we saw a sight I have never seen before or after: an old sow grizzly and two little cubs were out in the water at the edge of the lake. She was picking up water in her paws and splashing it on her babies.

My father-in-law also had a great time on this trip, and talked about it for a long time.

Spook Lake and Ed

In some of my earlier years of packing and guiding, two of my neighbors, Leo David and Ed Sias, worked for me off and on during the hunting seasons. Both of them were good guides and good mountain men, and both had some Indian blood. Ed had a lot of stories for our hunters and most, or a lot, of them told for the truth.

Elk Lake, a big beautiful mountain lake with a glacier hanging in it, was virgin of fish until I planted it about 1938. These trout grew very fast and got real big and the lake became a prize place to fish. One evening in our hunting camp, Ed told us a story about him and Leo camping on the edge of this lake one night.

As he was peeling potatoes for supper, he started to toss the peelings into the lake and a big fish started coming into shore and getting all the potato peelings. Ed said, "I threw a big potato out into the water, and I saw a great big fish coming after it. I got ready and when he grabbed that potato, I jumped, straddling that big fish, and that darn big fish started right for the middle of the lake with me on him. But Leo was right on the ball with his lariat rope, and he threw it out and got me. And he pulled me and that big fish right up onto the bank."

Then Ed told about he and Leo camping at a little lake about a mile north of Elk Lake. This pretty little lake lays under some big high cliffs. Ed told us that as it started to get dark that evening, a voice came from across the little lake, from under the foot of the cliff. The voice said, "Hey Ed! Hey Ed! Hey Ed!" and a big ball of fire came out of that cliff, rolling right across the lake, right at us.

"Boy," said Ed, "We packed up quick, and got the devil out of there." I then started to call this little lake Spook Lake, and the name has carried on now for over fifty years.

Snowed In On Crazy Horse in 1938

A fellow that I had been working with had been bugging me to take him into the Crazy Horse area for a long time. He had a large family to feed, so finally I consented for him to come along with me and my brother-in-law, Herman Byrd. He had told me of his many hunting experiences and I was led to believe he was a good woodsman. He told me that he would use his own horse, which he had borrowed from my neighbor, Ernie Landquist; it was a good mountain horse that had once belonged to an Indian.

By the time the plans were all made and we were ready to leave, the sky had started to cloud up. I told my companions that I didn't think we should go, as I knew what a storm was like in these mountains. But the others felt that since we had everything ready we should go ahead, so we went into the Crazy Horse again.

It was starting to snow before we were half way up the mountains, and by the time we got to the divide on what we call Goat Foot Pass, there was a good foot of snow, and it was still coming down, and turning cold as well. I started down the back side of the divide with a few horses. The trail went down a steep side hill, and as soon as my horses came down the trail, it froze very quickly.

The other two fellows started down behind me, their horses having a hard time holding their footing on the icy trail. I hollered to them not to come down, and that we had better turn back. But it got so slick my horses were unable to get back up there, so I walked back up to the others. I tried to talk them into turning back, explaining that I would go on by myself and come out over a lower pass. They refused to let me go alone, so we had to try to get the rest of the horses down.

The first horse we tried to take down was a very nice, young horse that I had raised. We only got him a short way down when he lost his footing and away he went, sliding down the mountainside and over a cliff. He landed on his feet, but broke three legs, and I had to get my gun and go around the end of the cliff to shoot this beautiful horse. We only had an empty saddle on him, so I took it off and carried it to my other horses, and I sure did hate to try to take more horses over that slick ice.

Herman and I started down again, each with a horse. We got quite a distance past where the first horse had fallen when another one slipped, and went down the steep sidehill just like a bullet. We were far enough down that we were past the end of the cliff, and when the horse hit the bottom of the slope, he simply got back onto his feet. Before we finally got all the horses down, four more had fallen, sliding about two hundred yards down the mountainside.

It was a good thing the snow was soft and fluffy. Each time a horse slid down, it boiled up into a cloud of snow. One of our good mares slid into a big boulder about the size of two cars. The impact should have killed her, but she had a pack on her back and she slid with her back downhill. She was sliding so fast that when she hit the rock, pack first, it flattened the saddle under the pack. Her back puffed up so badly that she looked like a camel and she was in poor condition, but able to follow along with the other horses.

When we finally got all the horses down and ready to go again, we still had several miles of bad trails to go over. But the other fellow had not come down, so Herman and I went back up to the top of the divide to see why he wasn't coming. We found him shaking and crying, scared half to death. He said he just couldn't go down that trail, yet only a couple of days before, he was telling us about all his rugged mountain experiences. But to get out of there, he either had to come with us, or go back on foot, alone, which he was afraid to do. Herman and I pleaded with him, explaining that it really was not that dangerous as long as we were on foot.

Finally I said, "Come on, let go, or we won't get out of this canyon today." I took him by the hand and Herman got behind him, and we started down the trail again. He just crept along, hanging on to the uphill bank of the trail. When we got to where the horses had slipped off the trail, he started to slip a little, so he just sat down in the middle of the trail. It was a good thing he had on a good heavy pair of canvas pants, because I grabbed hold of him and started pulling him down the trail on his seat.

Herman came along behind him, ready to grab him if he should go over the edge of the trail. Once, as I was skidding him along, Herman's feet slipped and he slid into this fellow's back end a little bit. The guy started screaming and swearing that Herman was going to knock him off the trail. We finally got him far enough down that we were able to get him back onto his feet and over to the horses.

Eventually, we managed to get the horses all lined up and the packs straightened out. We had to put the pack that was on the mare with the injured back on another horse. One of our good horses had a broken nose from sliding into a rock and others were skinned up quite badly.

In spite of the trouble and delay, we managed to get to our camp ground by nightfall and unpacked the stock and gave them a feed of grain. The snow was already so deep the horses couldn't do much pawing for grass, so they mostly ate snowbrush (as horses can eat a certain amount of it).

We had a hard time kicking out enough snow for a spot to put up our Indian tepee, but we got it up and started a fire in the center. Herman was real good help, but "our man" as I will call him, never once lifted a hand to help us with anything. I guess he was pooped, and must have stayed pooped on the whole trip, because he never offered to help with anything. We even had to saddle his horse for him.

Many, many times he would say, "I never dreamed these mountains were this big!" By the time we got our wood all gathered for the night and also enough for the next morning, Herman and I were as pooped as "our man." It had been a long, hard, miserable and sad day, and we knew we had more rough days ahead of us.

We had a fair night's rest and were up before daylight to find that the snow had let up a little, but was very deep on the ground. Our horses were still close by, and I think they were also anxious to get going, as they could not get at the grass to eat. We packed up again as fast as we could. We had to get out of the deep snow so that the horses could get something to eat.

We also had to get our man out of there, as he was already starting to act a little bit strange, and we had only been out one day. He asked me over and over again if I was able to find my way out of these mountains. I did my best to assure him that we would get out all right.

We started down the canyon and I told the fellow that all he had to do was let his horse have his head and follow along behind us. He was riding a good horse that liked to follow right up close and we were making fair time even though we had to pick our way through a lot of fallen timber and thick brush, and cross several streams, as there was no trail of any kind for several miles. Every little way our man would cry and say that we were never going to get out. He was a man of about forty years, but he acted like a little boy — and he kept telling Herman that he was sure I didn't know where I was going and that we were going to die in there.

We were starting to get down to where the snow wasn't so deep when I came onto a bunch of very fresh elk tracks, which led up onto a nice bench where I had killed elk before. I stopped my horses and told Herman; then we tied our horses up and got our guns out. Our man had been lagging behind a ways, but not waiting for him to catch up we started to climb up to the bench two hundred yards above us. I sent Herman one way, and I went beyond him so that we might have a better chance at the elk.

We had been hearing a roaring sound in the sky for a few minutes and just as we were ready to break over onto the bench where I though the elk might be, a very hard wind started to blow. Trees were falling everywhere, but thank goodness it only lasted a few minutes and was over.

Our man had reached the horses, and started to scream bloody murder, and then he shot a couple of shots into the air. Well, I forgot the elk and, thinking maybe a tree had fallen on him or some of the horses, I ran back down as fast as I could. Herman had the same thought in mind and we both got back to the horses at the same time. Our man was standing among the horses, still screaming. The horses were all nervous, but I couldn't see anything wrong. We asked him what was the matter and he said, "I thought you guys had left me here to die with all these horses."

By this time Herman and I were starting to get aggravated with him, but I think Herman was a little more so than I. While all this was going on, a mule deer buck walked out in right in front of us and since we didn't have any meat yet, I grabbed my gun to shoot the deer. Our man ran and grabbed me around my body and gun and started hollering, "Don't shoot! Don't Shoot!"

By the time I got free of him the deer had bounded off, and I was beginning to realize the guy's mind was slipping a little. I would tell him of landmarks we would be coming to so that he would realize that I really did know where I was going, but Herman had told him several times already to shut his mouth and leave me alone, as I knew where I was going and had been through here several times before.

The hard wind that had just passed had blown down a lot more trees, making it that much harder to get through. We had to jump the horses over a lot of logs that we couldn't get around, and because it was easier for them to get over the logs on their own, I turned two of our horses loose and let them follow along behind. Our man was supposed to sort of haze those two horses along.

It was getting late in the evening and the guy had been lagging behind, so I stopped to wait for him to catch up. When he caught up with us, the two loose horses were not with him. I asked him where they were, and he said, "I don't know, I didn't see any horses today."

I replied, "Well, you have been following them all afternoon. You told me you would haze them along." He said again that he hadn't seen any loose horses all day. By this time we were getting fairly close to the government trail, so I explained to Herman where it was and told him to go on until he hit the trail while I went back and tried to find the two pack horses. I went about a mile and a half back up the canyon to find them standing alongside our pathway. From the looks of the tracks, our man had ridden right past them and left them there.

I caught up with the others just as they were just getting to the government trail — and what a relief to be on a trail! It was getting dark, but I knew of a level spot with some grass for the horses about three hundred yards down the trail. When we got there, I had to help the guy off his horse.

We sat him on one of the packs, then cut a few tepee poles — just enough to hold our tepee up to shelter us. Herman and I put it up right over the top of our man, as he was unable to move out of the way.

Then I chopped into a big dead tree to get dry enough wood to get a fire started, as everything was so wet. By then it was very dark and we didn't have any kind of a light with us, but we needed a bucket of water, and the stream was not too far away, so I set out to get some. I could hear it plainly and knew I would be able to feel my way to it and back again, with water to cook with and to drink.

When I picked up the bucket to go out of the tepee, that fellow started to holler and cry. Sobbing, he said, "Don't go, Bud! You will never get back. No, no, don't go!" By this time, Herman was losing his cool. He doubled up his fist and started for the guy. I had to stop him, as I felt it would only make matters worse, and we already had all the problems we could stand. Then I went out and managed to get what water we needed.

Things were getting aggravating and discouraging, in fact, the whole situation was pitiful.

The next day we went down to Elbow Lake, now called Lindberg Lake, as we had decided to cross back over the mountains by taking an old Indian trail over the North Fork of the Jocko. There was no snow at Lindberg Lake, but the horse feed was very short even though we camped in a little meadow on the south side of the outlet of the lake. In the morning we discovered that our horses had gotten rested up and had taken off. I took off on foot to look for them, finally locating their tracks on the bare ground where they had gone up the big ridge that had been burnt over a few years before. It was not hard to track them as the ground was soft from rain.

I followed the tracks a long way up this big ridge by just going through the woods, not following any trail. The horses finally crossed over the ridge and went right over the old Indian trail. They may have gotten thirsty and gone down the steep ridge to the lakeshore, because when I caught up with them they were feeding along the lake. I had been on their trail all day.

I caught the two bell mares, as I had only two halters with me, and jumped on one of them bareback and started for camp. Fortunately, the rest of the horses followed. Suddenly I realized I was hungry, as I had left camp before breakfast and had no lunch with me.

When I got back to camp around five o'clock in the evening, the storm was finally over and the sky was nice and clear. I suggested to Herman that we pack up and leave that night, because there was no more horse feed and the horses would leave again. So he started catching and saddling the horses while I got a bite to eat, and a half hour later we were on the trail again. It was a beautiful night with a full moon and the stars shining on the snowy peaks.

Our man was constantly mad at his horse, even though it was a very good horse. He was continually swearing at it and threatening to kill it. We had to take his gun away, because he got it out to shoot his horse. Several times he got big rocks and tried to hit the horse in the head and it was a good thing the horse was able to duck away from each of his blows.

When we crossed back over the divide the snow was quite deep, but the going was not dangerous like Eagle Pass. We finally got down to the foot of the mountain about four in the morning. We got to the road at a spot called Shovel Camp, and went to a little meadow about a quarter of a mile up the road and unpacked the horses, letting them feed while we laid down and slept for a few hours. After breakfast, we were starting to pack up again when I heard a car coming, so I went out to meet it.

The driver was a Reclamation man, checking ditches. He told me he was going to St. Ignatius, and I asked him if he would mind taking our man that far. He agreed when I told him the trip had been a little hard on the guy. The driver ended up taking him clear to his home in Ronan, having realized the fellow was having problems — and a good man he was, too, to take him that far.

Herman and I got home early that evening.

What a trip! We never did stop to do any hunting, so we came home empty-handed. Our minds had constantly been on trying to get that man home and I don't think he ever went hunting again. And, a trip like that should have stopped Herman and me too, but it didn't.

Adelle's First Trip Over Eagle Pass.

Not too long after Adelle and I were married, about 1934 or 1935, we decided to go hunting over Eagle Pass and into the Crazy Horse again. George Moore had never been in this area, so he, his wife, Fern, Thurman Trosper, and Adelle and I made the trip. George and Fern's big German Shepherd also came along.

Adelle and Fern were good, rugged gals. We had seen a lot of grizzly sign around our camp, and the second day we three men went out hunting while the girls stayed in camp. We had a tepee set up.

About mid-forenoon, Adelle and Fern were sitting in the tepee reading when all of a sudden they heard a loud noise from a little ways out. That big dog of George's let out a few yipes and went flying past the tepee and up the trail we had come in on, like something was after him. The girls both knew there was a grizzly out there because they were sure nothing else could frighten that big dog like that.

So, one grabbed the .22 rifle and the other grabbed the only other weapon left — the butcher knife. They were both afraid to go out to see where the bear was for quite a while, but when they finally got nerve enough to venture out of the doorway, they discovered what had happened. The night before we men had piled all of our saddles on top of each other in a high pile and the dog must have been sleeping by the pile when it fell over onto him, scaring him out of his wits. Sometime later the dog came sneaking back into camp, looking sheepish.

On this same day George shot and killed a very large bull elk. I don't remember how many points there were on the rack, but I do remember what they looked like. They were shaped in an unusual manner and extra heavy beamed. As I mentioned before, in those days we never ever brought out any horns, but when seeing this big bull we figured that George had shot the old man of the mountains. I sure wish I could get another look at that set of horns now; during my years of hunting and packing in this area, I have taken many large elk with that same type of horn, which has led me to believe that they were all from the same family line.

Lure of the Mountains

I have never been able to figure exactly what it is that attracts me to this place time and time again over the years. The Mission Mountains are a rough area on people and livestock. I am an old man of seventy-eight years now, and yet I am still attracted to them.

I was through there two summers ago with son, Buddy, grandsons Matt and Monty, a granddaughter, Laurie Jo, and a great grandson, Garrett. And last August my son, Buddy, his wife, Laurie, my granddaughter, Laurie Jo, and Eneas' granddaughter, Jeanette, and great grandson, Arnold, went with me on a trip through the Mission Range. I have always wanted to take some of Eneas Conko's descendants on this trip and let them see what it was like when I went in there with their grandfather.

We followed the route where the old Indian Trail used to be, camping in the same spots where I had camped with the old ones as a boy. It was a difficult trip, and before we returned, we were in snow and rain, and all had the chance to see how rugged these mountains are. I am sure that Eneas and Sofia's spirits were with us, guiding us and smiling their approval.

Hunting Our Winter Meat on Little Salmon

In 1937, we decided to go into the Bob Marshall to Little Salmon to hunt for our winter meat. It was getting a little late in the season for that high trail over Smith Creek, but we got our gear and horses ready and loaded the gear into our 1937 Chevy sedan.

Herman and I took off early in the morning with all the horses, going on the Crow Creek trail over the Mission mountains. We planned to meet Bernida and Adelle at Condon Ranger Station the next day; they would go in the car.

We rode all day in the rain and snow and I wanted to stop at my old campsite, but it got too dark before we reached it, so we had to stop along the trail and tie our horses up and wait for daylight.

Bernida and Adelle left the morning after we did. They drove as far as Flathead Lake where they got a flat tire and the jack was under all the gear, so they tried to pry the car up with poles, but didn't succeed. They went to a nearby house, and the man there helped them change the tire, so we got to Condon about the same time they did.

Old Henry Thall, the ranger, advised us not to go as the weather was very bad so we camped that night at a small meadow near the trailhead. As we got ready to leave the next morning, my brother-in-law got bucked off, Rex, a horse that belonged to my brother Floyd. He was a fine horse, but didn't mind bucking someone off now and then. The cinch broke and Herman had a soft landing, saddle and all, in a brush pile.

Near the top of Swan Divide the trail cuts through a big rock cliff on a narrow bench and there is just enough room for the horses to walk on it single file. The edge of the trail drops straight off several hundred feet below. Before we reached this spot, the snow and water had run off of the rocks from above, onto the trail, where it froze again, making it very slick for the horses. Of course we all got off and walked across this part of the trail, but as we were coming along the ledge one of the horses slipped and fell. It appeared as though the horse's feet were over the edge, but it managed to get back up without going over.

The incident scared Adelle's horse and it knocked her down and ran over her, stepping on her hand and rolling her right near the edge. My sister was not brave of heights, and seeing all this happen in front of her didn't help with her, either.

We got the horses across this ledge and around the point of the cliffs. It was still snowing hard and we waited for my sister to come for what seemed like a long time. We were just going back to look for her when all at once she came around the bend of the cliff, screaming bloody murder, a gray blanket she had been riding with, squaw fashion, pulled over her head. It looked like a scene from the movie "Lost Horizon", where the young lady crossed over the mountain and turned into an old woman!

We went down the Little Salmon to about the seven-mile sign, where we made our camp. My sister, Bernida, didn't hunt, but she did a big share of the cooking, and also, I think a big share of thinking about having to go back over that high pass.

Adelle and I shot and killed two large bull elk near the top of a high ridge. The following day the girls made sandwiches for our lunch and all four of us went to pack them down to camp. After cutting on that meat, my hands were all covered with blood and when it was time for lunch my sister asked if I was going to wash my hands. I said no, because it was two miles down the canyon to water. So, she went down the mountain a ways to where she couldn't see me eating my sandwich with bloody hands.

Before we could get off the ridge, night fell quickly and it got so dark we couldn't see a thing. One side of this ridge had a sheer cliff that ran a couple of miles long and we were all walking and leading our horses; it was so dark that I got off course a ways, and the horses that I was leading finally stopped and refused to go any further.

As I tugged on the lead rope, a young horse that we had left tied to a tree that morning so it wouldn't follow us nickered quite a distance to our left. I turned to go where I had heard him, and my horses came right along. The young horse kept nickering and we finally found him and got down to the main trail. I started to feel all the horses to see if our packs were still riding well, and found that we were one horse short.

We managed to get to camp in the dark, and early the next morning Herman and I headed back up to find the missing horse, which had half of an elk on it. We found the horse, but she seemed to be afraid and wouldn't let us catch her. We finally got her wedged with the pack between two trees and caught her, and then unloaded her as she must have been tired from carrying that pack all night. We called this horse Babe. She was young at the time and a very good animal and she eventually became the great, great, great grandmother of a lot of our horses.

While coming down the mountain the night before, Herman had lost his good wool jacket off of his saddle horse. After finding Babe, we both went back up to look for it by following our horse tracks along the way we had come down during the night. It scared us when we came to where my tracks were on the very edge of the cliff; if I had taken one more step that night, I would have fallen four or five hundred feet down. Thank goodness my horse refused to come any further! We found Herman's jacket along the edge of the cliff, and realized that we had been following along that edge for some time without knowing it.

That afternoon Herman shot and killed a young bull elk.

I took Adelle goat hunting up Chasm creek the following day and we spotted a big goat up in some cliffs. A good goat trail that went along a narrow ledge was the only route for the goat to go from one area to another, so I parked Adelle on this narrow ledge while I left to go way around the goat and chase it to her so that she could have a close shot.

I went all the way around and above the goat, and it took off for the ledge and when Adelle saw it coming she decided that there was not enough room on that ledge for her and that big billy goat both, so she climbed up a little indentation in the cliff. She melted herself into the rock and let the big billy go by without even attempting to shoot it! I did get a smaller one though.

When we came back out, the weather was quite nice and we had no problems, so when we got back to our car we spent the night there. We had three elk and a goat, plus camp gear to load onto the car. When we got that car loaded it was squatting down like a mother hen getting ready to lay an egg. I think Herman was afraid to get into it, so he and Bernida offered to bring the horses back over the Mission Mountains.

I was also afraid to get into the car, we didn't even have a spare tire. The Lord had to have been with us, because we made it home without any problems and Herman and Bernida brought the horses into our place in record time, getting home not too many hours behind us.

But our work was not done yet. We had no electricity or refrigeration, so early the next day we took the meat up to the Mollman place where Bernida and Herman were living. We started to cut and cook and can all that meat. We fried meat in three or four big frying pans and then put it into jars, and we roasted some, and also put a lot of it into jars raw. Then all of the jars were boiled in boilers of hot water in order for it to keep through the winter.

One time Adelle and I were going up a steep mountain trail with four other men, leading enough horses to pack out a couple of elk. On a steep section, Mr. Trosper, my friend's dad, told Adelle to take a good hold of the tail on the horse in front of her as it would help her up the mountain. So she proceeded to get a good hold and was going right along when all at once that horse let out a blast of hot air right into her face! I don't know why, but nobody could persuade her to take a new hold on that horses tail. She was so embarrassed that she stayed her distance from that horse!

Making Trails

In the early days I had to go over Crow Creek Pass to get to the Swan or the Bob Marshall, which made quite a distance. In about 1937 or 1938 I decided to make myself a trail from Mollman Pass and down the head of Elk Creek where the Indians already had a trail a short way down.

I couldn't afford to hire anyone to help me, so I went over there all alone with a crosscut saw and an axe. I cut the trail down the south side of North Elk Creek to below the big cliffs, and then crossed back onto the north side all the way to the government trail. After using this trail for a few years it got real muddy in several places as there were lots of little streams to cross, so I decided to make a new trail up on the ridge, which is still used. When cutting this trail, two of my neighbors, Ed Sias and Leo David, came and helped me for a couple of days. They were good woodsmen and I really appreciated their help, and both guided for me in later years.

Our two older kids, Buddy and Viola, were with me on this trail for a couple of days. They were still quite small then, but were able to throw rocks and brush out of the way.

When I started taking my horses over the first trail that I built, I would pack all of my camp gear from home on my horses all the way to the Bob Marshall.

I didn't even own a truck, nor were our camps as elaborate as they are today. One fall my oldest son, Buddy, helped me take our horses over to Holland Lake. It snowed hard all the way over the Missions. Buddy was only about six years old, and when we got to where we were going to camp that night I remember telling him to get off his horse. He just fell off, because he was too cold to manipulate his body.

I think it was the following year that, when I got ready to take my horses over, I had a good number of them to take but I also had a lot of volunteers to ride with me. My mother, my youngest brother, Adelle's two younger brothers, and Viola and Buddy all came along, and there may have been another one or two people. It sure did help to have all those riders.

I had borrowed a little horse from my friend Thurman, as we used each other's horses real often, and somehow this little horse slipped off the trail and slid down the mountain back first. He stopped just at the edge of a little cliff about twenty feet high. He was ready to go over, so I tied his four feet to a tree with my lariat, but we couldn't get him back up the hill. I took a bunch of ropes off of my empty pack saddles and tied several together. Making sure the horse's legs were tied together well, so he couldn't struggle too much, I wrapped a couple of ropes around a solid tree and edged him over the cliff, down to the bottom.

Once there, I untied him and he got to his feet and I had to take him some distance to get around the edge of the cliff and back up to the trail; I sure didn't want to lose my friend's horse.

My mother had been in the mountains quite a lot, but she couldn't believe that we would be able to save that horse's life. The horse made it fine, but by the time that bunch of kids got to Holland Lake, there was a lot of blisters and moaning and groaning!

Camp At Bartlett Creek

I started to camp near the mouth of Bartlett Creek in the South Fork area in 1937 and set up the camp on the south side of the creek, as this was a nice, cool place to keep our meat. I also would often put a spike camp up the head of Bartlett Canyon near Cluster Creek.

At that time our camps were pretty simple, but we had good tents, with a stove in each tent. For the first few years we cooked on what they called the Kimmel Stove, which had an oven on the back and also one above the regular part of the stove. The Forest Service was using the same type of stove at the time. Most of the hunters we took in those days were self-sufficient, and furnished their own food. We all pitched in with the cooking and there were always some who were willing to help with the wood and sometimes some would try to help with the horses. Most of the hunters hunted in pairs, but a few preferred to hunt alone. I often took a group to the top of a mountain, and then they hunted back down with a couple of men on each ridge. We didn't use saddle horses much for hunting, unless we were going across the river.

When I first started to hunt here, I hunted from Scarface Peak to Bullet Nose Peak, and any place on the east side of the river. George Moore was up near Gordon Creek, so there was plenty of room to hunt. Babe Wilhelm was up near Shaw Creek, and Russell and Roy Fox were on Big Salmon Creek and Murphy's camp was at Murphy's Flats near the White River.

Soon, Ed Crawford started coming in and camping on a little flat across the creek from me.

Sometime later, two men came into my camp with pots and pans rattling on the outside of their packs. They wanted to know how I put on my packs, so I spent most of the afternoon showing them how to make up my packs, and how to tie the knots. The following year, they came with a bunch of hunters and camped just a mile down river from me — so here I was, sitting between two other hunting camps. It got to be discouraging, as the horses were getting mixed up, and the hunters kept running into each other.

When we first decided to start taking hunters, Mr. Erkhart was the Forest Supervisor at Kalispell and he gave us a lot of encouragement to go ahead with our plans, and he thought Bartlett Creek would be a good spot for us, although there were no regulations on where a person could camp, so others could come there too. On several occasions when hunting was slow, I took a group into Holbrook Creek. The rangers didn't bother any of the packers — in fact, they were all real cooperative. Henry Thall was ranger at Big Prairie when I first started camp at Bartlett.

The main reason I left the Little Salmon was that later in the fall it started to snow for real at times, and we couldn't get out through the trail, as the snow would slide and pile up. We would have to go by Big Salmon, and in the early days there was no trail in Holland Canyon. The trail then was high on the south side and went along just below the rocks on the high peak.

The Bartlett Bear

For several years the same group of hunters came with us on the first hunt of the season and we always went in a day early to set up camp. A hunter named Milo Jensen was a good friend and ambitious as could be. One morning, all of the guys went fishing, except Milo and me — we were busy.

Milo was working in one tent, and I was building a good log and dirt footing for the cook stove to set on in another. I was on my knees when I heard Milo in the doorway, and I turned to say something to him, but there, almost in my face, was a big, beautiful brown bear with a white diamond on his chest. It sort of startled me, and without saying anything, I ran him out with my axe. He walked right over to the other tent and stood outside the doorway.

The door flaps were down, so I called to Milo that he had a visitor. He pulled the tent flaps open and there stood that big bear! We would run him off a ways, but he would turn and come right back.

A little while later the game warden and another man came riding into camp. Now this warden was kind of an obnoxious, know-it-all type of fellow, and when we told him we couldn't get rid of the bear that was then sitting on his fanny on the side of the hill about fifty yards away, he said he would get rid of it for us. He took out his

Son Buck and a trophy mountain goat.

pistol and emptied his gun by shooting over, under and alongside of that bear, until it finally got up and ambled slowly up the hill.

Sometime later, Frank Mager, one of our fishermen, came back into camp with a big mess of fish. The bear was nowhere in sight, but we told Frank about him and he sort of chuckled, and said that he'd heard a lot of bear stories lately. Then Frank took his fish downstream from the tent a little ways, laid them out and squatted down to start cleaning them. Milo and I were watching, and soon we saw the bear coming down the hill and it headed straight for Frank and the smell of fish meal. It came up right behind him.

Frank thought he heard one of us behind him, and when he turned to look, he looked straight into that bear's big face! With a blood curdling scream, Frank jumped right out into the middle of the stream, spilling part of his fish into the water. That big old bear started grabbing and eating the fish. Frank was still screaming, so Milo and I each grabbed a club and ran the bear off and rescued the fish.

It took poor Frank quite awhile to get calmed down; between the scare and the cold water, he shook for some time. When the rest of the guys came in with their fish, some of them had to keep fighting the bear away constantly — and later that evening we used up almost all of our firewood throwing it at the bear to run him off. He kept getting a little more aggressive all the time and all the farther we could run him away from camp was a big tree at the corner of our tent.

I finally decided that we just couldn't fight him all night, so I saddled a horse and started for the ranger station, which was two and a half miles away, to tell the warden that we were going to have to do something with that bear. I got about two-thirds of the way when I heard, "Bang, bang!" I was quite sure what had happened, and I went on to the station to tell the rangers what was going on, and what I thought might have happened after I left camp — that the marauding bear had been shot a few hours before the official bear season was to open.

The warden said he would be over to our camp first thing in the morning and, as it turned out, the guys had shot the bear inside the tent while I was on my way to the station.

The next morning the warden showed up and made us dig a big hole and bury that nice, fat bear with a beautiful pelt that would have made a prize trophy. Sometimes it doesn't seem worthwhile to be honest and follow the law; I think we all felt like we should have shot the bear and not reported it. The warden knew the problem we were having with the bear, and he could have let one of the hunters take it out, as the season had opened at midnight. But, instead, he forced us to bury it and the bear was wasted.

Grizzly At The Clay Lick

Early one evening when we were at our Holbrook camp, I took one of my hunters horseback to a meadow with a clay lick in it, to watch for elk. We got off of our horses and tied them up about a quarter of a mile from the meadow.

There was about four inches of fresh snow on the ground. We walked to the far side of the beautiful little meadow and sat down on a log just inside the edge of the timber, where we were well out of sight of any game that might come into the meadow to feed. We had been sitting quite comfortably for about fifteen minutes when I saw a movement across the meadow, near the spot where we had come from a short time before.

"It is a grizzly bear," I said. The bear was coming along with his nose down in our tracks in the snow. He was a big, beautiful gray-colored bear.

While coming to the clay lick, we had made a couple little circles before we came across the meadow. We watched as the bear made the same circles that we had, all the time sniffing our tracks with his nose. At this point I thought he would leave our tracks and go on his way, but no, here he came, right across the meadow, directly toward us.

I didn't have a gun, and I didn't know what kind of shot my hunter was, and I knew he didn't have a grizzly tag. When the bear got halfway across the meadow, I told my hunter, "We better let him know we are here. Let's walk out to meet him." My hunter kept saying, "I can kill him, I can kill him." I said, "No, we can't shoot him."

Then I started talking to the bear, telling him to go on and get out of there. The grizzly looked at me and turned his big head one way and then the other way while I was telling him to leave. Then, when he was about fifteen yards from us, he stopped, cocked one of his hind legs up, and urinated in the grass. He came a few feet closer, my hunter saying repeatedly, "I can kill him!" I said, "Don't shoot unless he wants to fight."

The bear looked both of us over good, and then turned slowly and took a few steps away from us. Finally, he turned, and looked at us again, and again, and again, and then he slowly ambled away.

When we got back to our horses they were on the nervous side, looking toward where the big bear had gone. His big tracks in the snow showed that he had come

Mick leads a packstring on an easy stretch of trail at the head of Holbrook Canyon.

within eight steps of our horses, circled completely around them, and then followed our tracks to where we were sitting. What a sight! What an experience! And no camera! My hunter said that this was the biggest thrill of his life, much more so than killing all the elk in the woods. I have seen many grizzly, but it was also a thrill for me.

A lot of people would have shot this bear, and called it self defense — and I might have been more concerned if the grizzly had been bristled up, but he didn't appear to be a mean bear to me.

A Blizzard In The Missions; I Almost Gave Up

I don't remember for sure, but I think it was about 1939, after I had brought my last hunters out of the Bob Marshall, when I almost gave up my life. I went back in by myself to pick up my camp and bring it out, and to do this, I had to take my horses across the Mission Mountains.

I left Swan Valley with about twenty or more horses, knowing that the snow was going to be deep. All of the stock were saddled, and I was leading most of them, although I left a few loose to follow behind. I put three of my best horses on the tail end of the pack string, so that they would be fresh when we crossed the last part of the mountain. And, when I got about a half a mile or so from the top, I moved my three best horses to the front of the string to break trail.

Early each fall I would stand poles up at the end of each switchback, so that if the snow got deep I would still be able to tell where the trail was. On this particular day it was snowing and blowing fiercely and I was wearing a long raincoat over my clothes, and a wool scarf around my neck to keep the snow from blowing inside my clothing.

I decided that I would try to take just one horse up to the top first, so I started up leading a good, big, strong horse called Chip, who belonged to my brother Floyd. The snow was sort of packed from the wind, so part of the time I didn't sink to the bottom, but the poor horse did. In many places the snow was so deep that he had to jump and lunge, until he finally just lay in the snow.

I would coax him and he would lunge again and by the time I got Chip to the top, I was already very tired. I left Chip and started back down the trail; our tracks were already filled in with snow and only once in a while I could see evidence of where we'd come up the hill.

I got down to my horses and started up again, this time with two horses, and had to do the same thing over again, coaxing them along. Before I got those two horses to the top, I was so tired that I was starting to think of giving up. I finally got them to the top, with the snow still blowing in hard gusts and I sat down in the snow for a few moments and thought about laying down and letting the snow cover me up.

Then a powerful thought hit me: I couldn't let all these horses die up here in the snow. I managed to get back onto my feet and tied the halter ropes up on the two horses, so that if they wanted to go on they could.

Fighting exhaustion, I started back down again, and once again our tracks were almost covered up. I succeeded in getting back down to the rest of the horses, and this time I took three or four and started up again. I kept calling the rest of the horses, hoping they would follow, and a few of them came a ways until they hit a spot with a deep drift where they would have had to lunge to get through. Here they stopped.

I felt like crying, but realized there was no use in doing that! Several times, as I was leading the horses where they had to lunge in the snow, they almost jumped on top of me because I was too tired to get out of the way. I was getting to the point where I sort of wished they would trample me down, but again I made it to the top and turned the horses loose. I rested a few minutes, thinking I would leave the rest of the horses down there, but even as I thought about leaving them, I knew I just couldn't do that.

So, I got onto my feet and started back down for some more horses. Before I got to them, I just had to stop and rest, and I sort of laid down, and I very nearly didn't get back up — I felt so peaceful lying there. I wanted so badly to let the snow cover me up, but once again I thought of all the horses, and then of my family, and having to leave them to wonder what had happened to me.

At the time I had not been attending any church, and it didn't occur to me to ask God for help, but sometimes when I think back, I wonder if He was trying to tell me something. Thinking of leaving my family spurred me to get on my feet again and down to the horses.

The first horse in the trail was a long-legged black mare that I called Midnight, who I had been riding earlier in the day. By this time, even though it was snowing, the snow was a lot looser in the trail, so it was not as hard for the horses to get through, and I led Midnight and a few more horses that I had tied together through the deepest drifts, all the time calling to the loose horses to follow. This time all of them came as far as that bad drift before they stopped.

Again, I wanted to cry, but instead I went on and had not gone very far when I decided to ride as far as the next drift. Midnight was a tall horse, so I led her to some large rocks and I was in the process of trying to get on her, but because of exhaustion I was having trouble climbing onto the rock, when one of the horses nickered, and Midnight answered it. By the time I managed to get onto Midnight, the rest of the loose horses were coming. What a relief it was to hear! It was so dark that I was unable to tell if all the horses were there, but I was hoping they were.

I rode Midnight through three or four of the deep snow drifts where she had to lunge through before I got to the real bad drift. Then I had to get off and lead her to where I had left the rest of my horses. When we got there, all of the horses I had turned loose were gone.

I untied Chip, did up his halter and turned him loose, too, and he took off up the trail, following where the others had gone. I managed to get back on Midnight and started up the trail behind Chip. I had gone less than a quarter of a mile when I caught up with the horses that had taken off ahead of me. They were stopped in the trail between two of the Mollman Lakes, where the stream flows through the rocks to the lower lake. The stream bed was full of drifted snow, and the horses were afraid to cross.

I tried to force them through it, but they wouldn't go so I got back off my horse, and started to tramp snow to pack it down enough to get the horses through it. I sure needed a shovel right then, but I tramped snow until I started to play out again.

A horse I called Nig was close to where I was tramping, so I tried to lead him across, but he refused. Again, I started to get a sick feeling in my stomach that I was not going to get them across. I decided that my only chance was to try to bring Chip, who was back a ways on the trail, across. I brought him up, but he, too, refused to cross the streambed. I tried a couple of more times to get Chip moving, and all at once he acted like he might try it — and then he decided to cross. The snow I had trampled didn't hold him up, and I thought for awhile that he was going to be stuck, but he kept lunging until he got out the other side.

Then Nig, who'd seen his mate make it through, was willing to try, with a little coaxing on my part. Then, one at a time, the loose ones went through on their own. I tied Chip's and Nig's halter ropes up and let them go, and they took off up the trail. I coaxed my saddle horse and the few others I was leading across the streambed, and with some difficulty climbed back on my horse by mounting from the wrong side.

By now the snow was letting up, and the wind had calmed down a little, and enough moonlight was filtering through the clouds so that I could see quite well. I had reached the summit of the divide, and although there were a few more drifts to work through, none were as bad as those we had already labored to cross. All of my horses were now working just like soldiers, with those in front of me keeping a steady gait as they broke trail — and even in all the deep snow, they always knew exactly where the trail was.

By now the horses were hungry, and both they and I were quite sure that we would make it home, which we did, sometime in the middle of the night.

When I got there, I told myself and my family that this was my last year to do packing — that I was never going again. But when fall came again, I was back on the trail!

There were two other trips after this experience on which I got into extremely bad weather coming over the mountains. Once I was with my brother, Jim, and another time my two older sons, Buddy and Buck, were with me. We started up the east side of the Missions and had climbed half way up when the snow got too deep, so we turned back and went around by Seeley Lake and Jocko Pass. That makes for an eighty-mile trip, but that is always a lot better than fighting the deep snow.

Big Black Bear At Holland Lake

In about 1941, I set up my base camp, which is where I picked up my hunters, near the Forest Service cabin at the lower end of Holland Lake. I had a large tent there to provide a place to sleep and keep our extra supplies.

On the day that I was to bring out a group of hunters, Adelle would come from home to the base camp with a new supply of groceries that we would use on the next hunt. On one occasion when she got to our camp with the supplies, she noticed a big hole torn in the back end of our tent, where I had about a half a ton of rolled grain for my stock stored.

A huge black bear had come in and made a mess of everything. He had dragged every sack of my horse feed out into the woods, and torn the sacks on logs and roots until every sack was empty. What a mess to have to clean up!

When Adelle saw this mess, she was afraid to stay in the tent, so she sat in the truck until we came in just as it was starting to get dark. And, after riding out of the mountains for thirty miles, everyone, including me, was dead tired.

The hunters all decided to stay overnight and since it was a beautiful evening they just rolled their sleeping bags out under the trees and went to bed. The meat of the kills was put up into the truck and covered and Adelle and I finally got to bed, on the ground, inside the tent. I was so tired that I went right to sleep, but within a few minutes Adelle woke me up. That old bear was sniffing at our heads through the canvas tent; he was only six or eight inches from us.

But I was so tired I told her to go to sleep, that the bear would soon leave, but I would just start to go back to sleep when she would get after me again to get up. After several occurrences of this, I finally decided if I was to get any sleep, I might just as well get up and get rid of the bear — so I got up, slipped into my pants, and picked up my rifle. Bare-footed, I went out of the tent with my flash light and shined it around; a big bear standing right over one of my hunter's head, Stanley Scearce Jr., and it looked as if that bear was licking his face.

The bear finally walked away from Stanley and when he got a little distance from him, I shot it. The bear went down, but was not quite dead.

All the hunters came back to life. Stanley burst out of his sleeping bag, crawling on his hands and knees in his long underwear, so excited that he was crawling right towards the bear, and the bear was crawling towards him.

I hollered at him, "Bear! Go the other way!" and Stanley turned and started crawling the other way without even trying to get onto his feet. Then the bear fell over dead and the adventure was over, except for the mess we had to clean up the next morning.

Floyd Rolling Pack String and Grizzly After Him on Cardinal

One fall, about 1945, for some reason I was unable to take my last few hunters into the hunting camp, so my brother Floyd took them for me. After they got into camp, it started to snow and it just didn't let up — and by the time they came out, the snow was very deep. As they brought the hunters over the Holbrook Divide and started down a very steep sidehill, one of the packhorses stepped off the trail and pulled about four more packhorses over with it.

Down they went, head over heels, into a deep ravine. While Floyd and someone else were getting this bunch of horses out of this mess and back up on the trail, a fellow hunter by the name of Frank Mager, who had hunted with us for many years, offered to take the rest of the pack string on down to lower and flatter ground to wait. But he went around another bend in the trail where something happened, and he lost every horse in the pack string. They all went down a very steep sidehill like lightning, with the snow boiling up all over, and slid for about a hundred and fifty yards, all one on top of each other in a pile right in the bottom of the creek. All of these pack animals on top of each other made a perfect dam in the narrow stream and the water started to back up, and began to rise steadily.

One of our hunters, a big, strong, ambitious fellow by the name of Milo Jensen, went down with Floyd into this deep, steep canyon to try to save these animals, and Milo went out in the water and held two horses' heads at one time out of the water to keep them from drowning.

Meanwhile, Floyd took the packs off of the animals and got them up and onto their feet. When they got up, they were stepping on the ones underneath them, sometimes stepping right on each other's bellies and legs. It was a terrible mess, and it took them a long time before, finally, Floyd and Milo got them all back on their feet.

There was not one broken leg among the horses, but they did have a lot of cuts and bruises. Old Babe, one of our best old mares, had her tail broken next to the rump bone, so her tail was useless the rest of her life. And a lot of the gear was damaged, with several of the saddles being badly torn up.

The sidehill at the crash site was so steep that the stock had to be taken, without the packs on them, a long way up this canyon to get them out to the trail. Then all of the packs had to be carried and pulled up the steep mountainside, back up to the trail where they could load them once again.

It was getting dark by the time they got the last pack up to the trail, even though the wrecks had occurred early in the forenoon. From here, they traveled down the trail about three-fourths of a mile to a spot that was quite flat and kicked out a patch of snow so they could camp for the night. The fellows who had helped with getting the stock and packs out were wet and all played out, so they built themselves a big fire and managed to get their clothes partially dry.

That night in that hastily-set-up camp, Floyd, who was just four years younger than I, said that this was his last year to do this sort of thing, and I don't think he ever went back in there.

Floyd was a top hand and he had his share of great experiences in the mountains. He was once charged by a big grizzly bear that was trying to claim an elk that one of his hunters had shot the day before. Floyd was alone and as he and his two packhorses got to the elk, the grizzly charged from behind. The spooked horses knocked Floyd down and ran over him, but he managed to get up and was able to kill the bear. Then, one fall Floyd and another younger brother, Jim, were pulling out one of my camps and had a very hard time coming over the Missions in very deep snow, taking several days to accomplish what normally was a one-day trip.

One Of My Hunters Took A Shot At Me

One year I was a little short on saddlehorses for the number of hunters that I had coming for this hunting season and a friend of mine had a fair saddle horse for sale, so I thought about buying it. But I didn't like the horse's color, a buckskin.

There is nothing wrong with a buckskin, as they are usually good, tough horses, but that color is too much like an old bull elk. I took the horse, and we used him along the main trails going in and out of the hunting camp, but we didn't use him while we were hunting, as I was always afraid some other hunter might take a shot at him.

During our last hunt of the season, though, I saddled and rode old Buck, since there were no hunters besides ours left in this wilderness. All of our hunters, plus the guides, went up to hunt out a certain area and when we got to the area to be hunted, the other guides and their hunters got off of their horses and tied them up; they all went on foot from there.

Two of the hunters and I were going to ride another half mile further up the trail and we hadn't ridden very far when it felt like someone had blown on the back of my neck. Then I heard the rifle shot. I'd almost been shot!

I hollered at my hunters to duck, "I think someone is shooting at us."

The hunter who took that shot at me had said before we left camp that he didn't want an elk unless it was a big bull, and I must have looked like a big bull to him. He was about to take another shot when my son, Mick, who was further up the mountain above this hunter, hollered at him not to shoot.

The hunter felt very bad when he found out that he had shot at me. He went back to camp and put his gun away, saying he was done hunting, and when we finished for the season I got rid of the buckskin horse.

Moving Camp

I believe that 1946 was the year I decided to move my camp on Bartlett Creek. With hunting camps located on both sides of mine, I felt that there was too much pressure on both hunters and game.

I talked to Holinger, who was the ranger at Big Prairie at the time, about the impact of crowding in my hunting area and he suggested that, if I would like to, I might move my camp down to Holbrook Creek, as Murphy's group only made one hunt a year down there, and some years they didn't come in at all.

Or, he suggested, I might move to Burnt Creek. I had hunted both places, but had camped on Holbrook quite a lot, so I decided I would relocate my camp there.

In the earlier years, any packer could go any place they wanted, so when, or if,

Hunters and crew at the camp on Upper Holbrook in 1957.

the hunting got a little slow, I would just move my camp to another area. One time when I had moved my camp to Upper Holbrook, I left a few things at my Bartlett Camp and later, on my way back to pick up what I had left, I saw a large grizzly digging around as I crossed the air strip.

It was quite late when I reached the old camp so I turned my horses out to graze on the opposite side of the creek from the air strip where the bear had been. I didn't have a sleeping bag with me, so I laid out my saddle pads and put my pack saddles on each side of my bed-to-be. I kept all of my clothes on, even my jacket, and rolled up in one of my pack mantis, and covered over with another one. I had a little food wrapped inside of my rain coat and tied on the back of my riding saddle, which I had laid right at my head.

When I woke up in the morning, my saddle had been moved a couple of feet away from my head. That bear, or some other bear, had taken what food I had out of my raincoat and eaten it right there. And by the time I got packed up and back to camp, I was every bit as hungry as that bear must have been during the night.

Bears Have A Feed

After we moved onto our new ranch, we started to hunt in both the Bob Marshall and the Mission Mountains. Usually, we hunted the Missions first and moved our camp into the Bob later in the season. There used to be a lot of good trophies in the Missions before the roads were put in.

At the start of hunting season in 1964 we had our camp all set up in the Missions.

This particular year we had made up all of the grocery order at the ranch, about $800 worth, which was quite a bit at the time, and sent our two sons, Buck and Mick, in with the packstring, leaving from the ranch to go over the top of the range and to our campsite. When they reached camp, they left all of the groceries, which were done up in the packs, in the cook tent. The next day, they brought the packstring down to our corrals on Glacier Creek, leaving the upper camp unattended for the night.

Adelle and I were bringing the hunters, coming from the Swan side by car and after we arrived, we packed all the hunter's gear, saddled their horses for them, and headed up Crazy Horse Canyon to our main camp. When we got close to camp, Adelle, who was riding ahead of me, said, "Where is the cook tent?"

The cook tent, always her main interest, was flat on the ground, torn to ribbons. What a sad-looking mess!

In addition, one of the hunter's tents was nearly down, and big grizzly tracks showed where a bear had gone up the side and caved it in. All the packs were torn apart and scattered all over the place. The pack boxes were all smashed up, and every last can of food was smashed and opened — in fact, several of the cans looked like some kind of professional had taken the tops off with a can opener.

Practically everything was ruined. The bears had even bit holes in the Joy soap, just to let us people know that we had encroached on their territory! The bears ripped up the tents, and tore most of the sleeping bags in the sleeping tents, and punctured every one of the twelve air mattresses. Actually, the boys had left the two air mattresses they had slept on full of air and it looked like the bears had played ball with them; they were completely torn to shreds, we surmised that it had probably been fun to hear the air going out of them.

We had to send out right away for a new supply of food and another tent, and we were lucky to have all good natured hunters with us on that first hunt of the season. They pitched right in to help clean up the mess and we put the tents back up the best we could. I had a good supply of nails, so we pinned the cook tent back together, as well as we were able, and covered it with a plastic fly. After we had all gone to bed that night, we could hear those grizzlies mumbling and grumbling in the darkness — and I think they were put out because we had spoiled their fun.

The season for bears opened the next morning, but wouldn't you know it, there wasn't a bear in sight. All the hunters, except one, killed their mountain goats the first forenoon of the season, so I spent the afternoon packing out their goats. One of the hunters, Dr. Skinner, hadn't gotten a goat yet, so Bill, another hunter, stayed with Skinner on top of the mountain until he did get one that afternoon.

We had heard them shoot, but it was getting late in the evening and they still hadn't come back to camp, so I got my saddlehorse and went looking for them. I had just started out when three fast shots went off straight ahead of me, about a quarter of a mile away, and when I met them, Skinner, who had wanted a grizzly quite badly, was sort of put out with Bill.

Bill had been walking in front as they came out into a meadow and met up with five grizzlies. Bill got so excited that he hollered, "Grizzly! Grizzly! Grizzly!" and fired three shots right up in the air, so the bears all ran away before Doc could get a shot.

Our camp was completely torn up by the grizzlies.

After Grizzly

Our next group of hunters were having fair luck with goat and elk, and one morning when we had nice tracking snow, so three of the fellows decided they wanted to go for grizzly. I took them toward the head of the canyon, and when we had gotten about two-thirds of the way up we came onto a very big grizzly track.

I sent two of the men up to the pass on their horses, telling them to tie the horses up and for each to get into a position where they would be sure to see anything that came through. They were to stay there until the other fellow and I also got to the pass. But, when the two men reached the top of the pass, they found a big, wide trail of very fresh bear tracks, and they were afraid to tie their horses up or leave each other.

Meanwhile, the other hunter and I started to track this big bear which might cross to where the other two guys were if we failed to get it. After tracking the bear a ways, I was wishing that I had taken one of the other men with me instead of the big, young fellow who had come with me, as he had a loud voice and I couldn't keep him quiet.

I did my best to explain to him how it was important to keep quiet, but he kept on talking all the time. Then we found where the bear had been laying, until we'd scared it out of its bed, and we could see by his tracks that he would go a ways and then turn around and sit in the snow to wait for us. When we got close, he would go on again.

The bear finally crossed the divide, but quite a distance from where the other men were stationed, and I finally gave up on the bear and this talkative fellow, and we went to join the other men. When we got there, I could tell by looking at the tracks there were several bear in the immediate vicinity, but I couldn't be sure how many there were. We followed the grizzlies on horseback for a ways, and then I thought I might know where they were headed, so we tried to ride ahead of them, with the notion of then letting them come to us.

When we got to the spot where I wanted to be, we tied the horses on the back side of the ridge, and I had the fellows come with me. I posted them each a little way apart, in positions which were perfect to shoot from and where we could peek over to watch the other side.

I put the noisy fellow up the ridge a short distance, so he wouldn't be talking to anyone, and I also warned the guys to let the bears come out into the open so they'd have good shooting. We were there less than five minutes when I could see seven of them. I whispered to Dr. Carmon, who I had placed right beside me, to get ready for them to come out into the open. Just then, the loud-mouthed fellow jumped up, yelling, "Elk! Elk!"

There were no elk, of course, and like lightning, the bears disappeared back into the timber, and no one got a shot, even though it was a perfect place for all of them to get a grizzly.

I thought that those bears just might go right back to where they had come from, so I quickly got the guys back onto their horses and we rode to where there were two long slide areas which the bears had crossed earlier in the day. We tied the horses back where they wouldn't be seen, and then I started to place two fellows on the edge of the big slide where they would be able to see all the way down the canyon. I wanted to put one man, alone, in a spot I thought would be good, but he hemmed and hawed, and finally said he would rather be up on the hillside where there was a good-sized tree with a lot of limbs on it, and a lot of brush around it. I told him it would be quite a long shot if the bears crossed in the same place they had before, but he said he wanted to shoot a long ways, and he wanted to be where the bears wouldn't see him, so I left him there.

I took Dr. Carmon to another spot where I thought I would like to be if I were the hunter. I had planned to take the other man with me and get behind the bears, chasing them to the guys I'd positioned, but when I started to leave Dr. Carmon protested. "You're going to leave him with me, aren't you?" he said. I had planned to take the other hunter with me, but Dr. Carmon replied that he didn't want to stay there by himself, so there was nothing else to do but leave both of them there.

I hurried back around to where we had seen the bear before, and realized that I had only three shells in my pocket for my old 30-30 rifle. I put one of the shells into the gun, which I only used as a single-shot, and started down through the timber where I thought the bears had gone. I had only gone three or four hundred yards when I came to a fairly level area with lots of good-sized spruce trees, which were sort of spaced out, park-like. The bears had dug themselves a nice nest in the thick needles under the trees, and bedded down.

They were all down in this bed like a bunch of pigs on top of each other, and they saw me about the same time I saw them. They jumped up, one at a time, and ran off over a nearby bank. They were all adults and the last one to get up was huge, but instead of running away with rest, it stood up on its hind feet and started to bellow, walking toward me. I sure didn't want to shoot it, but it got down on all four legs, came a little closer, and then stood up again.

I was afraid to run, and it was only about thirty yards from me by this time. I felt the grizzly wasn't going to leave, as it increased the volume of its bellow, so I thought I had better shoot it while I had a good chance — but the bear had moved so that half its body was hidden behind a big tree, and I wanted to hit it center in the chest. I had to hold the sight close to the tree and make sure the bullet didn't touch the tree. I shot the bear and it let out a loud bellow and rolled over onto its back.

I reloaded my gun as fast as I could, keeping the third and last shell in my hand. I backed up a little, because I thought that some of the other bears might come back after hearing the big one bellow. All of a sudden, the bear jumped up and also ran over the edge of the bank.

I checked where it had fallen and there was a lot of blood, so I started to follow the tracks. Then the other fellows started shooting, and there were bears bellowing again.

The bears were going toward the men, as we had figured they would, but as soon as they appeared at the edge of the slide the guys began shooting, even though they were still a long way off. The bears then turned and went farther down the canyon, without getting hit.

I met the other fellows and we trailed the bears. Dr. Carmon was sure the bear I had hit wasn't going to get very far, because it was losing so much blood, and he was right. We found the bear in a short distance, and then trailed the rest of them back over the saddle where they had crossed that morning to make sure that none of them were hit, and they went down into the lower elevation.

A Description of Our Camp

For several years after our boys were old enough to help, and able to do the packing, Adelle and I would go into hunting camp with the plan of staying in for the full season. Each fall, when we set up our camp, we would take along all of our grocery order, except the fresh meats, bread and fresh vegetables. These would be brought in with each new group of hunters. Most of the food was bought in case lots.

Each group of hunters were in the hunting camp for eight days, including the day in and the day out, leaving them six days of hunting. After the boys took a bunch of hunters out, they would lay over for a day and then bring in another group. That gave Adelle and me three days, between groups, to ourselves in camp.

It seemed that even between each group of hunters, we didn't have much leisure time. We had wood to cut and haul in, gas lanterns and saddles to repair, horses to shoe, and there was always trail work to be done. We also cleaned up the hunters' tents, washed up their pots and tables, and I split and piled all of the wood needed for the next eight days.

We always had two tents for our hunters. One was fourteen by twenty feet, and the other was fourteen by sixteen feet. When we had couples in for a hunt, we gave them a smaller tent of their own. We always had a guides' tent, a tent for grain and hay, and a large cook tent. We usually had one more tent set up when the boy's wives came in, and we also had a big tepee set up.

The cook tent had a sixteen-foot fly at the entrance where we kept our food supply

A wilderness camp in the Mission Mountains.

and tools. Each tent had a bunk made of logs on the ground, just high enough to sit on to dress, which ran the full width of the tent. The bunk was filled with straw or hay, and covered with a tarp, so that the beds could be rolled out onto it to make a good, warm bed.

Each tent had a place made to stand all the guns in one corner, and a table with folding chairs, or wooden blocks for stools stood in the middle. We put a stove up in each tent with a pole frame set up over it for a clothes drying rack. The tent was equipped with a water bucket and dipper, cups, glasses, a tea kettle, a large pan to heat water in, a dish pan and a wash basin, and even a looking glass and a comb. Each tent also had an axe.

In the corner of the cook tent, for our bed, I built a pole bed frame with a headboard, and filled it with hay. We had to be close to the food in case the bears came in looking for a midnight snack.

For several years, we had an old-fashioned wood cook range with a water reservoir on one end and Adelle also used a big propane grill with two burners on the end. She had a propane oven, and the oven in the old wood range. Her cupboards were made from the pack boxes, and she had two work tables to do all her kitchen work on. There was a long eating table with split log benches on each side.

Adelle did all the baking, from rolls, biscuits, pies, cakes, cookies and some bread — and she put out awful good food.

We had two log outside toilets that we used for several years, until the Forest Service made us take them out. One toilet was for the hunters, and one was for the cooks. After hunting season each year we moved them to a new location, covered the old hole with dirt, and stored a lot of our camp equipment in these log toilets so we wouldn't have to pack the gear in and out.

One fall, we had a grizzly that kept stealing meat from us and one day, after the boys had taken the hunters out, I went to get what horses we had left in camp. I couldn't find them, but late in the afternoon I found where their tracks had hit the trail about a mile above camp; they were headed for the home ranch. I rode back to camp and told Adelle that I was going after the horses, and that it might be late before I got back.

I was riding a horse called Smokey, and I trotted him wherever the ground was level. It took me about five hours to travel the thirty miles to Holland Lake, where I caught up with that bunch of horses, about a mile from the corrals. It was already dark when I got there, so I stayed all night and started back with the horses at daybreak.

Now Adelle was alone in camp all night with that grizzly, and before it got dark she brought in a lot of wood and filled the gas lanterns so she could keep the stove and the lights going all night. She also kept her little radio blaring all night, and as you might expect, she didn't get much sleep but she wasn't bothered by the bear.

We always got up about four o'clock in the morning, and the morning after I got back, I was out at the corrals while Adelle went out to the toilet. As she settled herself down on the toilet seat, she could hear something right behind the toilet. I don't know if that noise hurried her along or not, but there was a skiff of snow on the ground and when it broke day I discovered that the bear had gotten away with a quarter of meat from under our fly. I trailed him right to the toilet, where he had laid down behind it, and was eating on the meat while Adelle was sitting there.

Occasionally the bears would steal a lot of meat. Sometimes when we had bear problems and the hunters had a grizzly tag, we rigged a horse bell in the hunter's tent with a long rope attached to it, strung the rope out to the meat pole, and fastened the end of the rope to the meat. When a bear tugged on the meat, the bell would ring in the tent, and on occasion a hunter would get a chance to go after the bear.

Once, a group of hunters camped just across the creek from us accused us of stealing their bacon. On that particular morning, Joe Fort, one of my hunters, shot a big brown bear and when he cut the stomach open, there was the full slab of bacon, well chewed but still in one piece. Joe took the bacon over to the other camp and threw it on their table, exclaiming, "Here's the damn bacon we stole from you!" Those guys were pretty surprised because the bear had to have stepped right over two of them to get to their bacon.

Mick and the Butter-Butt Bear

One afternoon we rode into our hunting camp on Holbrook Creek. There was enough snow on the ground to make good tracking and as we came into camp a brown bear ran out of our cook tent. The bear had not done too much damage, but we had a case of margarine and a case of pure butter — and the bear had eaten all the butter, but had not touched the margarine.

Our son, Mick, who was about eleven or twelve years old, said he would go try to get that bear, and took off tracking it. He finally caught up with the bear and surprised it, so it went up a tree. He shot it, hitting it in the jaw, and the bear came down the tree after him. Mick shot again, this time killing it.

That was Mick's first bear, which we came to call the Butter-Butt bear. The butter he'd eaten had gone right through the bear, and his rump was all plastered with it.

What Has Happened to the Montana Grizzly?

The question of what has happened to the Montana grizzly that has bothered many of our outdoorsmen. Most people, when they hear the word grizzly, first think of a killer of man and of all other animals. This is not true.

During my life among these animals I have made my own study - especially about their eating habits — and I firmly believe that most grizzlies will live out their full lifetimes and never become a killer.

Don't get me wrong, I respect all bears, especially if they have young close by, and the grizzly are extremely protective of their young. The older sows will protect the younger bears until they are mature, up to two years old, and older than that if they don't have new cubs. Even the males will come to the aid of the younger bears if they believe them to be in distress, and if you should happen to make a young bear bellow, be very careful of others coming to its defense.

From experience, I've come to the conviction that a "killer" bear usually gets started by first feeding on dead animals in the woods and around the ranches near their habitat. After acquiring a taste for meat, they begin killing to obtain it. And they develop a taste for sheep, as sheep are a very easy animal to kill, and this is where many bears start. After that they like goats, pigs and often, when a cow hides her baby calf a bear may step in and get it.

We have watched our cows and mares many times run big bears out of the meadow and into the woods; a bear will never kill a calf if the cow is nearby. I have never known of a bear to kill a mature animal such as a cow or a horse, or deer or elk, although there have been countless numbers killed that have been blamed on the grizzly.

It is a natural thing for any bear, large or small, to eat on a dead animal of any kind. That's part of their role in nature, and most people who find one of their animals dead and eaten on by a bear mistakenly assume that it was killed by the bear. Most often, however, the animals bears feed on have died a natural death, were hit by lightning, or killed by other causes. I have seen this happen many times.

One time a neighbor came to me, all excited. He wanted me to help him get rid of all the bears, claiming the grizzlies had killed six of his cows and a large bull. I told him I was sure he was wrong, but I accompanied him to where the animals were. I looked them over closely, and only one of his dead animals had a small mark on it. And, upon looking into the tree above the cattle, I found the mark of the killer — one of the trees had a small lightning split.

A few days later, however, the grizzlies did find the dead cattle, and they feasted for some time.

Another neighbor had an 1,800-pound horse killed, and the blame was laid on the grizzly. The warden sent the government trapper to catch the bear. After having set the trap, several days went by with no catch, so the warden asked me if I would go with the trapper and show him how to set it properly. One of my sons and I went, and that night they caught a small brown bear.

I regretted that I had helped. When we first went to the spot, the bear had eaten only a small portion of the horse, which was proof that no grizzly was involved, but by then the horse was getting ripe, and bears began to come feed on it. Several bears ended up being destroyed there for no reason.

Upon coming out after hibernation, the bear, and especially the grizzly that hibernates high in the mountains, finds the snow still deep and food hard to find. In order to locate food, it comes down to the foot of the mountains and to the edge of the valley, where the snow is gone. The bears will naturally eat all of the dead animals such as elk, deer, and domestic animals, that are near their habitat — and while they are looking for dead animals, they feed on many of the tender plants that are beginning to grow.

They eat the young grasses of different kinds. They love rose petals and nearly all blossoms, and the glacier lily is another favorite, along with dandelion and clover blossoms.

Bears also feed on several types of roots. They like the sunflower best just before it blooms, when it is still tender, and they will eat the bud of the plant, and all of the stem. (When I was a kid, we ate a lot of these ourselves. My mother stewed them with gravy.)

The grizzly feeds on grass more than other bear. In the high country, there are two kinds of grass that the bear eat, and I have often seen them eat this grass just like cattle or horses. One kind of grass grows from about four to eight inches high and the leaf part is about one half inch wide all the way up; the other is a fine stem grass that gets little seed pods on the ends later in the fall. Both of these grasses grow from about 6,000 feet and up, doing best on the high ridges and little basins.

As the berries begin to ripen in early June, the bear turns to them. First come the strawberries, and then the serviceberries, followed by huckleberries and chokecherries. The higher in the mountains, the later the berries ripen, so the bears have a constant supply of berries from June into September in good years.

After the berries are gone, the grizzly starts on pine nuts. The limber pine nut tree grows best from 6,000 to 9,000 feet in elevation. In comparison with ponderosa pine, limber pine have a smoother bark, lighter color, and the needles are shorter. Mature trees are up to three or more feet in diameter and they have heavy, long limbs with a wide spread. The cone is similar to the ponderosa cone, with the nut, or seed, about the size of a pea. They lay right next to the core, and are very tasty to eat after being dried, like any other nut.

There are many people who have never seen these trees, cones or nuts, and for some reason, these trees are not producing any cones, and haven't been since the late Thirties. Many of the trees are dying and one time I asked a forest ranger if he knew why these trees were not producing cones anymore. He replied that he didn't know that this kind of tree ever produced cones.

Once in a while, nowadays, we find a few cones, but they are small or deformed. A lot of the trees are dying, and very few new ones are coming up.

All bears feed on insects such as ants, grasshoppers, lady bugs and most other species. Every loose rock on our ranch is turned over annually by the bears because, in the cool evening, bugs of many types will gather under the warm rocks. The bear will lick the bugs from on and under the rocks.

In the late summer, the grizzly like to go high on the mountains where, during the hot part of the day, they like to lay up against the cool of the glaciers, sometimes getting right up on them. At this time of the year there are two types of insects, the lady bug and a slender green bug, that gather by the millions on the rocks located on the tops of the highest peaks, mostly in the cool of the evening. When that occurs, you can see the grizzly coming from the cool glaciers to get their evening meal.

All of the aforementioned foods are not enough to sustain the big body of the grizzly, and I believe the decline of grizzly bears in Montana is directly related to the decline of the limber pine, and the nutritious nuts it provided the bears for high country food.

Over the same time that I've noticed that the limber pine was not producing nuts, we've observed the decline of the grizzly, and those that are around are not as large and as fat as they had been in years past. I believe that most, or at least a large number of these bears have died in hibernation, for the simple reason that without these nuts, they were unable to put on enough fat to be able to survive the winters. The Canadian camp robber and the blue grouse are also disappearing in these parts, and they also fed predominantly on the limber pine nut, which were at one time in great abundance.

Until about the late 1930's the grizzly from the Continental Divide, the Swan Range and the Mission Range moved into the pine nut areas from early fall until hibernation time, which is about the first of November. The pine nut areas are at the edge of the timberline and it was here the grizzly would feed nearly 100 percent on pine nuts.

From my first pack trip in 1924 until the mid-Thirties, these trees produced in abundance. The trees, from six inches in diameter to the very large ones, would be hanging with cones.

It is interesting to watch the grizzly eat these nuts. They hold the cone between their paws and, going right around the cone with their teeth, they take all the shell off right next to the nuts, spit the shell out, and then go around one more time to take all the nuts off in one pass. It takes them only a few seconds for each cone.

In the early part of the nut season a lot of the cones have pitch on them, and the bear's paws and forearms and nose become covered with pitch, but by hibernation time most of it has worn off. The later the season, the drier the pitch becomes on the cones, and by this time of the year the grizzly droppings were nearly 100 percent pine nut. Today, what few droppings that can be found are all grass, roots and berries.

The few grizzlies that survived in the Mission Range after the limber pine quit producing cones are the ones that came down the west slope of the mountains to the foothills. Here they feed on chokecherries and wild and domestic apples.

During the mid-1920s, logging was taking place along the base of the Mission Range and in this area, where the loggers ate their lunches and threw their apple cores away, many apple trees sprang up. Many of these trees are producing a good supply of apples, which the bear have enjoyed for many years now.

On the high ridges the grizzly did have some competition for food. You would think that this part of the mountains would be a very quiet place, but it was not. In fact, is was one of the noisiest places I have ever heard in the mountains. The first competitor was the *"Snalkk"*, the Indian name for the Canada jay, also called the camp robber. There were thousands of these birds, and it sounded as if each and everyone were squawking at the same time while feeding on the limber pine nuts. The pine squirrels were chirping noisily and were very busy, some in the trees, cutting and dropping the cones to the ground; others were scurrying back and forth as fast as they could, carrying cones to their caches. There were squirrels in great numbers then, too, and all seemed to be very busy and very noisy.

The blue grouse were very plentiful during those days. We would find covey after covey, clucking to each other as they fed on the pine nuts. It was great fun and easy for my friend, Bill Conko, and me to supply the camp with chicken when we were kids, since it was our job to provide the camp with grouse and fish. These grouse were so large and fat, and heavy, from eating the limber pine nuts that they had difficulty in getting off the ground to fly, and most of them would not fly unless pressured.

As the season drew to an end, the grizzly would start to rob the squirrels of their caches. They would turn logs over and tear them apart to get the cones out, digging big holes when the cones were hid under the ground. I have seen many places where very large areas were all torn up. I could still take you to some of these areas, although the evidence is getting dimmer each year as the holes are filled back in by rain or snow. They are covered by grass and trees grow in them, and most people seeing these holes would not realize what caused them or how they got there.

The next and least of the competitors were the Indians. When we went to pick the pine nuts it was a fun time for all. Everyone in camp would go, traveling on horseback and taking pack horses, wending our way to the tops of the high ridges. The younger and more active men would climb the trees and shake the limbs to break the cones off the branches, and some used sticks and long poles to knock off the cones. The women did most of the picking and sacking of the cones in burlap bags.

Everyone was laughing and hollering, and they thoroughly enjoyed themselves, and it didn't take long to pick each packhorse load.

In doing this work, our hands would get covered with pitch, and when we were through, we rubbed our hands in dry dirt to keep from being sticky until we got back to camp. Then we would use lard or animal fat to take off the pitch.

The Indians sometimes shelled some of these cones in camp, but if they were still green they would take them home and let them dry for awhile, and then shell them. The nuts were sacked and put away for the winter, when they were doled out to each member of the family. The nuts were rich, and, I believe, very nourishing.

At this time of the year the high ridges were abounding with grizzly bear, all fat and roly-poly, ready for hibernation. It was a common thing to find eight or ten in one group, bears of all sizes — like a family.

If you were quiet and a little sneaky you could go along the ridge where they were working and hear them jabbering and talking to each other, just like a bunch of kids; it sounded as though they had a language of their own. They were just about as noisy as the Indians, and it was very exciting to listen to them. When they sensed they were being watched, however, everything got very quiet.

I am very concerned about the disappearance of the limber pine nut. They are the first of the plant life that I have seen go and as I ride through these beautiful mountains that once were so lush and are now fast changing, with many of the plants and trees looking sick or dying, I am saddened. I am also afraid as I view these changes — if the plant life goes, so will we, and all other animal life. We should all be very concerned.

Bud Cheff (in white shirt) and his five sons at the home ranch in 1993. From left are Buck, Buddy, Kenny, Bud, Mick and Happy.

Bud Cheff in 1993 on his registered Tennessee Walker Stallion.

Part Six

WILDERNESS TRAILS

Pack String Washing Down Crazy Horse Creek

One time when I was moving our camp into the Missions, with some of my sons, one of our Ohio hunters, Cliff Thostenson, was along. We'd had a very heavy snow, and then a warm rainstorm. At the time I had a trail on the west side of Crazy Horse Creek, and as we went to cross the creek, we could see the water was very swift, and running over the banks.

I was riding a tall, strong, black horse, and I managed to get across with part of the packstring, but when some of the smaller, younger mules in the back of the string hit that deep, swift water they were swept right off their feet. A pigtail, the rope that ties a mule to the other mule's saddle, broke, and four of the mules went rolling down the creek.

Luckily, they rolled close to the bank and I was able to jump into the icy water and cut the pigtails on the back of each saddle, to free the mules from each other. Cliff, my good and faithful hunter, also braved the icy water to help me and I still don't know how we managed to get those mules all out without any of them drowning.

We drained as much water as we could from our wet packs, but everything was soaked and heavy and we were sopping wet from top to bottom. We still had to ride all the way to our camp area and put up the tent before we could get a fire built in a stove and change into dry clothes. And I'm sure, now, that none of us, including the mules, thought this was a bit of fun.

We finally quit packing into the Missions because of the Forest Service logging and road building, which enabled people to walk right into the area we hunted, and also into our camp. So, we decided to do all of our hunting in the Bob Marshall Wilderness, which saved us the hassle of moving our camp in order to gain a few days of hunting time.

Cleaning Out Trail

The same year that Buddy was outfitting over at Moose Creek in Idaho, we had a rough trip into the Bob Marshall. We had finished our hunts in the Missions, and were going to move our camp into the South Fork, and Mick and I moved our horses and mules from Glacier Creek to Holland Lake. I had called the Forest Service about the condition of the trail into Holbrook Creek, and they told me not to worry, as they had the trail all cleaned out and in good shape.

This was something new, and I was pleased because we had always cleaned the trail out ourselves in the past. Mick, Adelle and I were going in with the camp and all the supplies, and in the morning we had every animal that we owned loaded, except for our saddlehorses. We must have had thirty-five to forty head of stock between Mick and me, way more horses and mules than only two men should have been trying to handle, when we started up the trail in the rain, which soon turned to a miserable, wet snow as we got into the higher elevations.

Considering the number of packs we had, we were making good time until we got to the Holbrook Divide. As we started down into Holbrook Canyon, we began to run into all kinds of downed timber across the trail, which obviously hadn't been touched since we had come out the fall before. At that time it was still legal to use a chainsaw in there, and luckily we had brought one along with us. So, we had to clean out the trail ourselves, while that miserable, wet snow was still coming down.

Mick went on foot with the chainsaw ahead of Adelle and me, and started to cut the logs out of the trail while I took his pack string and saddlehorse, and tied mine onto the back end of his. I had Buddy's little white mule, Micky, as the caboose mule. A full pack string is considered to be nine mules and a saddlehorse, and I was leading about thirty-five or more pack animals.

We were lucky that our horses and mules were working well together, as that many animals strung out in single file makes for an awful long pack string, and I could only see the white mule on the tail end of the string once in a great while. It was quite a job to try to watch that many pack animals at all times.

There were so many logs in the trail that we didn't get very far down in the canyon before it started to get dark, and we still had thirteen miles to go before we reached our campsite. I stopped to check all of the packs and make sure everything was secure and riding well. We had one flashlight between us, and it soon played out as we slowly progressed down the trail. We had some gas lanterns in a pack, which we could have used for lights, but we didn't know which of the sixty packs they were in. Luckily, we had packed our saw gas and oil on our lead mule.

Mick had to feel his way down the trail with the chainsaw in his hand, to keep from running into logs. He had to clear the trail by luck and by chance, being careful not to get his saw stuck in a pinching log when he cut through it, and being wary of a log that might have had an overhang and snap upwards, or go sideways, and smash into him. He was also in danger of having timber come sliding down off of a steep side hill onto him, after he had cut some logs off.

I felt so sorry for Adelle, who would only ride when she was either coming or going from one of the camps, and so was not used to riding like we were. She had climbed into that saddle about seven o'clock in the morning, and it had rained and snowed all the way. And, as we came down that long, dark canyon, I was hoping and praying that Mick up in the lead would not get injured sawing those logs in the dark.

I was also hoping that none of my packs would turn over, or that any of the string would get off the trail, or get tangled up in some way.

We finally got to our campsite somewhere between two or three in the morning, wet and very tired, and Mick had endured the roughest job of any of us on that arduous trip, carrying and working that chainsaw for thirteen miles in pitch darkness.

When we reached camp, Adelle seemed to have melted right down into her saddle, and I had to help her down off of her horse. We managed to find the mule with the bedrolls, and I rolled out our bed and put Adelle in it, while Mick was unloading the mules, who were as tired as we were, after carrying those wet, heavy packs for such a long time. After we got the animals unpacked and the saddles off the stock, we covered everything as best we could in the dark, then turned the stock loose without their usual feed of grain, to let them go out to pasture.

We tied a long pole to a tree by one end and threw a plastic tarp over it for shelter for the rest of the night, and crawled into our sleeping bags.

It seemed like we had only just got to bed when daylight came. We started sorting out our packs, and got ourselves some breakfast, then started to put up some tents. Thank goodness the rain had stopped, but I was still grumpy after our all day and all night trip into here, and still aggravated with the Forest Service for telling us that our trail was cleaned out for us when they hadn't even touched it.

About 9:30 in the morning, a young, smart-alec assistant ranger came riding up to our camp. He got off his horse and tied it to a tree right in the middle of our camp area where we never allowed horses to be brought, and strutted around there a little bit, and then started giving me orders.

First of all, I was to move the location of both of our toilets. He showed me where to put one toilet, taking a stick in his hand and scratching a square mark in the dirt about three feet away from a big fir tree that was about four feet around. He marked right over the top of a big root that was about a foot or more in diameter.

I told him I could dig a hole there, but did he really want me to damage that big, beautiful tree?

"Oh, no!" he said, "Don't you dare damage any of the roots on these trees."

"Well," I said, "There is a big root going right through the middle of the marks you made on the ground."

He wanted to know how I knew that, so I explained that anyone could tell by the bulge on the trunk of the tree where the root started, and could follow it on out by the way the ground was humped up the full length of the root.

"Well, he said, moving about eight feet away, "You can move it over to here."

He had already moved us about fifty feet closer to the stream, and this was the year that all the outfitters were supposed to dig a new garbage pit. He walked around a little and picked out the rockiest spot in the whole area, a spot with a lot of big boulders, and said, "Dig your pit right here, and be very sure that you build it six by six by six feet deep, and that it's square and all the walls are lined with logs." He added that the pit had to have a log top with a trap door in the middle, and that I had better have it finished by the end of my season, before we went out.

If you don't think I didn't have a lot of fun working on that hole every spare minute I had that season! I had to pull a lot of big rocks out of there with a chain and a work horse. What a job! After finally getting the hole dug, I had to go cut logs and skid them in from out in the woods. Bud I did get it finished by the end of the season — and it was a good thing I had the boys to help me with it.

But how heartbreaking it was. We always wanted to do the right thing, to do our best to get along with the Forest Service, but wouldn't you know it, the very next year, after all that hard work, they announced that we outfitters couldn't use these garbage pits anymore, and that we had to fill them back in. They told us we would have to start hauling our garbage out, which I didn't mind doing, but why they didn't do this before, instead of putting us through all that trouble and work, I'll never understand.

A couple of years later we had to take all the caches out. For many years we had left an old-fashioned wood range in there. We then took in another one, but later were forced to haul them out, and it seems as though the Forest Service does everything possible to make it as hard as they can on the outfitters, and it does get discouraging.

More Trouble On the Trail — Cleaning More Trail

Another fall when Adelle and I were going in to set up our hunting camp in the Bob Marshall, we had a rough time getting in — thirteen miles of the trail had not been cleaned of fallen trees and logs since we had come out the previous fall.

This particular year three of our sons were with us: Buddy Jr. with his new bride, Laurie; Kenny; and Buck with his bride, Cheryl.

I had two of the boys ahead of the packstrings, one with a chain saw and the other with a good sharp axe. In those days it was not as difficult to clean the trails as it is now, since we were permitted to use a chainsaw. Nowadays, however, we are forced to use the old crosscut saws, and it is very hard to find anyone outside of our family who knows how to use one properly.

On this trip we ran into so many logs that had to be cut out of the trail that, by the time we got half-way down Holbrook Canyon, night was starting to come upon us. We decided to camp in a little meadow in the creek bottom where I used to put up a camp, many years before.

It was a nice night, with no rain or snow, so after our supper was finished, we rolled out our sleeping bags on tarps, not putting up tents. Before going to bed, we picketed a couple of horses and a young mule that we had just started to break for packing and riding. Everyone was tired, and sleeping soundly when in the middle of the night, suddenly, we woke to the sound of hooves pounding. Some of the horses nickered, and some of the mules began to bray, but no one knew what was happening until the young mule we'd picketed came flying into our camp, right through the sleeping bags, with most of us still in them.

The mule had gotten its picket rope around a little green fir tree and pulled the tree out by the roots, which frightened the young mule half to death. As she came flying into camp, the little tree whipped back and forth behind her, hitting buckets and pans, and the clatter scared her all the more. She ran between and over the sleeping bags as everyone scrambled, trying to get out of her way.

The meadow was small, and the mule kept running around it, charging back and forth through our camp, kicking and bellowing at the little tree dragging behind her. Each time the mule made a run through our camp, Adelle and the daughters-in-law screamed as they tried to get out of the way. But the mule finally got so tired that she stopped, and turned to face that little tree. With her long ears forward and eyes wide open, she watched to see if the tree would take off after her again and, as she stood there trembling, we managed to get hold of her and free her from the tree.

The new wives got a taste of what can happen on these trips.

Adelle Cracking Her Pelvis

One fall, after they had taken the last group of hunters out, the boys came back in to help me tear down the camp and pack it up to take out, as it was the end of the season. The morning we left, we got the main pack strings packed up and the boys left with them while Adelle and I stayed behind and made sure everything in our campsite was cleaned up and in good shape. We were the last two people left in the Bob Marshall that year, as the other outfitters and rangers had already gone out.

We started up the trail for home with three or four mules and had gone up the trail only about five miles when we ran into trouble, at a spot where we had to cross a real bad, boggy section of the trail that was well frozen, except where some of the stock ahead of us had broken through in a few spots. Adelle's horse must have stepped on a frozen clod or something, which caused it to make a double stumble, something that happens very rarely. Her horse went down in the bog head first, throwing her up against the saddle horn, and as it struggled to get up, its head hit Adelle in the face, breaking her glasses and nearly knocking her unconscious. The horse managed to get up with Adelle still on its back, but she looked like she was going to pass out.

I knew that if I took her off her horse I would never be able to get her back on again so, in spite of the fact that she was in incredible pain, we decided to try to make it out with her on the horse.

Our options were incredibly limited. It was twenty miles back to the ranger station, but there was no one there, and our sleeping bags were on the boys' pack strings, and there was no way I could leave her there to try to get a helicopter to fly her out, and it was still twenty-five miles to Holland Lake.

We thought her pelvic bone might be broken, but there was nothing we could do but try to make it out of there, so she had to keep right on going on that horse's back. We had to cross over two divides, and I think it was harder on her going downhill than it was going up. I felt so badly for her because she was in so much pain, and before we got to Holland Lake she wanted to get off that horse, but we just had to keep going or she wouldn't make it. At times, she said later, she wished that her horse would go between two trees so she could take a hold of them and let her horse go out from under her.

After we got to our corrals, it was a real job to get her off of the horse — and when we got her to a doctor, we found out that the pelvis was badly cracked, but not broken. The doctor said he didn't see how she could have ridden so far on a horse, in that condition. But, she healed up, though even today, many years later, the injury bothers her.

Kenny on Dynamite

Early one morning in the hunting camp, our second son, Kenny, and Buddy, the oldest son, walked up to the meadow in the dark, each with a halter and a feed bag to catch a horse. Then they rode bareback and brought the rest of the horses into camp before daylight.

We had two brown horses that we rode, Dynamite and Smokey. Dynamite was a trained bucker that could be ridden as long as nothing went wrong, or if he didn't have a flank strap on. As Kenny called the horses, Smokey was the first to get to him, so he gave him a few bites of grain and put the halter on him, and then jumped up onto his back.

Kenny later said he could feel Smokey's back starting to hump up a little, and Buddy said he could hear Kenny, in the dark, say, "What is the matter with you, Smokey! Smokey! Quit it, darn you, Smokey, quit! Smokey, Smokey, Smokey!" and bang, Kenny was laying on his back out in the meadow — and Buddy was laughing his head off. Kenny thought all along that he had Smokey, but instead he had caught Dynamite, the trained bucker.

My boys practiced riding on him before the rodeos and Nels Jensen, one of my guides, also had an experience on Dynamite, and once he had been bucked off and dragged a little ways. My boys knew that horse and could handle him, and ride him, but a person had to watch him close and make sure nothing went wrong.

Micky and Mark

In the fall of 1971, the boys got ready to take some hunters out at the end of their hunt, a thirty-mile ride. Mick's wife, Karen, went with them, planning to bring their two small boys, Micky and Mark, back to camp with them when they brought in the next group of hunters.

The weather had taken a turn for the worse, and Adelle told Karen that if it was storming, she had better not bring the little ones in, and, sure enough, when they got ready to come back, the weather turned bad and quickly became the worst storm of the season. However, Mick rigged up a pair of panniers with plywood bottoms, and put them on Bunny, a good mule that liked people better than she liked other mules, so the kids could ride on her. Bunny was a good, safe mule, and one that all the kids could pile onto and ride.

At the time, Mark was just old enough to talk well, and Mickey was a year older, and Mick and Karen put these two little boys inside the panniers, one on each side of the mule. They gave them some toys to play with, closed the lids, and they were comfortably set for their thirty-mile journey.

Mick and Karen mounted their saddlehorses and took off up the mountain, with Mick leading the ten pack mules and Karen, just ahead of him, leading Bunny with the two kids in the panniers.

They had traveled about fifteen miles and were about half-way to camp when they met a packstring and hunters coming out from another camp. Mick and Karen stopped to talk to the packers as they passed. and all the while the two little boys in the panniers were talking to each other. Now Mick had not mentioned that there were kids on the mule, and as the other packers continued up the trail, they kept staring back at that mule — and word got out that Mick had a talking mule.

When they arrived at our camp, Mick told his mother that it was too stormy, they hadn't brought the boys in, and Adelle said, "Oh good." Karen had stayed back a little on the trail, letting Mick go in ahead of her, and when she came into camp Adelle told her she was glad they hadn't brought the little boys in that storm. About that time the two little boys threw open the lids on the panniers, stuck up their heads and yelled, "Hi, Grandma!"

Those two boys had the time of their lives in there and it didn't seem like any time at all before they were both grown up, and helping with the packing business.

Nine Hunters and Brothers

Also in 1971, we had nine hunters booked for an our elk hunt during the first of the season and two of our sons took a group of hunters out to Holland Lake and were to bring back a group of nine hunters, all from the Detroit area, for their hunt. Mick's packstring was the first one in that evening, and along with him was one of my nephews, and one of my brothers. Adelle and I had walked out to the hitchracks to greet everyone as they came in off the trail.

Another nephew and two more brothers came in next, followed by my brother-in-law, Herman Byrd, and then two more brothers. I was starting to get worried, wondering where we were going to put all of my relatives when we also had nine hunters coming! I looked at Adelle, and she had a very worried and puzzled look on her face. She said, "How am I going to feed all of these people? You know I have all of my food planned for nine hunters, and the closest store is thirty miles away!"

I was starting to feel like my brothers were sort of imposing on us, with ten or eleven of them coming into camp without letting us know in advance, but Adelle rushed down to the cook tent to start preparing more food for supper. I was still waiting for the hunters to ride in when I finally asked one of the boys, "How far back on the trail do you think the hunters are?"

He said, "They are all here. They all came in a little while ago." I finally realized that my brothers were the nine hunters, and had booked the party under different names. What a nice surprise!

We were all having a great time, but one evening as several of us were bringing in a six-point bull elk that my nephew, Dwight, had shot during the day, we had a turn of bad luck. As we got about a mile from camp, we noticed that one of the packs was not riding quite right. Now Mick was riding a wild mule that he was breaking and as he stepped off the mule to straighten the pack, the mule that was carrying the elk horns bumped into Mick's mule, scaring her. She took off, running a little ways into the woods, and some of the fellows started to go after her, but Mick and I both told them just to let her go because we were afraid that strangers would just scare her father away. A lot of mules don't trust just anyone.

We told them she would follow us into camp if she was left alone, so we started out again with everyone walking, even Mick who was leading two pack mules. My brother, Vela, and Herman were lagging along behind when Mick's saddle mule came from behind them. Vela caught her by her rope, and told Herman that he was going to ride her on into camp, but he had no more than got on that mule when she took off with him, bucking him head first into a thick group of pine trees that were about ten to twelve inches in diameter.

We had to rig up a stretcher to carry him into camp; he had a bad head injury, some broken ribs, and was unconscious. Mick saddled a fresh, long-legged sorrel horse that was an exceptionally good traveler, and, in the dark night, started for the ranger station some eight miles away. There, he would call for a helicopter to come and get Vela at daybreak and transport him to a hospital.

Mick didn't know that, the previous spring, high water had washed the trail out for quite a distance, leaving a straight down bank of nine or ten feet and, when he got to that part of the trail, his horse didn't see the bank and went head over heels off the bank with Mick on top of him. They landed hard at the water's edge in a

The "crew" in the Cheff's wilderness hunting camp. At table (from left) are sons Buck and Hap, and guide Gene Lefthand. Standing are daughter-in-law Sandy, son Mick, and Bud and Adelle.

pile, but, fortunately, neither Mick nor his horse were hurt, and Mick continued to the ranger station.

The chopper was called shortly after daylight, and in the morning came to pick up Vela, flying him to a hospital in Kalispell hospital. This accident, which happened twenty-two years ago, left Vela in bad condition, and he is still limited in what he can do.

A Foolish Climb

At the end of another fall, after we had taken all of the hunters out of the mountains, Adelle, Mick and I decided to stay another day to do some hunting for ourselves before we brought the camp out. As a rule, we never hunt for ourselves when we have hunters in with us.

Again, we were the last three people to leave the wilderness, as everyone else had already gone out — and it still makes me shudder to think about the chance Mick and I took. We each saddled a horse and rode to Burnt Creek, following it up the canyon. Then we decided to go up into what we called the "High Pocket," which lies just above the first big layer of high cliffs that run from near the bottom of the canyon all the way to Scarface Peak.

We tied our horses at the bottom of the lower end of this long, high cliff, and started on foot up the narrow canyon which led to the High Pocket. About half-way up, we spotted a bunch of mule deer on top of a high cliff, which was at least five hundred feet high. Mick said that he was going to climb up a small ravine to the top of this part of the cliff, instead of going about a mile up the mountain, and then around to the head of the cliff.

However, the snow was quite deep and it was hard walking, so I told him that no way was he going up that cliff, and that he should come with me. Then I walked about a hundred yards or so back to where I could get a good look at that cliff, and I could plainly see that there was no way anyone could possibly climb the cliff on these conditions. There were patches of snow here and there on the face of some of the rocks, and it had thawed a little the day before, and then had frozen, leaving a lot of ice on parts of the rocks. But, by then, Mick was already climbing.

I tried my best to talk him into coming down, but he kept on, so I started to follow him. Before I started, I was feeling that I would soon have to find a place to go to the bathroom, but I was still trying to talk Mick out of going on up as, the higher we went, the worse it got — and the weather was several degrees below freezing.

In many spots we only had small crevices and outcroppings to hang on with, and our fingers were numb from the freezing cold. We had our guns slung over our backs, and we each had a thirty-two foot cargo rope with us. Finally, we got up so high that it probably would have been impossible to get back down by the same route, as we would not have been able to see where our foot and hand holds were.

Sometimes we had to take our gloves off so that we could hang onto the rock better, and if Mick had slipped and fallen, he probably would have taken me with him, as I was directly below him. If I had fallen, Mick would likely have tried to climb back down to me, in spite of the risk — and no one but God knew where we were. We hadn't even told Adelle which way we were going, and I started to get worried, not for myself, but for Adelle. If I should get killed or badly hurt — and, more likely killed as we were already several hundred feet up the cliff — what would she do? If we didn't come back she would be left alone in the middle of this wilderness, wondering what had happened, and not knowing what to do.

Once in a while, we would find a little bush or tree growing out of a crevice, and that would help us some. Several times Mick gave me his gun, and then climb up farther, and drop his rope to me. I would tie the guns on, and he would pull them up. And, sometimes, he would tie his rope to a bush or little tree growing out of the rock, and I would climb with the rope.

We finally got to a place where we couldn't go any further. The next fifteen feet of rock face sloped outward past vertical and there was not a hand or foothold anywhere on this sheer outcropping. Mick was still ahead of me, and we were standing on a little ledge about four inches wide — and it looked like forever down to the bottom. The higher we had climbed the more uncomfortable I had become, and by this point I desperately needed to relieve myself but couldn't figure how a person could get into a squatting position on a four-inch ledge.

At the upper part of the cliff, a little fir tree about three inches in diameter was growing upward out of the rocks. Mick handed me his gun, took his rope from around his waist, and, curling it up small, tried to throw it up and over the trunk of that little tree. Now it was an extremely difficult task to balance on the narrow ledge by leaning against the rock while trying to throw a rope around a little tree that was growing only six inches out from the rock. Finally, after several attempts, he got about five or so feet of the rope over the tree trunk, and, by cautiously flipping the rope, he managed to get enough over to catch ahold of the other end.

We had no idea how well the little tree was rooted into the rock, so Mick tested it with his weight a couple of times, and then he climbed up the rope to the tree. He managed to get himself up and over the tree, but there was only room enough for one of his feet to fit on the little trunk where it came out of the rock. Then, I tied the guns on to the rope and he pulled them up, and, finally, he helped me to get up. And, when I reached the little tree, he had to get off and work his way up a bit further, to make room for me to put my foot on the tree. From this point we were able to make it on up.

As soon as we got to a spot where it was feasible to squat, I did just that, and for the first and only time in my life, I didn't care who might be watching me. It was a double relief to be at the top of the cliff, and to finally be able to answer nature's call.

Nowadays, Mick always kids me about that climb scaring the ---- out of me, but it was a good lesson for us both. We could have easily lost our lives, and by the time we got to the top of the cliff, the deer were all gone anyway.

Three Spike Bulls And A Lost Hunter

Things can happen while hunting that a person doesn't expect. In my years of guiding, I have had several of my hunters kill more than one animal with one shot but, as far as I remember, I have never done this in the many years that I have hunted.

But one year before Hungry Horse reservoir was in, my oldest son, Buddy, and I were hunting on Doris Mountain, he on one part of the mountain and me on another. I was near the top of this mountain when I saw a spike bull about 250 yards uphill from me, just walking slowly away. I took a shot at him and he disappeared in the patchy brush. I moved toward where he'd been when I shot and then I saw the young bull quite a ways further up the hill, still walking, so I took another shot at him. Again, he went into the brush, which was just a little higher than the elk's back. Once again, I moved up toward the new location I got about half-way there when I saw him again, this time quite a distance up the hill.

I thought I was sure doing some poor shooting, as it usually only took me one shot for an elk. The elk stopped and was looking down at me. I was standing right by a little tree, so this time I took my time and anchored the rifle against the tree so that I would not miss him. Again I shot, and this time the elk came tumbling down the hill.

When I got up to the bull, there was only one bullet hole in it. I cleaned him out and got him propped up and open to cool. But while I was cleaning the animal, I was got to thinking that I had hit the bull when I fired my second shot so I decided on my way down to check the spot where he had been standing the second time I fired.

When I got there, in the edge of the brush lay a spike bull — I hadn't missed, after all. I cleaned this bull out and, after finishing, wondered if it could be possible that I might have hit with my first shot, too, so I decided to stop and check. Back in the brush a short ways lay another spike bull and by now I was getting sort of panicky as I had already put my tag on the first bull and I had two more down, and no tags. All I wanted was one elk and I felt terrible about what I had done.

Buddy had heard me shoot and came up, so he claimed one of them and, upon getting home, I told my brother, Chris, about what I had done. He said, "You sound like a darned liar, but I will go up and help you pack them out, and put my tag on one of them." I hated for him and Buddy to have their hunting stopped, but we didn't want to waste the elk. If I could of, I would have kicked my own rump.

Packing Out Three Spike Bulls

The next day, my sons, Buddy and Kenny, went with me to pack out those spike bull with some of my horses. When we got there we found that a grizzly bear had already started to bury one of the elk, covering it with dirt and spruce needles. We didn't have enough horses to pack all three elk out on one trip, so I left Buddy and Kenny there to guard the elk while I took one load down.

They each had a stick, as well as their hunting knives, to scare a bear off with and Buddy told Kenny to "Get a bigger stick!" That morning they could hear the bear grumbling off a ways in the brush, but it didn't come in close. About midday, it started to snow and by the time we were coming down off of the mountains with the rest of the meat, late in the afternoon, it was starting to snow very hard. It was not going to be long until dark and we were about two mile from the road when we saw a fresh man's track.

As there was only a little bit of snow in his tracks, I knew that he had been there a very short time before. I thought this was odd, as it was so late in the day and the tracks led away from where the road was, and it was snowing very hard.

A short time after we got home with our meat and horses, and had taken care of them, we were eating supper when a special news bulletin came on the radio, reporting that a hunter was lost on Doris Mountain. I told my family that the boys and I had just seen the missing man's tracks, and that he was going in the wrong direction. If I had known that this man was lost, I could have stopped him by just calling for him but at the time I didn't think of anyone being lost in those hills.

The radio said that a search party was to gather at 7 a.m. at the Doris trailhead. My brother and another man offered to go with me to help look for this lost man, as we knew where to find his tracks. We were at the trailhead a little before seven in the morning and by then the snow was getting very deep.

We waited until after 8 a.m., but no search party showed up, so I decided not to wait any longer. I was riding Honey, a fine big powerful mare and as we went up the mountain, the snow got deeper and deeper. The other two fellows finally gave up, but I kept on going. Before I could get to where I had seen this mans track's, the snow was up to my horse's neck and she finally played out.

I tied her up and tried to go on foot but there were a lot of trees bent down across the trail from the heavy snow and by the time I got to where I thought I had seen his tracks, I was also played out. I tried to do some hollering, but all that soft snow muffled the sound. This was the heaviest, fastest snowfall that I have ever seen, and winter set in for good.

After several attempts, the official search was called off until spring.

When spring came and the snow started to go off, a few people started again to look for the lost hunter and they finally found his remains, but a bear had eaten his body.

I will tell you what I believe may have happened.

I don't think they ever found his knife, and his gun was found with the bolt out of it. He most likely had an encounter with the same big grizzly that my son, Buddy, had in the same area the following fall. If he did, he may have gotten excited; to reload the type of gun he carried, he would of had to have his finger on the trigger for the bolt to have come out — and this is the only way that bolt could have come out. (We are quite sure that bear did not take that bolt out later.) This man would not have been able to shoot without the bolt in his gun, and that could have been why he lost his life — and I have always felt bad that if I had only known that the man's tracks I had seen late that evening were of a lost hunter, I'm sure that I could have saved his life.

During the next hunting season, one year later, my oldest son, Buddy, was guiding a young hunter from Minnesota who shot and killed an elk right near where the skeleton of the lost hunter was found.

Buddy took the pack animals early the next morning to go up and pack the elk out, the hunter going with him, following the same trail that we had used the fall before to get to the top of the big ridge. When they got on the ridge directly above where the elk was laying, they tied their saddle horses there and set out with the packhorses to go down and get the elk. The hunter also left his rifle there to avoid having to carry it, as it was about a quarter of a mile down a steep sidehill to get to the elk. Young Bud had his 30-30 Winchester on the side of one of the pack animals.

They started down the steep and heavily-wooded sidehill on foot, leading the two packhorses, and when they got a hundred yards or so from the elk they heard some mumbling and grumbling. Then they saw this big, sort of brindle-colored grizzly bear come up the hill toward them. Young Bud didn't think the bear was coming after them, but he did get his gun down off of the horse, thinking that when the bear got a little closer he would run him off. But the closer the bear came, the louder it grumbled, and it started to blow. Buddy didn't want to have to shoot the bear, but decided that if it came across a large log a few steps in front him that he would. He yelled at the bear, and the bear started to bellow — and when it started coming over the big log, Buddy shot the grizzly, then walked down to him. The grizzly jumped up and tore one of Buddy's coat sleeves off before he could shoot it again; that shot put the bear down for good.

This big grizzly was one of the ugliest bears that I have ever seen and it is my belief, based on the way it came after the guys, that this bear had been in a fight before with a human. It was on the fight from the time it first heard or smelled them. The end of the bear's nose, the black part, had been cut about three-fourths of the way off some time before and the cut piece was hanging outward from the nose. It was a smooth, slick cut like a knife would make, and I believe that had been cut come from a fight with another bear it would have been a jagged.

My theory, or belief, is that the hunter that lost his life the fall before got excited when he encountered the bear, which most people would, and tried to reload his gun with his finger on the trigger. This would have caused the bolt to come straight out the back of the gun, which would render the rifle useless. Then, the man probably tried to fight the big bear with his knife, and cut the end of this bear's nose before the grizzly got him. His hunting knife was never found.

Over the years I've found that any animal — a dog, bull, a bear, or any other animal — that gets hurt some in a fight will then be more aggressive in a subsequent fight, and I think this was the case with that particular grizzly.

Whatever, I asked that young hunter if he was nervous during the encounter and he said he was scared almost to death, and was sure that big bear had Buddy.

The Bull of The Missions

One year in the early Sixties, we had a group of California hunters who had made several past trips with us into the Bob Marshall and the Missions. This particular year they were having good luck with goat, bear and elk.

Late one afternoon we were all on horseback, bringing down some mountain goat we had killed in the high country, when we heard a bull elk bugle quite a distance up the side of the mountain. Soon he bugled again, and I told the fellows that the bull was coming down to see us, and that someone had better get off his horse and up on a little ridge about twenty-five yards above us. One fellow behind me quickly dismounted and climbed up there. He had no more than gotten in place when that huge bull came charging down right toward us. The hunter who had climbed above us fired one shot, so we tied up our horses, and I started up to where he was at.

I could hear this fellow talking to himself. "Damn, damn, what a bull!"

I had seen plenty of real big bull elk, but this was the largest ever. It had nine points on each side and its body was absolutely huge. Interestingly, my wife's cousin, George Moore, had killed a huge bull elk with the same type of horns thirty years before, about two hundred yards from where this one was taken, and I had shot the biggest cow elk I had ever seen not too far from this same spot.

We had to use the biggest pack animals that we had to pack this big bull out, and we weren't able to put the horns over the packs like we usually do, because the horns came nearly to the ground. Instead, we had to build a bunk on the rump of the pack animal to support the horns, yet they still came to the back end of the pack animal.

We only had three or four miles to go to reach the truck when we packed the meat out, but those hind quarters of meat were so heavy that the pack animals sure worked up a sweat getting there. If I remember correctly, its weight was 690 pounds of meat, and we had to cut the neck off short. The meat cutters said they had never seen a bull elk like that.

Unfortunately, as some of the group told me later, the taxidermist made a very bad mount of the head, as the cape was much too big for the form, and he didn't fill it out like it should have been. Instead, he just rolled the skin up on the top of the neck.

The hunter who shot the elk was not so lucky after all; he was killed the following year when he fell off of a cliff on a fishing trip in California.

In my sixty-seven years of going into this area, we killed a lot of real big elk, and a large share of them had horns very similar to this big one. I believe this herd of elk was one that had utilized the area for decades. I don't believe there are any left in there now because the area became too accessible when the roads were put in and

Our packstring struggling through deep snow.

I think it's sad that logging roads were put into that particular area. It was too small an area for the hunting pressure that came after the roads were built.

My older sons, Buddy and Kenny, helped me a lot when we were getting these big elk, so they got in on part of the guiding, as well as packing those big brutes out of there. Buck and Mick also helped the last couple of years that we hunted in there.

The Hunter With Uncommon Courage

One year, a young man from back east some place wrote us to make plans for a hunting trip into the Bob Marshall Wilderness. While making his plans, he was laying in bed in a hospital with cancer, and he said that the doctors were doing some sort of experiment on him at the time. He told us that he would be out of the hospital by the time hunting season was to open.

It was this young man's life-long ambition to go on a pack trip to hunt for elk, and we thought he must be a brave young man to want to come and take a thirty mile ride into our hunting camp. But come he did, and he made it into camp without any complaints, although I am sure he was hurting.

I wanted very badly for this fellow, whose name was Dick, to get an elk, but his climbing ability was limited. On one particular day of that trip, the others in this group of hunters were going to hunt a steep, heavy wooded area and my plans were to take this young man horseback up the canyon, beyond where the rest of the hunters would be. So, we rode about four miles up the canyon and then tied up our horses.

It was a slow process, but we hiked up the side of this mountain about a mile or so to where I knew of a good game trail, away from where the other hunters would be. We finally got about forty yards from this game trail. There happened to be a nice log that we could sit on comfortably, with another larger log just in front of us, and it both hid us from view and offered a real nice spot to shoot from. I told him that if anything came along to let them get as close as possible before shooting.

We had only been in this spot a very few minutes when it seemed that, from out of nowhere, a big bull elk appeared. I had told Dick beforehand to shoot just behind the shoulders and a little below center of the animal's body. The big bull came walking along slowly and then, when he got directly in front of us, it stopped. I think he sensed that we were there — but he offered a perfect shot.

I was beginning to think that Dick was not going to shoot, when "Bang!," he did. I saw the bullet hit, and it was a perfect shot. Dick started to jump up, but I grabbed his arm and said to him, "Dick, it's lunch-time. Let's have a sandwich and then we will go after him."

Just ahead of us, and in the direction the bull was going, were some cliffs and a very steep sidehill — and I sure didn't want the bull to roll down that sidehill because it would make it extremely difficult for us to get it out. Now, it was very hard to get Dick to eat his lunch because he was hyped up and wanted to go after that bull. But I knew that if the bull was not dead yet and we should appear, it would flounder around and probably go down, over that steep hillside.

We finished our lunch and I said, "Okay, let's go get him. Keep your eyes open and be ready to shoot."

But that big bull had only gone about fifty yards and was laying there, dead. When Dick saw him he hollered, "I got him" over and over, and he grabbed me around the neck while he was jumping up and down, and I thought for a minute that he was going to kiss me.

This is the best part of guiding, to see the hunters get so thrilled when they get their game, and it's made more special when someone like Dick puts something extra into the hunt.

Happenings In Camp

One year, one of my old schoolmates and a life long friend, Sidney Roullier, was working for me in our hunting camp about eleven miles from the South Fork of the Flathead River on Holbrook Creek. On a dark, rainy day, I sent my oldest son, Buddy, and Sidney with a chainsaw, as we could use a saw in those days, to clean the logs out of the trail that had blown down in the past year. They had eleven miles to clear out to get to our main camp on the South Fork of the Flathead River, and there was a lot more to cut out than we had thought.

About half-way down, they came to a huge tree on a very steep sidehill that had been uprooted just above the trail, and were unable to cut it out. However, they managed to get their saddlehorses up the steep bank and around the up-rooted tree, so they figured we could grade out a new trail with our digging tools later.

By the time they got down to the river it was almost dark, so they turned around and started right back up the trail to cover the eleven miles to camp. It soon was so dark that they were unable to see anything and that cold, miserable rain pelted them, the horses managed to stay on the trail.

When they got back up to where they had to go around that down tree, it was too steep for them to ride and the horses stopped. Buddy knew that they were even with the big log, though they could not see a thing, so they got off of their horses, with Buddy in the lead, and started feeling their way up and around this downed log. Sidney had turned his horse loose ahead of him; he was climbing up and around the log when he walked right into the horse, with his hand out feeling in the pitch dark. He could feel a horses rump, and right tight against the horse's rump was the face of another horse.

Sidney asked Buddy, "How in the hell did you get that horse turned so short and bent around like that?" He didn't know that Buddy had dropped his reins, and that his horse had turned around, and was standing facing the opposite direction, tight against the other horse. In spite of their miserable situation, Buddy couldn't help but laugh.

Sidney was a great entertainer. He was always happy and he kept everyone else happy and laughing at all times. He was good for my hunters, and it is sad that a man with so much talent in so many ways should die young, as Sidney did.

Tux

We had a group of hunters from Michigan that came with us for several years, including Tuxbery, who was the fellow who always got the group together, a fine fellow. We all called him Tux.

One evening he brought my wife, Adelle, a fake, life-like fried egg and asked her if she would make Dr. Hill a fried egg sandwich for the next day's lunch out of this plastic egg. Adelle made up the lunches and put the egg in Dr. Hill's lunchbag and let Tux carry an extra real sandwich with him.

At lunch time, we sat under a big tree to eat the lunches. Tux knew that Hill was not to fond of egg sandwiches and when Dr. Hill opened his lunch sack, he asked Tux, "What kind of sandwich have you got in your lunch?" He wanted to make a trade. Tux said, "An egg, same as yours."

Dr. Hill said, "As hungry as I am, and I get a damn, cold egg sandwich." But he was hungry, so he took a bite. He said he didn't know an --- --- egg sandwich could be so darn tough! Then Tux started to laugh and Dr. Hill took a good look at his sandwich, and started cussing Tux. Tux pulled out the good sandwich and gave it to him.

This group sometimes liked to stay up late and play cards. One night, Adelle and I could hear them getting quite loud over in their tent at about midnight. A couple shots went off over in their tent and I jumped out of bed, jerked on my clothes, and ran over to their tent as fast as I could. We both thought that they had gotten into a fight.

When I got over there, they were all laughing. I said, "What in the world is going on over here!" One of them had a bad case of hiccups, and one of the others said he knew of a good cure for the hiccups. When no one was looking, he took his .45 caliber pistol and fired two quick shots right near the fellow, but out of the tent. It almost scared them all to death, but there were no more hiccups. It scared them out of him, too.

—220—

Adelle and Her Monkey Boots

Each year after our hunting season was over, we had to pack our hunting camp out of the Bob Marshall, and some years the snow got very deep on top of the passes. The horses and mules going over the trail every few days packed the snow down, but if one should happen to step off the trail it would have to do some lunging to get back onto it.

One particular time that I remember, all of that deep snow on the top of Holbrook Pass made for a beautiful sight and Adelle and I had only a few loaded mules on the way out. Our boys were somewhere behind us with the rest of the mules and the camp. We were within a hundred yards of the top of the pass when Adelle's horse stepped off the trail with her and the horse started to lunge in the deep snow.

Adelle was not too brave on a lunging horse after being bucked off a couple of times in her younger life, so she jumped off her horse. Her legs are not very long, so when she jumped off into the deep snow, about all I could see was her stocking cap sticking out of the snow. I helped her get out and onto the trail, but she said she would walk the rest of the way to the top.

The horses had been stepping in each other's tracks, and each track was like a deep hole. Now Adelle was wearing what I call monkey boots, big, round insulated boots, and when she tried to step from one horse track to the next one, she would become high-centered between them. And, when she tried to pull a foot out of the track, her boots would stick tight and start to come off; the expression of frustration on her face could never, ever be duplicated.

I finally told her, "Adelle, you've just got to get back onto your horse." The snow was crusted, but not too hard, and I had Adelle stand on the crusted snow while I brought the horse up to her. The stirrups were only about four or five inches above the snow as I brought her horse into position for her to step into the stirrup, but just as she raised one foot the other foot broke through the crust. So here she was, one foot down and the other on top of the snow, and she tried three or four times to reach the stirrup, but each time she broke through the snow. She was crying, she was so frustrated, and I felt sorry for her, but it was so funny that I had to try to hide my face. I didn't want her to see me laughing at her.

I said, "I will lift you on." But I lifted her almost too far, and she nearly went on over the other side of the horse. She said several times, "How can anybody be crazy enough to come in here! I should have my head examined!"

But the sun finally came out and it was a gorgeous day — though it was hard on the women, horses and mules.

Our Daughters-In-Law

One of our daughters-in-law, Karen, who is married to Mick, often came into the hunting camp and helped Adelle with the cooking. Adelle always appreciated having her there with her, and on this one particular day, Adelle was sitting at the end of the table reading a book, after they had all of their work done. Karen was directly behind Adelle, laying cross-ways on our pole bed with her feet dangling over the edge. Both were reading, and probably were about to go to sleep, when all of a sudden Karen let out a blood-curdling scream, and she would not stop.

It startled and scared Adelle, and she turned around to see what was wrong with

Karen, who kept screaming. Adelle thought for a minute that Karen had gone off her rocker. Finally, Adelle said, rather crossly, "what in the devil is wrong with you anyway!" About that time, Adelle saw a chipmunk scamper out of the tent — this darned little chipmunk had run up Karen's leg on the inside of her pant leg. Then, with all the commotion and screaming, it had run back down and out of the tent, and it was probably as scared as Karen was.

Cheryl, another daughter-in-law, who is Karen's sister and married to Buck, another son, came into camp and helped Adelle on occasion. I always made a sweathouse, the same type as the Indians made, at our hunting camp, near a big pool in the creek a short ways from the tents.

The sweathouses, which are made by sticking willows in the ground and bending them over to make a round, dome-shaped structure about three to four feet high that is covered with canvas, utilize heated rocks on an open fire inside to create humidity, and sweat. After you get inside the sweathouse, you shut the flap doorway and sprinkle the hot rocks with water - and after sweating all you want, you run out and jump into the cold water to wash off.

One evening, while all of us men were in there singing and sweating, someone jumped, and yelled, then Kenny said, "Something poked me in the butt!" Then it happened again, and at first we all thought someone in there had a sharp stick — but we finally discovered that they were coming from the outside. Adelle and Cheryl had sneaked out there, and each had a stick and were poking us from the outside.

Laurie, Karen and Bear In Camp

One season we were having quite a lot of problems with bear. Buddy and Laurie, our oldest son and his wife, had their sleeping tent right behind our cook tent where Adelle and I were sleeping; we slept close to the food to keep the bears out should they come into camp.

This camping out was sort of new to Laurie at the time, and she was not too brave when Buddy wasn't there. Every eight days the boys went out with the hunters, and then they would bring a new group back in. Laurie took a pepper can and sprinkled pepper all the way around her tent to keep the bear from coming in.

One time Karen and Mick had their tent attached to the back of our tent so that they could go out our back door and into their tent. One night while Buddy and Mick had gone out with the hunters and were to bring more in the next day, we had gone to bed and were almost asleep when someone came into our tent. It was Karen, and she was too nervous to sleep out of sight of us by herself, so she brought her sleeping bag in and asked if she could roll it out by our bed to sleep, as she was not able to go to sleep out there in their tent, alone.

Bad Water

One fall, Buddy, our oldest son, got very sick in the hunting camp. The day before, while out hunting, he had become real thirsty, as he had given all of his water to his hunters, and even though he knew better, he took a drink out of an elk track — and we think that is what made him sick.

We had a doctor in our camp, and Murphy's hunting camp also had a doctor among their group of hunters. Somehow, the Murphys found out that Buddy was very sick, so their doctor came up to look at him. Our doctor was sort of reluctant to let the other doctor look at one of his patients, but they both laid their ears on Bud's stomach and listened to how it kept growling. They both said that we should fly him out.

A Forest Service wilderness air strip was only a quarter of a mile from our camp, and we got in contact with the ranger at Big Prairie Ranger Station. He called for a plane to come in early in the morning to pick Buddy up, but it started to snow and by morning we had ten or twelve inches of new snow. All of our guides and hunters, including the girls and Adelle, and some of Murphy's crew came up and helped to tramp down the snow on the runway so the plane could land, a gesture we've always been thankful for.

When the plane came, we put young Bud on a saddlehorse, as he had no control or balance what-so-ever. One fellow had to lead the horse while two others got one on each side of it, holding Buddy on so he would not fall off. It was hard to keep him on the horse as we had to go a hundred yards up a very steep bank to get to the air strip. We got him onto the plane and he was taken to the Kalispell hospital. Laurie went with him. They said he had about the same as typhoid fever, and would have died if we had not been able to get him to the hospital.

He had not shaved for sometime and looked quite rough. At the hospital one nurse kept bringing him pea soup every day, which he doesn't like. Finally, he told her that if she brought him anymore pea soup, she and the pea soup were both going to be thrown out through that window — and he heard her say to some of the other nurses that they should all be careful with him, because he was a vicious man.

Adelle Sneaking Candy And Toys Into Hunting Camp
Each fall we went into the South Fork of the Flathead a few days before the hunters came in so we could get our camp all set up. At first, I didn't know that Adelle was sneaking out boxes full of candy and little miniature toys, fishhooks, ribbons and you name it, for the grandkids at home.

When Adelle would have her work caught up in camp, she would make funny papers of all the happenings in camp for each of the kids, and never were any of them left out. She would have letters for each of them, and little gifts, ready at the end of each of the hunts — and the kids were always waiting to get their mail from grandma, who was back in the Bob Marshall.

Some of them wrote letters and sent them back into the hunting camp to her, and she loved to get their letters as much as she enjoyed writing them. In fact, she has most of those letters put away, as they are so cute she plans on giving them back to them someday, even though they are all grown now and most have their own families.

After the season was over, some of the little ones would ask her when she was going to go back in so they could get more candy, toys and letters.

Buck And Family Coming Up The Middle Fork
One fall, Buck, our third son, wanted to see the Middle Fork of the Flathead River country, as he had never been there, so he took his wife and six daughters along. He hauled his packstring and saddlehorses and packs all by truck on Highway

2 at the edge of Glacier Park to the trailhead, where he and his family unloaded the animals. They packed their mules and the girls all onto their horses and started up the trail.

Three days later they came into our hunting camp at the Holbrook Creek. They had crossed over the mountain at the East Fork, gone through the White River country, and then followed White River to our camp. After arriving at our camp, their youngest daughter, Dusty, had her first birthday, and Adelle baked a cake and had a candle on it for her. I very much doubt that Dusty remembers this.

A Noisy Hunter

Buck was guiding for me one fall. He is a big, husky, fellow, especially quiet while he is hunting, and he is a good hunter. One time he was guiding one of the hunters and they were following the fresh tracks of a bunch of elk and Buck was sneaking along as quietly as he could, expecting to see the elk at any moment.

Suddenly the hunter that was with him said, in a loud voice, "Can you neigh like a horse? I can!" and he started neighing like a horse. All of the elk jumped up and away they went, and Buck was so mad after spending all afternoon trying his best to get this hunter close to the bunch of elk, he didn't say a word, he just turned around and headed for camp.

Jim Got Killed

In 1969, while Adelle and I were in our hunting camp, late one evening the Forest Service packer from Big Prairie Ranger Station rode into our camp to give us the bad news that our son-in-law, Jim Ledesky, Roxy's husband, had been killed in a car accident by going off the road and into the Kootenai River near Libby Dam, where he had been working. The family had gotten word to the ranger station by short wave radio.

Daughter Roxy.

So, early the next morning, we saddled up and Adelle and I took off on the thirty-mile ride to Holland Lake. When we got about half-way out, we met one of our daughters-in-law, Buck's wife, and our youngest son, Happy, coming in to take our place in the hunting camp. We didn't know that anyone was coming but we were sure grateful to see them, as Cheryl was a good and capable cook, and while Hap was still quite young, he was also able to handle most anything.

We have been so fortunate, whenever anything went wrong, that there has always been some of our family or friends ready to jump right in and willing to help. That has been a real source of strength through the years.

The Help From My Family

Without the help and cooperation of my family, our outfitting business would never have been a success. We never did make a lot of money, but we always managed to pay our bills, and we made a fair living at it, along with the extra wages I earned working out as an ironworker during part of my off-seasons.

My dear wife, Adelle, got to be a super cook during her life, but after being bucked off horses a few times when she was younger, Adelle was not too brave while riding in the mountains. Still, she managed to bundle up her nerves and ride into the Missions over those rough, rugged trails into our summer camps, as well as make the thirty-mile trip into our hunting camp in the Bob Marshall. All of our hunters, and other guests, both in the mountains and at the ranch, praised her cooking to the highest and it has always been one of the greatest features of our business. Good food is one of the main pleasures in any camp, and a good, clean cook, and well-cooked meals always please everyone in camp.

All of the girls, our daughters and daughters-in-law, also got to be very good camp cooks under her tutorage. Adelle did a terrific job planning and getting her

Bud and Adelle Cheff (center) pose in 1993 with their family. From left are Karen and Mick, Don and Roxy, Laurie and Buddy, Claudia and Ken, Buck and Cheryl, and Hap and Sandy.

food supplies together to be packed into the camps, as well as handling all the paperwork and business end of the packing. And Karen has followed in Adelle's footsteps, accomplishing the same thing since she and Mick have taken over the business.

In the years that I packed and guided, I always had to hire extra help, but when my boys got old enough to help me in this business, they were always the best help that I could have, even though I had lots of good men through the years. Buddy and Kenny were the first two to start helping me, and then a few years later Buck and Mick grew big enough to help. When Buck and Mick worked together as pair, they could load a pack string faster than anyone I have ever seen.

I remember one fall an outfitter in the corrals adjoining ours told me they wanted to get an early start in the morning. Well, when we got up the next morning the other outfitter and seven or eight of his men were already in their corrals, hollering and swearing, and cracking a couple of bullwhips, trying to catch their horses and mules. Two of my boys and I caught our animals and got them saddled, the two boys started to throw the packs on the mules while I got the saddlehorses ready to go. The boys tied their pack strings together, and we started up the trail — and those other fellows, who had less stock than we did and twice as much help, were still yelling, snapping their bullwhips, and trying to catch the rest of their stock when we left.

Hap and his wife Sandy came in to help, and the daughters-in-law and, Roxy, our daughter, have been in here to help sometime or another, the rest of the family, including grandchildren, were helping hands, too. I could never afford to pay them what they were all worth, but still they were always willing to work for us — and we have appreciated it all.

Bud and Adelle in a formal portrait taken in 1993 on the occasion of their 60th Anniversary. Photo courtesy Dana of Denesen Gallery.

Part Seven

EPILOGUE

Retiring

In the year of 1980, on January 19th, Adelle and I went into town with Buck, our third son, and his wife, Cheryl, and sold them our old place, the first land we owned. At the same time we made out the papers to sell the Guest Ranch to our fourth son, Mick, and his wife Karen. I was sixty-five years old and Adelle was sixty-two, and we thought that we should be old enough to retire after spending forty-three years packing and guiding, and on the ranch.

For thirty-five of those years, I also worked as a structural ironworker, putting up steel bridges, buildings and power dams, and throughout that time I had been a member of the Ironworker's Union.

We built our retirement home right on the edge of a beautiful cold stream of water, not fancy, but we love it. It is in "Grizzly Country," and joins our old ranch. We have been retired now for thirteen years and the date today, as I write this, is May the 5th, 1993, and some of our old grizzly friends still come and visit us. There was one in our yard last night and he has been spending a lot of his time a half a mile away, up at the main ranch.

Each year they have come to visit us and our children on their places. Adelle doesn't like it when they come up on our porch and smear their noses on our plate glass windows because the smears stick like glue and are very hard to wash off.

One evening as Adelle opened the door, one of the bears was sitting just outside of the door, and when I went out to tell him to leave, he was reluctant to go.

A few years ago, a pair of grizzlies mated on our son Buddy's lawn, while their children watched, and again last year Buddy and Laurie looked on as a pair of big ones played there, and mated right in front of them. What a rare sight for anyone to see!

We live in a natural bear area, with six families of our children all within three miles of our home and they have all had grizzly experiences. But we try to discourage people from bothering the bears.

During our married life, I have raised and bred hundreds of horses. We have trained and broke all of the horses we used to ride, work and pack. I have used and worn out several generations of these good horses, but now, at my age of seventy-eight years, although I am still helping a little with the packing, and still raising and breaking a few horses, I am beginning to believe that sometime soon the horses are going to get the best of this old man.

And at this time I want to give my sincere "thank you" to Adelle, my lovely wife, and to all of our children, and their children, and all of their mates, and to Buddy, Laurie, Laurie Jo, Cheri, and others who helped with preparing this collection of stories. Without my lovely family, this would be an awful empty world — and I thank you, and I love you all.

Bud Cheff Sr.
Ronan, Montana
May 5, 1993